TRADITIONAL STEP-DANCING IN SCOTLAND

By the same authors

Traditional Dancing in Scotland
(Routledge and Kegan Paul, 1964. Reprinted in paperback 1985)

Traditional Step-Dancing in Lakeland
(The English Folk Dance and Song Society, 1979. Reprinted 1993)

TRADITIONAL STEP-DANCING IN SCOTLAND

J F and T M Flett

with an appendix

STEP-DANCING IN CAPE BRETON ISLAND NOVA SCOTIA

by F Rhodes

SCOTTISH CULTURAL PRESS

First published 1996
Scottish Cultural Press
Unit 14, Leith Walk Business Centre,
130 Leith Walk
Edinburgh EH6 5DT
Tel: 0131 555 5950
Fax: 0131 555 5018

British Library Cataloguing in Publication Data
A catalogue record for this book is available from the British Library

ISBN: 1 898218 45 5

The publisher acknowledges a subsidy from the Scottish Arts Council
towards the publication of this volume

Printed and bound by
Redwood Books, Trowbridge, Wiltshire

Contents

Illustrations

Editor's note: Numbered references in square brackers [ ] throughout the text, refer to the list of sources to be found on p. 212–14.

Preface

This book is dedicated to the memory of my husband, Professor Tom Flett, who died in 1976 at the early age of fifty-two. The dances in the book were collected by him in the 1950s and 1960s, when most of his informants were elderly with memories extending well back into the last century. He was the only person to collect intensively all over Scotland, and therefore the material is of the greatest importance in painting a picture of the social life of Scotland and recording details of one of the greatest pleasures of her people.

Tom was born in London of Scottish parents who were founder members of their local Scottish Society in Wembley, and at the age of seven he was sent to the dancing classes arranged by the Society. Expatriate Scots were perpetuating the custom, dating back at least two hundred years, that children went to dancing classes as a matter of course, not only to learn the solo dances and current social dances but, just as importantly, to learn manners and social behaviour. At the age of seven Tom thought that the classes would be 'cissy', but he soon changed his mind when he found that the teacher was an ex-Pipe-Major of the Scots Guards, Pipe-Major David Taylor, who whacked the children's knees with the wooden sticks used for the Sword Dance if they did not turn their knees out to the required degree! From this first lesson Tom was completely captivated and he danced all his life, not only Scottish dances but also English country dances and step-dances and both modern and old-time ballroom dances. At the age of seven we were in the same class at school and re-met when I joined the Wembley Scottish Society. We were both later taught by the well-known London teacher, Jack McConachie.

In 1948, whilst taking his Ph.D. in mathematics in Cambridge, Tom met Hugh Thurston, also later Professor of Mathematics and author of *Scotland's Dances* (London, 1954). Inspired by Hugh and by our increasing scepticism about the stylised modern form of country and Highland dancing we began our research into traditional dancing in Scotland. We read all the books on dancing and social customs that we could obtain and, in 1953, made our first collecting visit to the Hebrides to see whether any of the 'forgotten' dances were still known. To our delight the trip was very successful, helped by Tom's ability to make friends with those from whom he sought information, despite his innate shyness. Following this trip, I continued to read the literary background of Scotland's dances and Tom spent his university vacations cycling all over the mainland of Scotland, the Hebrides, Orkney and Shetland collecting. Tom was helped in his research trips by Dr Frank Rhodes, another mathematician, who had danced with us whilst a student at the University of Liverpool. Frank also spent some time collecting on his own in the Hebrides and Cape Breton Island, Nova Scotia.

Our book *Traditional Dancing in Scotland* was published in 1964 and reprinted in paperback in 1985. That book was only concerned with the dances performed by groups of people on social occasions and does not cover solo performances. During our research, however, we did amass an enormous amount of material on solo dances, both from literary and from oral sources. These dances were danced and taught by Tom up until his death, were kept alive by his pupils, their pupils and by our daughters. I am now publishing these here for others to discover and enjoy.

In the first part of the book we give the historical background to step-dancing in Scotland, describing how there was once a wide diversity of different solo dances performed all over Scotland which have now largely reduced to those commonly seen at Highland Games. We cover the full range of solo dance styles which we found, including dances in which the rhythm is sounded by beating with the soles of the shoes, or even clogs, as well as the 'Highland style' dances. The second part of the book gives the instructions for many of the dances we collected, where these were considered reasonably complete. There is also an Appendix describing Frank Rhodes' research into step-dancing in Cape Breton Island, Nova Scotia, which can be traced back to the dancing of emigrants from Scotland.

I have been extremely dilatory in preparing this material for publication – there is such a wealth of unique information in our records that the task of selection was overwhelmingly daunting for many years. Tom was meticulous in his collecting and in the writing up of information, always checking and re-checking whenever possible, despite collecting in an era before video and tape recorders. In presenting this material I have tried to be as accurate as he was but it is inevitable that after all these years there will be a few inaccuracies or occasional lack of clarity in the instructions for the dances and I apologise for these. I have made no attempt to compare or analyse the various versions of the dances. I feel that it is important to record the dances as collected so that others may analyse them if they wish.

I am particularly indebted to Frank Rhodes for his contribution to the Chapter on step-dances from the Hebrides and for the Appendix on dancing in Cape Breton Island. For helpful comments I am also grateful to Chris Metherell, Director of the Instep Research Team of the Newcastle Cloggies, one of the people who have helped to keep the dances alive. Our daughters, Lindsay (Smith) and Jane (Lloyd), have given me great support and Jane has helped with the preparation of this book. Tom would be delighted that she continues to play her fiddle, dance and help others to enjoy the dances which he collected.

Joan Flett
Sheffield, 1996

'Cutts and Capers – Flashes and flings'

John MacTaggart, *The Scottish Gallovidian Encyclopedia*
(Glasgow, 2nd edition 1876. First printed 1824)

1

Step-Dancing in Scotland from 1750 to the present day

In this first part of the book we give the literary and traditional background to Scottish step-dancing. We use the term 'step-dance' to cover all types of solo dance performance in which a dancer executes a defined sequence of foot movements. The term refers not only to the well-known Highland dances such as the Highland Fling and the Sword Dance, but to solo dances from all over Scotland which had varying styles, including those which are akin to tap-dancing or clog-dancing.

One of the results of the spread of Highland Games during the last hundred years has been the virtual elimination of all but a few of the many step-dances which were once current in Scotland. The selection of two or three dances as competition pieces was made originally for the convenience of the judges, but the intensive competition of the Games has inevitably led to a concentration on learning the selected dances, to the exclusion of all others. In 1819, the position was very different. In that year, the first of the Highland Games of the modern type was established at St Fillans in Perthshire, whilst Braemar Games was still in the future in 1832. At this time, the Sword Dance, one of the three popular solo dances at modern Games, was rarely performed outside the Highlands, and the other popular dances, the Highland Fling and Seann Triubhas (Shan Trews), were only two of the many step-dances in common circulation all over Scotland.

The heyday of step-dancing in Scotland was from about 1750 until 1850. Resident dancing-masters were to be found in every sizeable town, while the smaller towns and villages were visited by itinerant teachers who taught there for a few weeks and then moved on. A full account of these teachers can be found in our *Traditional Dancing in Scotland*. Most people attended dancing classes in their youth and step-dancing was a normal part of the lessons. The dancing-masters gave their pupils the opportunity to show their skills at the balls with which they concluded their sessions of classes, but apart from these balls there were few occasions for performing in public. In those days one learnt the dances for the joy of dancing; only later were there Highland Games at which prizes could be won and then, for many years, only professional dancers competed.

An excellent description of one of these dancing-masters' balls is given by

St Fillans Games

(From *Scotland Illustrated*, J M Wilson (London, 1849))

St Fillans Highland Society,
LOCHEARNFOOT, PERTHSHIRE.

NOTICE.

THE FOURTH ANNUAL GENERAL MEETING of the SOCIETY will take place, at the VILLAGE of ST FILLANS on the 30th day of August next, precisely at Nine o'clock, (morning,) for Electing the Office-Bearers, Examining the Accounts, and transacting the business of the Society, the Members to be dressed according to the Society's Regulations; and it is of the utmost consequence that the Members should attend when the Private Business of the Society is transacting—which must all be ended before the Competitions take place.

The following PRIZES given by MEMBERS of the SOCIETY.

BY THE RIGHT HON. LADY GWYDYR.
1. To the best SWORD DANCER—*A Suit of Drummond of Perth Tartan.*
2. To the best DANCER OF HIGHLAND REELS—*Ditto.*
3. To the best RUNNER OF A FOOT RACE, 150 Yards—*A Silver Broach.*

BY THE RIGHT HON. LADY PERTH.
1. To the best DANCER OF THE ANCIENT SCOTCH SWORD DANCE—*A handsome Silver-mounted Dirk.*

BY THE RIGHT HON. LORD GWYDYR.
1. To the best DANCER OF HIGHLAND REELS—*A handsome Sporran Mollach.*
2. To the person WEARING THE MOST CORRECT HIGHLAND GARB—*A Set of Silver Buttons.*

BY THE HON. CHIEFTAIN, WILLIAM STEWART, Esq. OF ARDVORLAICH.
1. To the best PLAYER ON THE GREAT HIGHLAND BAG-PIPE, who never gained a Prize Pipe in Edinburgh, nor at St Fillans—*A handsome Pipe.*

BY LIEUT. PATRICK DRUMMOND, R. N.
1. To the best JUMPER, AT A STANDING LEAP—*A Dirk, or Two Guineas.*

By the SOCIETY.

1. To the SECOND BEST PLAYER ON THE BAGPIPE—*A handsome Dirk.*
2. To the THIRD BEST do.—*A Sporran Mollach.*
3. To the SECOND, THIRD, and FOURTH, best DANCERS OF HIGHLAND REELS—*A Pair of Stocking Hose,* each.
4. To the GAELIC BARD who can produce the BEST SONG, or ESSAY, of his own Composition.—*A Gaelic Bible in 2 vols., and Ossian's Poems,* handsomely bound in Morrocco, and Gilt.
5. To the SECOND BEST do.—*Ossian's Poems,* in Gaelic, bound in Morrocco, and Gilt.
6. To the best SINGER of a GAELIC SONG.—*Ditto.*
7. To the SECOND and THIRD best JUMPERS, at a STANDING LEAP—*A Pair of Stocking Hose,* each.
8. To the best THROWER OF THE PUTTING STONE—*A handsome large Silver-mounted Snuff Mull.*
9. To the SECOND BEST do.—*A Sporran Mollach.*
10. To the THIRD BEST do.—*A Pair of Stocking Hose.*
11. To the best RUNNER AT A FOOT RACE—*A handsome Sporran Mollach, and a Pair of Stocking Hose.*
12. To the SECOND BEST do.—*A Sporran Mollach.*
13. To the THIRD BEST do.—*A Pair of Stocking Hose.*

The Competition for the above Prizes to commence immediately after the private business of the Society is over, (supposed to be about eleven o'clock.)

Competitors will attend to the following Regulations :—

1. Those intending to compete for Prizes will lodge their names with the Secretary, or Treasurer, at least twenty-four hours previous to the Competition, mentioning what they are going to compete for ; and meet the Committee, at St Fillans, by Eight o'clock on the morning of Competition, all equipt in the Highland Garb.
2. Pipers to lodge, in Gaelic and English, the names of 5 Phibrochs—any of which they may be required to play.
3. Gaelic Bards will each lodge Four Copies of the Pieces intended for Competition—each copy separately sealed, and the four put under cover, addressed to the Secretary.
4. None but Members of the Society will be allowed to compete for any of the above Prizes, (and they clear of all Arrears, and obtain a Certificate from the Secretary to that effect,) except the Pipe Prizes, and those given by the Right Hon. Lady Gwydyr, for which strangers are allowed to compete.
5. Boys intending to compete for Lady Gwydyr's Prizes, must be equipt in the Highland Garb, and not exceed 14 years of age.
6. Those who gained a First Prize will not be allowed to compete for the like Prize again, but they may compete for the Secondary Prizes.

By Order of the Committee.

St Fillans, 9th July, 1822.

DAVID TAINSH, Secretary.

STIRLING:—PRINTED AT THE JOURNAL OFFICE.

Programme for the fourth meeting of the St Fillans Highland Society, 1822

Major Topham, an English soldier, who wrote from Edinburgh in 1774–5:

> [Dancing-masters] who swarm in Edinburgh... are constantly exhibiting their scholars to the public. You know 'tis a custom in London for some of the principal Dancing-masters to have balls for their benefit; but here it is a general thing, from the one most in vogue, to the humble teacher of a reel to the drone of the bagpipe. Each has his ball... in the Assembley-room; where... each endeavours to show his own excellence and skill as a master, by the execution and performance of his scholars. It is incredible the pleasure and satisfaction the inhabitants of this City take in this diversion. They seem to enjoy it much more than dancing themselves...
>
> At these balls all the children dance minuets; which would be very tiresome and disagreeable, as well from the badness of the performance, as from the length of time they would take up, were they regularly continued. But the dancing-masters enliven the entertainment by introducing between the minuets their High Dances, (which is a kind of Double Hornpipe) in the execution of which they excell perhaps the rest of the World. I wish I had it in my power to describe to you the variety of figures and steps they put into it. Besides all those common to the hornpipe, they have a number of their own, which I never before saw or heard of; and their neatness and quickness in the performance of them is incredible: so amazing is their agility, that an Irishman, who was standing by me the other night, could not help exclaiming in his surprise 'that by Jesus, he never saw children so *handy* with their *feet* in all his life'.
>
> The motion of the feet is indeed the only thing that is considered in these dances, as they rather neglect than pay any attention to the other parts of the body [1].

Many of the step-dances in use during the period from 1750 to 1850 were composed by dancing-masters for particular pupils. Sometimes these dances were set to well-known tunes, for example, in Urbani's *A Selection of Minuets, High Dances, Cotillions, Scots Airs, ...* (Edinburgh, *c.* 1795), we find the tune 'Miss Forbes' Farewell to Banff' labelled 'Miss Robertson's High Dance or Miss Forbes' Farewell'. Others had music especially composed for them, and the names of a good many of these, for example, 'Mr Keith's Favorite High Dance', 'Miss Ann Cockburn's Fancy High Dance', 'Miss Honeyman of Armadale's High Dance', 'Pas Seul Miss Margaret Black of Forresterhill', can be found in the music collections of Urbani, Gibb [2], Stewart [3] and Duff [4].

The origin of the term 'High Dance' is obscure. It may possibly be a term used to distinguish a lively dance, one in which the dancer springs up from the floor, from the *basse dance*, or low dance of earlier years, which was composed of gliding steps in which the feet were hardly lifted off the floor. It was used during this period, along with 'Hornpipe' and 'Pas seul', to denote a solo performance. Even the Sword Dance, Gille Callum, was referred to as a 'Hornpipe' or a 'High Dance'. Major Topham compared the High Dance to a 'kind of Double Hornpipe' as an explanation to a friend in England where the term 'Hornpipe' was also used for a solo performance. The fashion of composing High Dances for favoured pupils seems to have been at its height about 1800. For example, A Gibb, in about 1798, gives a list of nearly fifty tunes with the names of the 'Miss Murray's Hornpipe' style, some of which are labelled 'High

Dance', and he notes, 'A Gibb takes this opportunity to inform his friends, that at desire he makes Steps for Old and New Tunes'. The fashion was relatively short-lived and we do not know of any references to such dances in the literature after 1812. It may be that it was restricted to those teachers who drew their pupils from the upper classes of society. We have collected just one dance, Miss Gayton's Hornpipe, from informants, which may possibly be of this type and we give the instructions for this later in Chapter 11.

There must have been a good deal of classical stage influence in these High Dances for the more prominent Scottish dancing-masters had studied in London and France. For instance, in 1764, David Strange, an Edinburgh teacher, adver-tised that he 'last season studied Dancing, under the celebrated Signor GALLINI at London: he is now returned from Paris, where, for some time past, he has been improving himself in the MINUET; and learned, at the same time, several NEW DANCES under the first two Masters in France, Monsieur MALTERE, Teacher to the Royal Family of France, and Monsieur VESTRES first Dancer in the Royal Academy of Dancing at Paris. From these Gentlemen he has acquired the latest improvements in the Minuet' [5].

Mr Strange was perhaps the greatest of the Edinburgh teachers of the time and became almost an institution. Felix MacDonough, writing in 1824, some twenty years after Strange's death, recalls:

> For how many years did the grotesque Mr Strange lead on his capering legions in the high dance, minuet and highland fling, not without grace and agility. How many mothers' hearts beat high with tender feeling, as Bell or Ellen was taken out to figure on the boards! What crowding, what squeezing, to get a peep at a favourite at these prac-ti-sings! [6]

The odd hyphens in the last word are explained by the fact that Mr Strange introduced vocal parts into the music of slow dances [7].

Other Edinburgh teachers took lessons in London during their summer vaca-tions in order to keep abreast of the latest changes in fashion. Thus, in 1800, a Mr Richie advertised that he had been 'in London during the Vacation and stud-ied under Galini and Fiervelle, first Minuet Dancers and Teachers in London, also Mess. Deshayes and Didelot, and Mmeselles Parisot and Rose Didelot (principal dancers at the Opera House) and Mr Degvelle (Ballet Master at the Opera)' [8].

Most of the dancers from whom the Edinburgh teachers took lessons were French ballet dancers who had also made their names as principal dancers at the King's Theatre in London. Auguste Vestris was born in Paris in 1760 and died there in 1842. He was Maître de Ballet at the King's Theatre and his son, Armand (1787–1825), was also choreographer there. Charles Didelot was a pupil of Auguste Vestris and appeared at the King's Theatre in 1796. Both his wives were called Rose; the first was Rose Pohl, or Paul, who died in 1808 and his sec-ond wife was Rose Colinett who was also popular in London. Andre Jean-Jacques Deshayes and Mademoiselle Parisot were also French dancers who found fame in London. J H d'Egville was, however, an Englishman born *c.* 1770 who was choreographer at the King's Theatre from 1799 to 1809 and also danced at Drury Lane. Giovanni Gallini was born in Florence in 1728 and emigrated to England in 1753 when he made his debut at the Opera House, Haymarket, London. The next year he was appointed principal dancer, then director of dance and finally stage manager. Over this period he also made his reputation as a dancing-master. During a tour in Italy he so impressed the Pope that he was awarded the knighthood of the Golden Spur. Although this gave no right to a title in England, Giovanni thereafter called himself Sir John Gallini. He retired from the stage *c.* 1789 and spent the rest of his life teaching dancing; he died in 1805. He published two works on dancing, *A Treatise on the Art of Dancing* (London, 1762, 1765, 1772) and *Critical Observations on the Art of Dancing; to which is added A Collection of Cotillons, or French Dances* (London, *c.* 1770).

It was not only the Edinburgh teachers who visited London, for so also did their colleagues in the country towns. For example, in April 1813, Mr Josiah Miller, who taught in Tain in Easter Ross, advertised 'that he intends opening School... on the 19th Current... and has just returned from London and Edinburgh, where he made himself master of the latest and most fashionable dances and figures' [9]. Yet others, such as Mr Dean of Inverness, merely contented themselves with a visit to Edinburgh [10].

In view of the close contact with French ballet dancers in London among the fashionable dancing-masters in Scotland, it is unlikely that many of the High Dances composed by such teachers would be purely Scottish and there would have been a great deal of classical ballet influence. Indeed, some teachers advertised that they taught French and English High Dances in addition to Scottish dances. For instance, Mr Martin, who worked under Mr Strange for more than twenty years before setting up his own business in 1783, advertised 'a variety of French, English, and Scots High Dances' [11]. On the other hand, these teachers were also familiar with the wide variety of steps used in the Highland Reel and would, no doubt, make use of movements from these in their High Dances, so that Scottish characteristics would be introduced.

That a knowledge of Reel steps was by no means confined to 'the humble teacher of a reel to the drone of a bagpipe' is shown by an advertisement in 1800: 'Mr D'Egville, late dancer at the KING'S THEATRE, Opera House, London, begs leave to inform... That he teaches the MOST FASHIONABLE DANCES, privately and publicly, in a peculiar stile, and agreeable to the most correct principles of the science, particularly the most favorite Scots Reels, Chantrouse, and Highland Fling, with all the other Caledonian Steps, in a very superior manner' [12]. Mr Richie, already mentioned above, also advertised 'a variety of Scots and Irish Reel Steps' [13]. It is of interest that in an almost identical advertisement in an English newspaper, the *Salisbury and Winchester Journal* for Monday, February 27 1815, 'Mr Read, Professor and Teacher of Dancing' includes 'Chantreuse' in his very extensive list of dances together with 'Scotch Reels,

Waltz, Irish Steps, Hornpipes'.

The step-dances of the 'Miss X's High Dance' type were probably ephemeral, rarely becoming known outside the social circle of the person for whom they were composed. There were, however, some step-dances in use during the period from 1750 to 1850 which achieved a wide circulation. These 'popular' dances, relatively few in number, were taught not only by the fashionable dancing-masters of the towns, but also by the itinerant teachers of the Scottish countryside. It is no doubt due to these itinerant teachers that the dances became widely known.

Itinerant teachers would travel from place to place, settling in one village or district for eight or ten weeks at a time, teaching there on several evenings of the week. If possible, they would also teach in neighbouring villages on the remaining evenings. They would begin with a 'trial night' to see how many pupils would attend. If the numbers were not sufficient they would either hold another trial or would move on elsewhere. Such teachers were still remembered until about 1970 by older country people but their repertoire of step-dances had decreased to a sad remnant of what it once had been.

John MacTaggart has left us a vivid picture of one of these country dancing schools in *The Scottish Gallovidian Encyclopedia* (Glasgow, 1824). His account refers to his native countryside round Kirkcudbright, about the year 1820. The order of the first two paragraphs has been inverted in the quotation:

> A *light heel'd souter*[1] is generally the dancing dominie; he fixes on a barn in some *clauchan*[2] to show forth in; he can both fiddle and dance, at the same time; he can cut double quick time, and *trible Bob Major*[3]: he fixes on, and publishes abroad when his *trial night* is to come on, so the young folk in the neighbourhood doff their *clogs*, and put on their *kirk-shoon*, these being their *dancing-pumps*; off they go to the trial, which, if it be a good turn-out, he tries no more, but begins teaching directly; if not, he has a second, and even a third trial; ...
>
> Commonly the first step dancing masters teach their pupils... [is] Peter a Dick's Peatstack,... performed by giving three *flegs*[4] with the feet, and two stamps with the heel alternately;... the noise the feet makes seems to speak... *Peter a Dick, Peter a Dick, Peter a Dick's Peatstack*[5]... when the Scholars become tolerable at *beetling it*[6], they are next taught to *fleup*[7] through the *side-step*; then *Jack on the Green, Shawintrewse*, and other *hornpipes*, with the *Highland Fling*, mayhap; these dances are all got pretty well by the feet in the *first month*, with sketches of *foursome*, eightsome reels and some country dances; but if the scholars attend the *fortnight* again of another *month*, they proceed at great length into the labyrinths of the art.

---

[1] Souter – Shoemaker.
[2] Clauchan – a small village.
[3] Bob Major – a type of change in bell-ringing.
[4] Fleg – a swinging blow with the foot.
[5] Peter a Dick – in Argyllshire a wooden toy similar to castanets was called Peter Dick. According to MacLagan the name Peter Dick was an attempt to express in words the sound made by the toy [14].
[6] Beetling it – presumably footing it, or stamping from *beetle*, a wooden club or machine for stamping cloth.
[7] Fleups – broad feet.

> [They learn] the 'Flowers of Edinburgh', mayhap; *Sweden* and *Belile's Marches*, with other hornpipes and country dances many;... yes, and they will even dare, some times to imitate our Continental neighbours over the water, in their waltzings, alimanging, and Cotillion trade; ay, and up with the Spaniards too, in their *quadrilles*, *borellos*, and falderalloes of nonsense; so out-taught, they become fit to attend *house-heatings*, *volunteer* and *masonic-balls*, and what not.

The reference to the noise made by the feet should not be taken to mean that the dances were necessarily all of the style later popular as clog or hard shoe dances or the modern tap-dancing. Up until the early years of this century only professional dancers wore the now ubiquitous Highland dancing pumps and MacTaggart notes that the young folk put on 'their *kirk-shoon*' which would have had hard soles and heels. These would obviously be worn for all the dances which today are danced in soft shoes but they would also be suitable for beating out the rhythm in particular dances.

The use of the word 'hornpipe' here does not mean that the dances mentioned were all danced to tunes in hornpipe rhythm or that they were all of 'beetling' type. By 1820 the term 'High Dance' had dropped out of use and 'Hornpipe' was being used to denote a solo performance. This is very clearly shown in the following letter, written in 1835 by one of the competitors in the Highland dancing competition held that year by the Highland Society of Edinburgh, and addressed to the secretary of the Society [15]. In this, even the Sword Dance, Gille Callum, is referred to as a hornpipe.

> A C MacKay took the liberty... to suggest – most humbly – to have some old highland hornpipes danced on the Wednesday... he moreover begs liberty to have the sword dance hornpipe played to by his native music – Edinburgh musicians may play well enough for Quadrilles and Micolanzes. But they are certainly insufficient to play gillie Callum. Highland Laddie and highland fling – with – over the Hills and far way – are in his humble opinion worth the viewing.
>
> Allan Cameron MacKay (Strontian)

Of the step-dances mentioned by MacTaggart and MacKay, namely Highland Fling, Shan Trews (Seann Triubhas), Jack on the Green, Flowers of Edinburgh, Sweden's March, Belleisle's March, Highland Laddie and Over the Hills and Far Away, three of them (Shan Trews, King of Sweden's March and Jack on the Green) were 'common throughout Scotland' in 'the cottage and the barn' in 1798 [16]. The others have all been recorded, in one form or another, in different parts of Scotland and all but Belleisle's March and Jack on the Green either still survive or survived until recent years.

Jack on the Green was performed to a triple time tune of the same name which occurs in many eighteenth century collections, the earliest occurrence known to us being that in Book I of Walsh's *Caledonian Country Dances* (London, 1733). Belleisle's March was presumably named after the Duc de Belleisle (1684–1761), a noted soldier who took a leading part in the closing stages of the War of the Austrian Succession. Earlier in that war he spent a year as a prisoner in Britain. He was Secretary of War for France during the first three years of the

Seven Years War, but did not live to see the end of the War in 1763. The tune 'Belleisle's March' was played by the bands of three regiments of Guards before George III when he reviewed his troops on 27 June 1763. As far as we know this is the earliest occurrence of the tune. Both tunes survived in England to be collected by Cecil Sharp, the folk-song and folk-dance collector, but we have no record of the dances subsequent to MacTaggart, although there is a possible survivor of Belleisle's March under the name 'Earl of Erroll' and we will refer to this later.

It is difficult to find a satisfactory theory to explain why this small number of step-dances should achieve such widespread popularity. There may have been other solo dances, like the many High Dances made up for favoured pupils, which were known only in a particular locality. One possible solution for the popularity of the recorded dances may be that some, at least, first appeared on the stage and became well-known by being performed by some famous dancer of the day. Once they had gained a certain measure of renown they would be taught first by dancing-masters in the larger towns and then be included in the repertoire of itinerant dancing-masters. Because of their small number they could easily be retained in the repertoire and be taught over a wide area, unlike the great number of social dances available from which different communities took and retained favourite dances to form a local repertoire. We have no direct evidence for this theory, but a number of facts bear out the suggestion. For example, King of Sweden's March, the full title of which is 'Charles, Twelfth King of Sweden's March' has already been mentioned as being 'common throughout Scotland' in 1798, and it appears in MacTaggart's account as 'Sweden's March'. The tune 'Charles, Twelfth King of Sweden's March', to which this dance was presumably performed, was well-known in the early eighteenth century and many popular songs were set to it.

The first mention of a dance to this tune is in the third volume of Walsh's *The Lady's Banquet* (London, *c.* 1733) where the tune appears under the title of 'The Swedes Dance at the new Play House'. It seems quite likely that this London stage dance, brought to Scotland either directly to Edinburgh or by itinerant dancing-teachers, was the forerunner of the various versions of the King of Sweden's March found in the Scottish countryside. The tune (and dance) probably took its name from a Jacobite song in honour of Charles XII of Sweden which belongs to the period immediately after the 1715 rising. After the defeat of the Jacobite forces in 1715, the Pretender began negotiations with Charles XII to persuade him to invade Britain. The Swedish King, on his part, was only too ready to strike a blow at the Hanoverians and undertook to invade Scotland at the head of twelve thousand Swedish troops, while James guaranteed a general rising of the Jacobites in England. This scheme became known almost immediately to the British Government which took the extreme step of arresting the Swedish representative in London. This action, combined with Charles' increasing military difficulties, brought the conspiracy to nothing [17].

The tune was also known as the 'The First of August', from one of the several songs of this name which was set to it. Under this alternative title it had Protestant connotations. The date referred to is August 1st 1714, the date of the death of Queen Anne. The succession of George I to the throne was regarded by the Protestants as a signal victory over the pro-Stuart Catholics, and the song was written to celebrate this event. We do not know which was the earlier of the two names of the tune. It occurs in the ballad opera *The Beggar's Wedding* (1729) as 'Glorious First of August' and in Wright's *Country Dances for 1734* as 'First of August'. As 'Charles of Sweden' it occurs in the ballad opera *Devil to Pay* (1731) and *The Rival Milliners* (1737). The tune was known by both names in Scotland and, no doubt, the same was true of the dance.

A dance called 'Highland Laddie' was known on the Edinburgh stage before 1781. This may be deduced from the title of a tune 'Highland Laddie as danc'd by Aldridge' in McGlashan's *A Collection of Scots Measures, Hornpipes, Jigs...* (Edinburgh, 1781). Robert Aldridge was born in Ireland and was a noted dancer and teacher in Dublin and London before opening a successful dancing school in Edinburgh. He died in Edinburgh in 1793.

The earliest instructions for step-dances known to us occur in a MS written by a dancing-master in a southern Scottish town for his pupils: 'The Dancing Steps of a Hornpipe and Gigg. As also Twelve of the Newest Country Dances, as they are performed at the Assembleys and Balls. All Sett by Mr John M'gill for the use of his School, 1752.' The MS is now lost, but some of the instructions in it were reproduced in an article in *Notes and Queries*, xii (1855), 159–60, written by the son of one of M'Gill's pupils. The article is signed W.J. and the author was probably William Jerdan, well known in literary circles in the nineteenth century, whose father was brought up in Kelso.

The hornpipe in the MS had sixteen steps and the 'gigg' fourteen. The second, third and fourth steps of the hornpipe were respectively 'slips and shuffle forwards', 'spleet and floorish backwards' and 'Hyland step forwards'. Other directions included 'heel and toe forwards', 'single and double round step', 'slaps across forward', 'twist round backward', 'short shifts' and 'back hops'. It is to be hoped that M'Gill's pupils could understand these instructions! The fact that the hornpipe and 'gigg' are unnamed is perhaps some indication that in 1752 the 'popular' named step-dances had not yet become widely known.

A number of the 'popular' step-dances have been preserved, either in manuscript or by oral tradition. We must emphasise here that there can be no such thing as a single 'authentic' version of any one of these dances. Versions of the same dance from different parts of the country may show quite wide variations from each other and, may indeed, be quite different dances although bearing the same name. Each dancing-master would make his own modifications to the dance in either steps or style, or both, and the cumulative effect of such changes could be quite large. What does appear to remain constant in most cases is the general character of a particular dance. For instance, the character of Flowers of Edinburgh always appears to have been in the 'tap-dance' style (beating out the rhythm with the soles of the shoes) although the individual steps varied quite widely from place to place.

The earliest written instructions for some of the better known step-dances occur in a MS which was brought to light in about 1942 by Dr The Hon. E Forbes-
Sempill, who later became Sir Ewan Forbes of Craigevar. It is a little notebook
headed 'Frederick Hill's book of Quadrilles and Country Dances, 22nd March,
1841', and contains instructions for various Quadrilles, Country Dances, Reels
and step-dances[8]. The writer was born in London *c.* 1824, but spent the greater
part of his life in Alford in Aberdeenshire where he was a tailor and it was there
that he learnt the dances described in the MS.

Some of the dances may have been taught to Frederick Hill by the 'Myren'
mentioned in the notebook, for Myren (or rather, Myron) was the name of a
family of dancing-teachers still remembered in Banffshire in the neighbourhood
of Dufftown in the late 1950s. Adam (Dancie) Myron, whose father and brother
were also dancing-teachers, was a typical peripatetic dancing teacher. He walked
from place to place 'wearing a big Highland cloak, his fiddle tucked under his
tippet in a poke' and held his classes in farm barns for which he charged 4/6 for a
thirteen week session. Like many other dancing-teachers he was a fine fiddler
and usually played for his classes although, when teaching in Dufftown he asked
a grand-nephew, Mr Charles Milne, to play for him so that the could give even
greater attention to his pupils. He died around 1915.

The Hill MS contains twelve step-dances: Marquis of Huntly's Highland Fling
(two 'sets' of this are given), Shan Trews, Flowers of Edinburgh, King of
Sweden, Highland Laddie, Blue Bonnets, Scotch Measure, Earl of Erroll, Dusty
Miller, Wilt thou go to the barracks, Johnnie, Irish Jig and Trumpet Hornpipe.
The first four of these are mentioned by MacTaggart in his *Encyclopedia*, whilst
Highland Laddie is one of the dances which A C MacKay recommended to the
Edinburgh Games Committee in 1835. We shall meet other dances in the MS
again later when we discuss traditional sources.

From the historian's point of view the most interesting dance in the MS is
Dusty Miller, for the tune is one of the old hornpipes played in triple time. In
earlier times the name 'hornpipe' was used for a tune in 3/2 time, 'Dusty Miller'
being a typical example. After about 1830 the term 'hornpipe' was used with its
modern meaning, i.e. for a tune in common time (4/4). In the interim the term
was applied to tunes in 3/2, 9/8 and 4/4, and these were distinguished by the pre-
fixes 'single', 'double' and 'treble'. This usage was not quite standard but a single hornpipe was usually 3/2 time, a double hornpipe in 9/8 time and a treble
hornpipe was similar to a modern hornpipe.

The tune 'Dusty Miller' is a very old one and occurs in the Blaikie MS of
1692 under the title of 'Binny's Jigg', and in Walsh's *Compleat Country
Dancing Master* (London, 1731) and *Caledonian Dances* (London, 1733) as
'Dusty Miller'. William Stenhouse remarked *c.* 1820 that the tune 'was, in former times, frequently played as a single hornpipe in the dancing schools of

---

[8] In 1955 the MS was in the possession of Frederick Hill's grand-daughter, Mrs B S Lorimer
     of Aberdeen. The present owner is her son, Commander T Myles of Crieff, Perthshire.

Scotland' [18]. 'Wilt thou go to the barracks, Johnnie' is possibly a corruption of 'Go to Berwick, Johnnie', another of the old 3/2 hornpipe tunes, but it is impossible to be certain of this. Only three steps of the Irish Jig are given in the Hill MS and the first of these bears a strong resemblance to the steps of the Irish Jig which is sometimes performed at modern Highland Games. Of the Trumpet Hornpipe we know nothing but a tune of that name is well-known to-day.

Three of the dances in the Hill MS have been published. The instructions for the Earl of Erroll were printed in the *Clan Hay Magazine* for January 1952. These are the original instructions from the MS and are of considerable interest in the study of the older step-dances. They make use of some obsolete terms such as *Shallie*, but once these terms are known, the instructions are quite clear and precise [19, 20, 21]. The instructions for The Earl of Erroll, the King of Sweden's March and Scotch Measure have been published in a booklet issued by the Royal Scottish Country Dance Society, the instructions here having been put into modern notation [22]. It is suggested in the booklet that the second is a woman's dance and the Scotch Measure has been arranged as a dance for two but there is nothing in the MS to justify this.[9]

The dances in the Hill MS are closely related to some recorded from traditional sources in the town of Peterhead in Aberdeenshire. There, a number of step-dances were preserved by a family of dancing-teachers, the Cruickshanks, having been passed down from one generation to another. The last of the family, Mrs Flora Buchan, who learnt them from her father before 1900, herself taught dancing in Peterhead for a number of years and included them in her lessons. One of the dances learnt by Mrs Buchan from her father, Flora MacDonald's Fancy, has been published in the booklet mentioned above. Mrs Buchan's version of the Earl of Erroll is by no means identical to that in the Hill MS but that is only to be expected.

The tune 'The Earl of Erroll' given in the booklet was taken from a copy written down by Mrs Buchan's grandfather, and, as far as we know, does not occur under this title in any printed collections. It does, however, bear a marked resemblance to the tune of 'Belleisle's March', one of the hornpipes mentioned by MacTaggart. It is possible that the 'Earl of Erroll' is an Aberdeenshire version of the latter, its name having been changed to that of a local dignitary in place of that of the long dead and forgotten Duc de Belleisle. There appears to be no record of the dance under this name earlier than the Hill MS.

Another Peterhead teacher, J Scott Skinner, later to become famous as a fiddler, included a number of step-dances in his repertoire. Versions of his dances do not appear to have survived the years but the names of the following appear in his *The People's Ballroom Guide* (Dundee, *c.* 1905): The Cane Hornpipe, White Cockade, The Bonniest Lass in a' the World, Highland Laddie and The Three

---

[9] D G MacLennan in his *Highland and Traditional Scottish Dances* (Edinburgh, 1952) gives his own arrangement of a dance called 'Scotch Measure'. He calls it 'A dance of the 17th century for couples' but gives no source for the dance. He also had a dance which we have in his own MS labelled 'Scotch Maker (Measure) Lady's Dance'.

'Dancie' Reid teaching at one of the early Summer Schools held by the Scottish Country Dance Society

(Taken from a film made by I C B Jamieson, c. 1930)

Graces (although this last may have been a dance for three). Scott Skinner himself wrote of them, 'A number of solo and exhibition dances that were once popular have now disappeared or are only occasionally seen'.

Versions of two of these 'popular' step-dances, Highland Laddie and Flowers of Edinburgh were preserved well into the twentieth century in Angus and Fife.[10] Mr James Neill, who taught in Forfar, and his pupil Mr John Reid who taught in the vicinity of Newtyle, both taught Highland Laddie to their girl pupils and Mr Neill's version is given in Chapter 11 together with details of Mr Neill's distinguished career. Another version of Highland Laddie was published by a well-known Dundee teacher, David Anderson, in his *Universal Ball-room and Solo-Dance Guide* (Dundee, *c.* 1899). Another Dundee teacher whom our informants believed to be a Robert Anderson, included both Highland Laddie and Flowers of Edinburgh in his repertoire in about 1910, but we were unable to obtain any details of his versions.

Both the above two dances were taught by Mr William Adamson who held classes throughout East Fife until 1953. Mr Adamson learnt the dances from his father who died in 1939 at the age of eighty. He, in turn, had learnt them from Mr Andrew Doag, a teacher in the Cowdenbeath district of Wester Fife in 1875. Mr Adamson remembered only one step of Flowers of Edinburgh but he taught us his version of Highland Laddie and we give this in Chapter 11. This is a simple version suitable for young children. Mr Neill, Mr Reid and Mr Adamson were all known by the sobriquet 'Dancie'. In fact, so well was 'Dancie' Reid known by this name that not one of our informants ever mentioned his first name.

'Dancie' Reid attended at least one of the early Summer Schools held by the Scottish Country Dance Society (later the Royal Scottish Country Dance Society). The illustration on page 13 shows him teaching whilst playing his fiddle in about 1930. It is taken from a film made by Ion C B Jamieson who at that time was a factor on an estate at Langshaw, between Lauderdale and Gala Water. Jamieson was interested in acquiring dances which he could teach to a young men's club which he ran and for his wife to teach at the local Women's Institute and he noted dances which he collected from workers on the estate. He was the source for the dances published in the *Border Dance Book* compiled by Elizabeth MacLachlan and originally published in two parts in London in 1930 and 1932. The film is a fascinating record of traditional dancing prior to its revival by the Royal Scottish Country Dance Society and was donated by us to the School of Scottish Studies at the University of Edinburgh.

The dances collected from oral tradition on the mainland of Scotland represent a minority of the number of step-dances taught over the last two hundred years. However, in the Hebrides a considerable number of dances, bearing names known from literary records, survived and they are discussed in the next chapter.

---

[10] A version of 'Highland Laddie' is also described by G Douglas Taylor, *Some Traditional Scottish Dances* (London, 1929), but Mr Taylor was unable to provide any information about the history of this version.

2

Dances from the Hebrides

Versions of a considerable number of step-dances were still well-known in the Hebrides in the 1950s. Some of them had become known to a wider public in 1924 when they were performed by two men from South Uist at a meeting of one of the Glasgow Celtic Societies. Shortly after, in 1925, a competition in these dances was arranged at the South Uist Games. The well-known Edinburgh dancer and teacher, D G MacLennan, attended the Games in the hope that they would bring to light other dancers who knew the dances and might have further information about them. Only the two men who had danced in Glasgow took part in the competition, although the dances were well-known to many people in South Uist and Benbecula. Mr MacLennan spent a short time in South Uist, but he talked to only one of the dancers, from whose information he drew the erroneous conclusion that the dances had their origin in France. The two competitors subsequently had a number of pupils to whom they taught the dances, thus ensuring their survival in the islands.

Our attention was first drawn to these dances by a fellow pupil of Jack McConachie, Miss Elma Taylor, who had visited the Hebrides in the mid 1940s and had learnt a version of the dance Over the Water to Charlie. Jack McConachie, himself, learnt some of these dances from John MacLeod of South Uist (see Chapter 9) and taught them at his Strathspey School of Dancing in London. After his death in 1966 his notes were published by Peter A White in *Hebridean Solo Dances* (London, 1972). In 1953 we visited Coll, Tiree, Barra, South Uist and Benbecula. On that visit, and several later ones to South Uist and Benbecula, we recovered versions of seven out of eleven dances which were once popular.

All but one of the dances from the Hebrides can be traced back to one teacher, Ewen MacLachlan. The exception is Aberdonian Lassie which had been known on Barra. On our visit to Barra early in 1953 we found traces of this dance from just one informant. This informant had been taught the dance by Mr Farquhar MacNeil, a native of Barra, then living in Jedburgh. On a subsequent visit to Mr MacNeil later that year he taught us the dance which he had learnt from his grandfather. However, at that time we were unable to trace any history of the dance nor have we encountered it elsewhere. Mr MacNeil's grandfather had learnt his dancing from two teachers. One was known as Ronald the Dancer and had come from South Uist to work on Barra and the other was a Mr MacLeod from Skye. Mr MacNeil's grandfather would only dance in private with friends and to Mr MacNeil's knowledge did not teach the dance to anyone else. The dance was always known by the English name, unlike other dances which were referred to by Mr MacNeil's grandfather in Gaelic. In the 1950s we felt that a possible explanation for the knowledge of the dance was that it had come to Barra with the great influx of people from the east coast of Scotland, including Aberdeen, during the summer fishing seasons. As well as the great number of fishing boats taking part in the seasonal fishing, other workers such as curers and coopers also came to the Hebrides and during the school summer holidays wives and children joined their men and mixed with the local people. In recent correspondence Mr MacNeil has also suggested the same theory. For some years Mr MacNeil has once again been involved in the teaching of dancing in Barra and we are indebted to him for his help.

The dancing-master Ewen MacLachlan was a very interesting character and our account of his history is condensed from a mass of information collected from many old people in South Uist and Benbecula in the 1950s by Dr Rhodes and ourselves, with help from Dr Alistair MacLean, then the island doctor. We consulted Mr D G MacLennan about his account of the dances given in his book *Highland and Traditional Scottish Dances* (2nd edition, Edinburgh, 1952) and we are indebted to him for general information about all aspects of dancing and for the kindness shown to us on several personal visits.

From an entry in the registration records of the parish of Boisdale, South Uist, we learnt the dates of Ewen's birth and death: 'Ewen McLachlin, Dancing master, single, 1879 80 years'. His father's name is given as Angus McLachlin and his occupation as 'sailor'. Census records give Ewen's place of birth as Greenock, Renfrewshire. At some time prior to 1840 Ewen came to South Uist to live with his sister Isabella at Loch Eynort. She had married an islander, Donald MacDonald, in 1830. Ewen is known to have held classes in Bornish which was cleared of inhabitants in 1840. Isabella died in 1844 but Ewen continued to live in various places in South Uist making his living as a dancing-master. In the 1950s there were many confusing stories about his background most of which have been impossible to check. His sister was sometimes referred to as Iseabail Reitealain – Isabella of Retland – and there is some evidence that the family had, at one time, lived at Retland on the south shore of Loch Morar, Invernesshire. It may be that when Angus MacLachlan retired from the sea he became a tenant of property at Retland where he is supposed to have been a man of some substance. It is now unlikely that the whole story of Ewen's background will be uncovered but it was possible to check some of the stories about his education.

It seems that Ewen was a man of considerable learning. D G MacLennan says that he received training for the priesthood at the Scots College at Douai in France and this story persisted in the 1950s giving credence to the story that his dances had their origins in France. However, this is impossible, for both Scots

Colleges in France, at Douai and Paris, closed in 1793 during the French Revolution and never reopened. We were told by a grand-nephew of Ewen's (Isabella's grandson) that he was trained for the priesthood in Spain, but this is also false, for the names of those who attended the only College in Spain, at Vallodolid, are known and Ewen's does not appear among them. Nor does his name appear in the records of Aquhorties or Lismore, the two Catholic schools and seminaries which existed in Scotland at that time. However, the records for Lismore are not complete so there is just a possibility that he studied there. There was, moreover, the fact that Ewen suffered from a deformity of the arms. Details of this deformity varied, some people saying that his hands were almost at shoulder level, others saying that only his hands were deformed. We understand that any deformity of the hands or arms would have made his acceptance for the priesthood most unlikely. For the information about Scots colleges and seminaries we are indebted to the Reverend William J Anderson, then at St Mary's College, Blair, Aberdeenshire, who searched the relevant records for us.

It is possible that Ewen received his education in a less conventional manner. The Reverend Father Campbell, then of Mingary, Moidart, suggested to us that he may have been a 'mass companion' to a priest. In those days the Roman Catholic Church in Scotland was not organised on a parochial basis and the priests went where the need was greatest. They often employed young men to carry their vestments and mass utensils for them and sometimes the priest would further the education of his 'mass companion'. The young men were often referred to familiarly as 'Mass John'. What is certain is that Ewen worked as a catechist among the people of South Uist and, in the 1950s, there was still some knowledge on the island of prayers and hymns he had taught to children.

Ewen was also a noted story-teller with a large fund of tales. Many have been recorded by The School of Scottish Studies in Edinburgh from the last of the great story-tellers, Angus MacMillan of Griminish, Benbecula, whose father learnt them from Ewen. Ewen was probably the subject of a reference in J F Campbell of Islay's journal for 1859. J F Campbell was himself a collector of folk tales and he noted:

> There is a dancing master without arms who is now in Barra and who has hundreds of Sgeulachd [stories]... One of his best steps is to leap up and extinguish a lamp with his heel without spilling a drop of the oil.

A number of our informants told us of Ewen performing this trick with a candle on the wall and we are indebted to Miss Marie Slocombe, sometime Recorded Programmes Librarian of the BBC, for the reference to Campbell's journal. It is of interest that this test of skill, known as 'Smàladh na Coinnle', smooring of the candle, was remembered by emigrant families in Cape Breton Island, Nova Scotia, as late as the 1950s (see Appendix on step-dancing in Cape Breton). 'Smooring' is also the term used for the process of covering glowing peats with ash to keep the fire in.

In his early days on South Uist, Ewen was a typical itinerant dancing teacher, although his activities were mainly restricted to that island. Thus, he would set up his dancing-school in a barn in one of the townships and lodge nearby until it was time to move on elsewhere. Later in life he seems to have settled in the vicinity of Daliburgh, in the south of the island. He died in 1879 and was buried in Daliburgh. After his death his books were left to his niece but subsequently they were burnt along with the house in which they were kept, after an outbreak of 'fever'. D G MacLennan records that he was told about books found in Ewen's cottage:

> Before leaving South Uist I had an interesting talk with a nephew of Ewen MacLachlan, a sailor, who told me about two particular books found in his cottage, one resembling shorthand, or Chinese writing. It was shown to this sailor, who had sailed the China seas, but he could not interpret it, – only the heading was Chorégraphie. That was an easy decision for me, for I possess several booklets on that very difficult system of writing down dance steps of the Ballet, invented by Feuillet, a Frenchman, in the 17th century – surely a proof of Ewen's artistic dancing ability.

The step-dances taught by Ewen MacLachlan were Highland Laddie, Blue Bonnets (known as Scotch Blue Bonnets on the island), Scotch Measure, First of August, Miss Forbes' Farewell to Banff (known simply as Miss Forbes), Over the Water to Charlie, Tullochgorm, Over the Hills and Far Away[1], Lads wi' the Kilt, Flowers of Edinburgh, Carraig Fheargus (or Maile a Chandonn), Bonny Anne and Jacky Tar. He also taught the Highland Fling, Shan Trews and the Sword Dance. Of these we have succeeded in recovering most of the steps of the first seven. We also found odd steps of Over the Hills and Far Away, Lads wi' the Kilt, Flowers of Edinburgh and Jacky Tar.

We recall that The First of August is an alternative name for the tune to which The King of Sweden's March was performed. This suggests that the dance taught in the Hebrides is simply another version of the King of Sweden's March and indeed, there is a distinct similarity between that and the version of the King of Sweden's March in the Hill MS. Flowers of Edinburgh was a dance in which the rhythm was beaten out by the feet of the dancer as were the versions of that dance taught in Dundee and in Fife, which we note in a later chapter. The general descriptions of Flowers of Edinburgh and Carraig Fheargus given by people who had seen them suggested that they were the same dance performed to different tunes. Jacky Tar was merely Ewen's version of the Sailor's Hornpipe. Of Bonny Anne we know only that it once existed, it is possible that it was not a solo dance but a set dance for several dancers.

D G MacLennan published descriptions of six of these dances, Highland Laddie, Blue Bonnets, Miss Forbes, Tullochgorm, Over the Water to Charlie and Jacky Tar, all of which he learnt from one of Ewen's pupils in 1925. Mr MacLennan told us, however, that the versions which he published are his own

---

[1] William Stenhouse *(op. cit.)* notes: 'This tune [O'Galloway Tam] appears in Oswald's *Caledonian Pocket Companion*, book 6th printed in 1742, [but] it is the old air of "O'er the Hills and Far Away" changed from common into treble time.'

GRAND CELTIC
ENTERTAINMENT.

THE CELEBRATED

PIPERS & DANCERS,

PATRONISED

BY

HER MAJESTY,

AND

PRINCE
ALBERT.

THE

Celtic Performers

Who had the honour of performing before Her Majesty and Prince Albert, and the Nobility of Scotland, at Taymouth Castle, have engaged to give

A GRAND CELTIC
ENTERTAINMENT,

IN THE MUSIC SALOON, WOOD-STREET, WAKEFIELD.

On MONDAY Evening, August 28th, 1843.

The following Performances will be brought forward, when the Performers will appear in full Highland Costume, equipped in the Order of their Clans. After the Performances, the Prizes received by the Performers in Scotland, will be exhibited.

PROGRAMME.

PART I.

Tune—My King has landed in Moudhard,.................. ...J. Cameron.
Dance—Cameronian's Rant, ...Archibald M'Donald.
Tune—Bonnie Charlie, ...Duncan M'Kay.
Dance—The Original Strathspey Step, ... Donald M'Dougall.
Tune—Over the Water to Charlie, ... Duncan M'Kay.
Dance—Marquis of Huntley's Highland Fling,................S. Campbell.
Tune—Lochiel is away to France, a quick step, ...J. Cameron.
Dance—Gillie Challum, or Sword Dance, ... Archibald M'Donald.
Tune—The Downfall of Paris, a quick step,................Duncan M'Kay.
Dance—Highland Reel, as performed at Taymouth
Castle, ...Four Characters.
Tune—The Young Prince of Wales, a quick step,...........J. Cameron.
Dance—Highland Laddie, ...S. Campbell.

PART II.

Tune--My ain kind dearie, a quick step, ...Duncan M'Kay.
Dance—Highland Fling,.. Archibald M'Donald.
Tune—Bonnie Annie, a quick step,...... ....J. Cameron.
Dance—The Original Reel of Tulloch, ... Four Characters.
Tune—Pibroch of Donald Due, a quick step, ... Duncan M'Kay.
Dance—The Original Tullochgorum,................ Donald M'Dougall.
Tune—Captain M'Kenzie's quick step, ... J. Cameron.
Dance—Gillean a Neilludh, or the lads with the kilts,...A. M'Donald.
Tune—Faskley House, a quick step,.......................... John Cameron.
Dance—Marquis of Huntley's Scotch Reel, ...Three Characters.
Tune—Lochaber no more, a quick step, ... Duncan M'Kay.
The whole to conclude (by particular desire) with a Dance in the Character of a Highland Shepherdess......... Archibald M'Donald

" A Company of Highland Pipers and Dancers, who performed before the Queen at Taymouth, and who are on a tour, have given four Celtic Entertainments in the Theatre, Sunderland, during the past week, to numerous and respectable audiences. They appeared in Highland Costume, and exhibited various Prizes, which they have obtained in Scotland for the Superiority of their Performances. No similar Performance has been given in Sunderland for many years which excited the same amount of interest, and obtained such unbounded applause: added to this, the extreme modesty and characteristic native simplicity of the Performers, have gained for them general esteem and admiration.—*Newcastle Chronicle.*

ADMISSION.-----Front Seats, 1s. 6d.; Second Seats, 1s; Third Seats, 6d.

CHILDREN UNDER TWELVE YEARS OF AGE, HALF-PRICE.

Doors to be Opened at Half-past Seven, Performance to commence at Eight o'clock precisely.

Tickets may be had of Mr. Wm. Briggs, the Golden Lion Inn, opposite the Old Church, and at the Doors of the Mechanics Institution

T. Wray, Printer, 18, Briggate, Leeds.

Programme from the Music Saloon, Wakefield
(From the John Cryer Collection, vol. 2238, by courtesy of the Wakefield Libraries HQ)

arrangements of the dances and are not identical with the ones danced in South Uist. He stated in his book that Ewen studied dancing whilst at the Scots College in Douai and then composed the dances himself, using the steps he learnt in France. This theory, which in effect implies that the dances are neither Scottish nor old, seemed to have been generally accepted and may have contributed to the lack of interest shown in the dances for many years. MacLennan based his suggestion on the similarity of certain of Ewen's steps to ballet steps and to steps which he had himself seen in Northern France. However, as we have seen there is no foundation for that theory; a certain degree of French influence is only to be expected in view of the close contact maintained by Scottish dancing-masters with London and France.

We do not know where Ewen obtained his dances. One of our informants told us that he taught dancing in Glasgow, another that he had danced on the Continent and his grand-nephew said that Ewen had studied dancing in Edinburgh and that Edinburgh ball programmes were among his effects. There did remain the possibility that he composed the dances himself and this was a reasonable theory as long as the Hebridean dances were the only known examples of Scottish step-dances other than those danced at Highland Games, as was the case when MacLennan put forward his suggestion. This is no longer the case. We now know that a version of Flowers of Edinburgh was known in Kirkcudbright in 1824, that Highland Laddie and Over the Hills and Far Away were 'old Highland hornpipes' in 1835 and that Highland Laddie, Flowers of Edinburgh, Blue Bonnets and Scotch Measure were known in Alford in Aberdeenshire in 1841. We also know that versions of some of these dances had been preserved in Aberdeenshire, Angus and Fife until relatively recent times. In view of all the fresh information which we have found it seems much more likely that Ewen learnt the dances on the mainland of Scotland, perhaps as a youngster when an itinerant dancing-master came to his home district, and then took them out to the Isles. Like most teachers he probably made his own alterations to the dances but the basic material was quite clearly that which was once the common possession of all dancing-masters in Scotland. The illustration on page shows the programme of a Grand Celtic Entertainment which includes several dances bearing the names of those taught by Ewen.

We give descriptions of the dances we collected which we can trace back to the teaching of Ewen MacLachlan in Chapter 9 along with the instructions for Farquhar MacNeil's Aberdonian Lassie.

3

The 'Games' Dances: The Sword Dance

In Chapter 1 reference was made to early Highland dancing competitions. A full account of these competitions is given elsewhere [23] but, briefly, the earliest competition of which we have a record is a piping competition held at Falkirk in 1781 under the auspices of the Glasgow branch of the Highland Society of London. In 1783 the competition moved to a theatre in Edinburgh and in the following year the Highland Society of Edinburgh was founded, but prizes at the competitions were still awarded by the Highland Society of London. Dancing, performed by the pipers, was first introduced in 1783, simply as an interlude to break up the long sessions of piping. For many years the only dances performed were Highland Reels.

The Sword Dance, Gille Callum, first appeared at the Edinburgh competition in 1832 when five men danced it. The minutes of the organising committee record that: 'The ancient Ghillie Challaim or sword dance over two naked swords was peculiarly gratifying, and was performed by John MacKay with a degree of precision and ease altogether extraordinary, considering the intricacy of the figures and the rapidity of the motions'. This appears to have been the first introduction of Gille Callum to the Lowlands although there are earlier obscure references to a form of Sword Dance in various places. We are greatly indebted to Lieutenant Colonel J P Grant of Rothiemurchas and Mr Archibald Campbell of Kilberry for allowing us to examine the manuscripts relating to the early piping competitions and to reproduce programmes.

In *A Collection of Loyal Songs For the Use of the Revolution Club* (Edinburgh, 1770) a copy of which we examined in Sir Walter Scott's Library at Abbotsford, there appears a poem under the title 'Highland Laddie', which has the refrain 'Bonny Laddie, Highland Laddie' between each line. The alternate lines read:

> When you came over first frae France
> You swore to lead our King a dance
> And promis'd on your royal word,
> To make our Duke dance o'er the sword.

PLAN

OF

THE COMPETITION FOR PRIZES,

TO BE GIVEN BY

THE HIGHLAND SOCIETY OF LONDON,

TO THE

Five Best Performers of the Ancient Music of the Great Highland Bagpipe;

TO BE HELD IN

The THEATRE-ROYAL, on WEDNESDAY, the 25th JULY 1832, *at* 12 *o'Clock Noon precisely*,

In presence of a COMMITTEE *of* JUDGES *appointed by the* HIGHLAND SOCIETY *of* SCOTLAND.

To commence with a SALUTE upon the *Prize-Pipe* to the HIGHLAND SOCIETY of LONDON, by JOHN MACKENZIE, Piper to the Right Hon. the EARL of ORMELIE, and who formerly gained the Prize Pipe.

A HIGHLAND DANCE.

ACT I.

COMPETITORS' NAMES.	TUNES.	TRANSLATIONS.
1. Charles Duff, from Dounavourd, Atholl,	*Failte Dheors 'Oig,*	Young George's Salute.
2. William Duff, Piper to the Perthshire Militia.	*Failte Phrionnsa,*	The Prince's Salute.
3. John Smith, Piper to the Hon. Colonel Grant of Grant—Gained 4th and 5th Prizes,	*Cille Chriosd,*	Glengarry's March.
	A DANCE.	
4. John Mackay, son of John Mackay, Piper to the Right Hon. Lord Willoughby de Eresby,	*Failte Mhic Ghille Challaim,*	Macleod of Rasay's Salute.
5. John M'Beath, Piper to the Highland Society of London—Gained 2d Prize for Dress,	*Glas Mheur,*	The Finger Lock.

A DANCE,—AFTERWARDS THE ANCIENT SWORD DANCE, CALLED "THE GHILLE CHALLAIM."

ACT II.

6. Angus Mackenzie, from Rasay,	*Cunıh' Mhicantoisaich,*	M'Intosh's Lament.
7. Roderick Mackay, Piper to James Moray, Esq. of Abercairney—Gained 3d Prize for Dress,	*Clagean na Pheairt,*	The Bells of Perth.
8. William Smith, Piper to the 92d Regiment, or Gordon Highlanders—Gained 4th Prize,	*Failte Chlann Dhomhnuil,*	Macdonald's Salute.
	A DANCE.	
9. Donald Macleod, from Rasay,	*Failte Chinn Loch Moidart,*	Kinlochmoidart's Salute.
10. John Macpherson, Piper to the Right Hon. Lord Gienlyon,	*Bratach Ban,*	The White Flag.

A DANCE,—AFTERWARDS A STRATHSPEY DANCE.

ACT III.

11. Donald M'Innes, Piper to Colonel M'Neill of Barra,	*Failte Bharraidh,*	M'Neill of Barra's Salute.
12. John Bruce, now Piper in the United Kingdom Steamship, formerly Piper to Sir Walter Scott, Bart.	*Failte Mheanairaich,*	Menzies' Salute.
13. John Scott, Piper to Archibald Butter, Esq. of Faskally—Gained 5th Prize,	*Blar Bhatarnis,*	The Battle of Waternish.
	A DANCE.	
14. George Murchison, Piper to Duncan Davidson, Esq. of Tullich, M. P.—Gained 1st Prize for Dress,	*Is leinne fhein a Ghleaun,*	Our own is the Glen.
15. Adam Macpherson, Piper to the Stirling and Bannockburn Caledonian Society—Gained 2d Prize,	*Leannan Dhomhnuil Ghruimaich,*	Grim Donald's Sweetheart.

A DANCE,—FOLLOWED BY A STRATHSPEY DANCE.

The Judges will then retire to determine the Prizes; and, during their absence, two Highlanders will display the Broad-Sword Exercise by Cudgel-playing. The Band will also play some favourite Scottish Airs, which will be followed by National Dances. On the return of the Judges, the *Prize-Pipe*, elegantly ornamented, with the other Prizes to Pipers, to the best Dancers, and to the Best-Dressed Competitors, will be delivered by their Preses to the preferred Competitors, in presence of the Audience, and of the *whole Competitors.*

TO CONCLUDE WITH A DANCE.

N. B.—At the previous Rehearsal in presence of the Judges, it was found necessary, in order to shorten the Exhibition in Public, that only the Competitors in the above Plan should perform. The following Pipers also appeared, several of whom are very creditable Performers, and have gained Prizes at various Competitions, viz.

John Cameron, from Glasgow.
Peter Maclaren, from Lochearnhead.
James Macintosh, from Aberfeldy.
Angus M'Innes, from Lochaber.

Angus Cameron, Piper to the St. Ronen's Border Club.
Roderick Macdonald, from Ross-shire.

Archibald Stewart, from Rannoch.
William Gunn, from Glasgow.
Murdoch Maclean, from Inverness.

The whole Pipers, Dancers, and Competitors for Dress, are attended to in the distribution of the Money collected from the sale of Tickets.

Plan of the competition held by the Highland Society of London at the Theatre Royal, Edinburgh, 1832

Many other early references to a Sword Dance refer to a dance in which the dancer brandishes the sword. For instance, Richard Rolt, in his *Memoirs of the Life of the late Right Honorable John Lindesay, Earl of Crauford and Lindesay* (London, 1853) writes, 'The earl of Crauford was not more remarkable for his elegance in dancing, than in his noble way of performing the Highland dance, habited in that dress, and flourishing a naked broad sword to the evolutions of the body'. The Earl of Crawford was born in 1702 and wounded in battle in 1739 and was thereafter unable to dance. In some references this brandishing of a sword becomes confused with the practise of 'cudgel play', which in former times was taught to young men as an exercise. In the revised edition of James Logan's *The Scottish Gael* of 1876, the additional notes give 'SINGLE STICK, or cudgel play, was formerly taught the youth from an early age, as a necessary preparation for the management of the broadsword, and they used it in certain dances to exhibit their dexterity'.

Some references give a description of a dance in which two men danced a mock fight[1]. Robert Ridell, writing of various forms of Scottish music says, 'When danced by two men, armed with a sword and Target [targe], they were called the Sword dance' [24]. Various writers refer to a Sword Dance either as a pre-battle dance or as a celebration over a beaten enemy. J G MacKay, writing in 1928 said,

> As all know, the Scottish Sword-dance, called *Danns' a' Chaidheimh* and *Gille Calum*, is danced over two swords or a sword and a scabbard, which are laid across each other on the ground. But few know that, though the dancer turns on his own axis sunwise, he goes round the sword *widdershins*[2]. As a Highlander would never dance ill-luck to his own clan, the conclusion is that the Highland sword-dance is a war-dance, which sought to bring about ill-luck to another clan and good-luck to the dancer's clan. That it was once a war-dance is clear from the fact that it was at one time danced with a sword in each hand [25].

So, the writer has combined two different dances to prove his theory. However, it is certainly a fact that up to hundred years ago, at least in some parts of Scotland, the Sword Dance was danced in a clockwise direction – 'the right way' – as one old lady in Benbecula put it. Even in 1955, Frank Rhodes was able to collect a version of the dance in Benbecula in which the dancer did go clockwise round the swords. An early set of instructions for a dance of this form is given in C N McIntyre North's *Book of the Club of True Highlanders* (London, 1880). We shall mention the type of dance where the sword was brandished in Chapter 7.

---

[1] D G MacLennan in his *Highland and Traditional Scottish Dances* (Edinburgh, 1952) refers to men fighting with dirk and targe and alternating this with dance steps. 'It was called in Gaelic "Bruichcath" or Battle Dance, and was a form of "duelling" dance – attack and defence'. He includes a sketch taken from a plate in the British Museum but gives no indication of the source or location of the dance. The piper featured appears to be playing a continental form of bagpipe. (See also Chapter 7.)

[2] Widdershins – opposite to the sun or anticlockwise.

The most exotic theory about the dance, perpetuated by some writers, was that when the Romans invaded Britain in 54 BC they saw the 'Caledonians' dancing in and out among upturned swords and spears. The authority for this was given as the Roman author Tacitus. However, the title of the work, written in AD 98, refers to young men 'who make it their diversion to dance naked amidst drawn swords...' is 'Treatise on the... inhabitants of Germany' (Revised Oxford Translation, 1870).

A curious reference to the dance occurs in the original of James Logan's *The Scottish Gael* (London, 1831): 'The ancient Caledonians had a sort of Pyrric dance over swords, which is not entirely unknown, but the Gille-Callum, which generally terminates a ball, is supposed to have but a faint resemblance to the ancient sword dance'. However, a clue to this odd statement is given in the annotated reprint of 1876: 'A favourite amusement of the Highlanders was the sword dance which was performed with a great degree of grace and agility, being usually introduced as a finale to a ball, in the manner of "bob at the bolster" of the Lowlands and the country bumpkin of England'. The same note refers to dancing 'Gille-Callum over a fiddle bow' and to the Sword Dance over sticks.

'Bob at the Bolster'[3] appears again and again in the literature in descriptions of dancing in the Scottish countryside, including Orkney, and in the north of England. The name varies from 'Ba¹ ¹ty Bowster' and 'Bumpkin Brawly' (brawl or branle being a dance of the Middle Ages) to 'Pease Straw' and 'White Cockade', the tunes to which it was often danced. Further confusion has been caused by the name 'Bumpkin' or 'Country Bumpkin', the name 'Bumpkin' being also the alternative name for 'The Ninesome', a dance for three men each with two partners. It is probable that the words 'country bumpkin' used by Logan refer, not to a yokel, but to the name of the dance used in England.

MacTaggart, in his *Encyclopedia*, defines Bumpkin Brawly as 'an old dance, the dance which always ends balls, the same with the "Cushion" almost'. The Cushion Dance dates back to at least Elizabethan times when it was danced in 'court and country' and 'all the company dances, lord and groom, lady and kitchen maid, no distinction'. In Playford's *The Dancing Master* of 1686[4] the description of the dance starts: 'This dance is begun by a single person (either man or woman) who, taking a cushion in hand, dances about the room' [26]. In later years a bolster or pillow case or a handkerchief often took the place of the cushion.

A description of this form of dance written in 1913 sums up the dance more concisely than earlier ones:

> It began by some smart man dancing round his pocket-handkerchief which he had
> loosely twisted into a rope and stretched upon the floor. After dancing one or two

---

[3] To bob – to dance (J Jamieson, *An Etymological Dictionary of the Scottish Language*, Edinburgh, 1808).

[4] The first edition of *The Dancing Master*, published by John Playford in London had appeared in 1651. It was not until the 7th edition of 1686 that the Cushion Dance appeared under the title Joan Sanderson or The Cushion Dance.

figures round the handkerchief, he picked it up and marched round the room, then approached some lady, kissed her, took her arm, and the couple pursued their course round the room. It was now the lady's turn to make a choice, and she would coyly toss the treasured handkerchief to some favoured man, who would promptly have his kiss as a reward, and join the march round the room. He in turn would select a lady, and this process would go on until the dancing space was filled... Hands were caught as in the modern Eightsome Reel, and the man who began the dance got into the centre, kissed his partner, and dropped out. The lady at once took his place, threw the handkerchief to her partner, was kissed and passed, and this process continued until only two or four couples remained on the floor, when the dance would end in an ordinary reel [27].

At first sight it would seem unlikely that actual swords were used in a 'finale to a ball' as Logan says. However, it must be remembered that at a dancing-master's 'ball' his pupils may well have demonstrated the Sword Dance during the evening's performance and therefore, in the general dancing following, in which all present would join, it would be possible for the concluding dance to be started using actual swords. On other occasions it is quite easy to imagine 'some smart man' who fancied himself as a dancer, performing a few steps of the Sword Dance over his handkerchief to show off. A twisted handkerchief is an easy substitute for a sword or even for tobacco pipes. In 1906, Cecil Sharp, the collector of English dances and songs, found in Oxfordshire that Bampton Morrismen had 'Greensleeves or Bacca Pipes danced over crossed tobacco pipes or handkerchiefs'. In Gloucestershire he noted that the tune 'Greensleeves' was played for dancing Bacca pipes or the Cushion Dance in 1909, and that in Devon a broom dance over a broom laid on the floor ended the dancing at a Harvest Home [28].

All the early references to Sword Dances are only vague and the first really clear reference to a dance of the now well-known type (i.e. where a single dancer dances over a sword and its scabbard laid flat on the floor to form a cross or sometimes two swords crossed) occurs in the copious 'Notes Explanatory and Historical' to an epic poem by Alexander Campbell, *The Grampians Desolate* (Edinburgh, 1804): '*Gille Callum da' pheigin*, is generally danced by one man, who performs it with great address over a naked broad-sword laid on the floor'. Campbell was born in Perthshire and his account undoubtedly dates from the latter part of the eighteenth century. The words 'Gille Callum da' pheigin' are from the first line of the *puirt-a-beul* or 'mouth music' used for dancing when no musical instrument was available. Often, as in the case of the Sword Dance, the *puirt-a-beul* was simply nonsense rhymes to fit the rhythm of the dance. Sometimes there would be extempore verses made up to suit the company but the well-known versions were handed down by oral tradition. In the case of the Sword Dance the words say (roughly) that the boy Malcolm has two pennies (two Scots pennies – a *bodle* – was a copper coin of extremely small value in the eighteenth century; some sources give it as a sixth of an English penny, some as a third), he shall get a wife for two pennies, a useless one for two pennies; he shall get a sweetheart for nothing, his pick and choice for two pennies. An early

'Gilli Challum', Ronald Robert MacIan (1803–1856)
(Courtesy of the Malcolm Innes Gallery, Edinburgh)

'The Gillies Ball', Egron Lundgren
(Courtesy of The Royal Collection © Her Majesty the Queen)

occurrence of written music actually labelled 'Gilliam Callum' is in John Walsh's *Caledonian Country Dances'*, published between 1730 and 1765. As 'Kheellum khallum taa fein' it was printed by Robert Bremner, also in London, in *For the Year 1769, A collection of Scots Reels and Country Dances* where a country dance was set to it.

Over the years many versions of the dance appeared, both in printed sources and in oral tradition. We have found steps and part versions in many localities but do not give any descriptions of steps in the later part of the book however, as we feel that the versions which we collected are not sufficiently precise to reproduce. They do indicate very clearly that there were many variations of the dance.

With the increasing popularity of the Highland Games and the increasing ease of communications particular selections of steps became more widely known and popular as dancers emulated the most successful competitors. This increasing standardisation was completed in the 1950s with the publication of *Highland Dancing,* the textbook of The Scottish Official Board of Highland Dancing (Edinburgh, 1955). The organisers of the Games had found 'That part of the programme which was concerned with Highland Dancing was a constant thorn in the flesh. Complaints were continually being made to them about bad or biased judging, or about unsatisfactory features in the conduct of the competitions'. There was, in addition, no authoritative body to which complaints could be referred. The first move to complete standardisation was made in 1949 when the Scottish Dance Teachers Alliance advocated the setting up of the Board. Whilst we appreciate the reasons for the standardisation, we deprecate the fact that this resulted in a lack of interest in other steps, not only of the Sword Dance but of the other 'Games' dances and did nothing to arrest the virtual loss of all other solo dances.

However, the Board did add, but only as a footnote:

> Originally it was intended also to provide a brief but authoritative account of the history of Highland dancing. Gradually, however, it became clear that the difficulties in the way of such an attempt are at present well-nigh insuperable: reliable evidence concerning origins and early development is scarce and scattered; in the general neglect of Scottish culture which has prevailed, until recently, in all four Scottish universities, Highland Dancing has been largely ignored by learned men; and as yet little or no serious research has been done. There is an opportunity here for academic investigators which, it is to be hoped, they will not fail much longer to exploit.

We hope that this wish is fulfilled, somewhat belatedly, by this present work.

4

The 'Games' Dances:
The Highland Fling

As far as we are aware, the earliest reference to the Highland Fling occurs
in 1794. From this date onwards references to it are fairly common, but
the first in which the reference *is clearly to a solo step-dance* does not
occur until 1824. The distinction here may seem, at first sight, mere pedantry,
but there is in fact good reason to be cautious. In the early nineteenth century
'the Highland Fling' was both the name of a solo dance and the name of a particular step used in the Highland Reel, and in many of the early references we
cannot be certain which of these meanings is intended.

The word 'fling' means literally a movement in dancing. The use of the word
is a very old one, there being numerous examples of it in the works of Scottish
writers from about 1500 onwards. For example, in a poem written in 1528, Sir
David Lindsay tells us that 'Sumtyme, in dansing, feiralie I flang' [29]. Again, in
the song 'Willy was a wanton wag', first published in Allan Ramsay's *The Tea-
Table Miscellany* (Second Volume, Edinburgh, 1726), the bride objects when the
bridegroom comes to take Willy's place in the dance:

> Bridegroom, she says, you'll spoil the dance,
> And at the ring you'll aye be lag...
> We will find nae sic dancing here,
> If we want Willy's wanton fling.

In its earliest occurrences in connection with dancing, the word 'fling' seems
merely to have meant a kick or some similar violent movement.[1] In later years,
however, the word 'fling' does appear to have been given to one or two particular movements. Thus, for example, Elizabeth Grant in her *Memoirs of a
Highland Lady* (London, 1898) mentions that at Kinrara on Speyside, *c.* 1804,
she learnt among other steps 'the single and double fling, the shuffle and heel
and toe step'. Later, when she describes her father's dancing at a Harvest Home
in 1813, she implies that 'the fling' is simply a turn performed in a particular
manner: 'My father's dancing was peculiar – a very quiet body, and very busy

---

[1] This meaning is still preserved today in the 'fling' (i.e. kick) of a horse.

feet, they shuffled away in double quick time steps of his own composition, boasting of little variety, sometimes ending in a turn-about which he imagined was the fling'. Whatever the 'fling' was, it does seem to have belonged primarily to the Reel. Alexander Campbell, for instance, speaks of it as 'the *fling* or gambol peculiar to the... Strathspey, or reel' [30].

Traditionally a Reel was a dance for three or more in which steps danced on the spot alternated with a travelling figure. In earlier times the travelling figure could be a simple circle with the dancers following each other or, in the case of the Threesome Reel, the travelling figure was a figure 8. The best known form of the Reel is the Foursome Reel in which four dancers perform steps of their choice on the spot and in the travelling figure trace the pattern of a figure 8 with an extra loop. Within living memory the first part of the dance was performed to a selection of tunes in strathspey rhythm and the second part to tunes in reel time. Nowadays the dance is more often in the form of the first part in strathspey rhythm following by the Reel of Tulloch which consists simply of alternate stepping and swinging by the pairs of dancers to tunes in reel time.

We have already remarked that the earliest mention of the Highland Fling known to us occurs in 1794; in that year the name appears in the title of a tune, 'The Marquis of Huntly's Highland Fling'. This tune was composed by George Jenkins, a teacher of Scottish dancing in London, and was first published by him in his *New Scotch Music...* (London, 1794). There is no indication in the book of the nature of the Highland Fling, but his choice of title for his tune does imply the existence at that time of some dance or dance step bearing the name.

The first reference in which there is explicit mention of dancing occurs in an 'extract' from Hannah More's *Strictures on... Female Education* published in the *Scots Magazine* in 1800. In the extract, complaint is made that young girls spend too much time in learning to dance: 'They are shut up all the morning, demurely practising a minuet, or transacting the more serious business of acquiring *the highland fling*'. It would not, at first sight, be clear whether this referred to a step or a dance. However, Miss More's book was printed in London and the wording in the extract appears to have been amended for a Scottish readership. Hannah More's original has 'a new step' where the *Scots Magazine* has 'the highland fling'. The indication that the Highland Fling was originally a step rather than a dance is amply confirmed by other references. For instance, the definition of Highland Fling given in Jamieson's *Dictionary* in 1808, is 'a name for one species of movement [in dancing] in which there is much exertion of the limbs'.

It is very probable that this step was the same as 'the fling' mentioned by Elizabeth Grant in her description of her father's dancing and that described by Campbell as a Reel step. Certainly the Highland Fling step, like the 'fling', was used in the Reel. A Colonel Thornton records that at Pitmain in 1804 he took part in 'a number of different reels, some of them danced with the genuine Highland Fling, a peculiar kind of cut' [31]. MacTaggart in his *Encyclopedia* gives 'Cutts and Capers – Flashes and flings'. So much was the Highland Fling associated with the Reel at this period that, in 1814, when a Russian envoy, Count Platoff, told Lord James Murray that he 'was very anxious to see the Highland Fling', he was shown a Reel. Lord James wrote of the occasion; 'I got Moon [Lord James's Valet] who dances very well, and some others to figure in a Reel, with which he was much delighted' [32].

This last quotation seems to imply that in 1814 'Highland Fling' and 'Reel' were almost synonymous, a possibility that must be taken into account in the early history of the Highland Fling. For this reason we cannot be certain in many early references whether they refer to the solo step-dance or to a Reel in which the step was used. This is the case, for instance, in a letter written by John Leyden from Oban in 1800: 'Here I am in great spirits, listening to the sound of a bagpipe and the dunning[2] of some very alert Highlanders dancing the Highland Fling with great glee' [33].

The same is true to a lesser extent of Robert Tannahill's poem 'The Kebbuckston Wedding', written some time before 1810:

> Sannie M'Nab, wi' his tartan trews,
> Has hecht to come down in the midst of a caper
> And gie us three wallops[3] of merry shantrews
> With the true Highland fling of Macrimmon the piper.

Here the linking of the Highland Fling with Shan Trews, the latter undoubtedly a solo step-dance, would seem to imply at first sight that the Highland Fling was also a solo dance. However, we cannot be sure that Sannie M'Nab did not first dance Shan Trews and then show off his 'true Highland fling' in a Reel in which others joined. The omission of any mention of a reel or of any other dancers might easily have been due to the demands of rhyme. For this and similar reasons we have to disregard a number of other early references to the Highland Fling and, as far as we know, the first unambiguous reference to the Highland Fling as a solo step-dance is that in MacTaggart's *Gallovidian Encyclopedia* of 1824. It is obvious from this that the dance had been in existence for some years when MacTaggart wrote of it. Not only does he refer to it along with other 'Hornpipes' but he gives the definition 'Hielan Fling – a rustic dance'.

The first instructions for the dance known to us are in the Hill MS of 1841, where the dance appears as 'The Marquis of Huntly's Highland Fling'. Another set of early instructions is given in C N McIntyre North's *Book of the Club of True Highlanders (op. cit.)*. According to McIntyre North this last version was derived from Sandy MacIntyre, a teacher in Perth *c.* 1850. In its early days the dance seems to have been performed to the tune composed by George Jenkins; this is shown by the title given to it in the Hill MS and by James Logan's mention of the dance as 'The Highland fling, in that style called the Marquis of

---

[2] To dunner – 'To make a noise like thunder', Jamieson *(op. cit.)*.
[3] Wallop – in a *Dictionary of Lowland Scotch* (London, 1888), Charles MacKay gives 'wallop' as an alternative spelling of 'walloch' defined as the 'Lowland name for Highland Fling or other dance'.

Huntley's' [34]. In view of this, it is possible that Jenkins may have actually composed the dance but there is no evidence to support the conjecture.

The Highland Fling was one of the dances at the Inverness Northern Meeting Games from their commencement in 1841. We have no record of it at any competition before that date even though dancing was introduced at the Highland Society of London's piping competitions in Edinburgh in 1783 and these competitions continued annually until 1826 and thereafter triennially until 1844. It would appear that, by this date, the solo dance was well-known. There is however, no evidence that it actually originated in the Highlands. It may equally well have been composed by a dancing teacher in the Lowlands or even in London. We can only speculate that it is a compilation of some of the steps used in the strathspey portion of the Reel. It may have evolved so that solo dancers could display their skills at the dancing-masters' 'finishing balls' other than in the Reel which required a number of dancers.

At this time the Reel was still a popular social dance (indeed, until 1875 it was practically the only dance in the remoter parts of the Highlands) and, as the knowledge of the solo dances spread, the teaching of both dances went together so that solo dancers could perform the Fling but equally, if not more importantly, so that those dancing the Reel had a selection of steps to choose from. The solo dance was therefore taught by a myriad of dancing-masters all over Scotland, from the most renowned Edinburgh teacher in his Dancing Academy to the humblest itinerant teacher in his barn. Every teacher, however, had his own version of the dance. Indeed, not all of the versions would necessarily have been derived from a common origin, some may well have been independent compositions. The variations between the versions of one teacher and another were often very wide; it was not uncommon to find the versions having only one step out of eight in common. We ourselves know of some sixty steps, either taken from printed sources, or collected from oral tradition.

The diversity and number of steps taught by dancing-masters is amusingly illustrated by the story told by Mrs L B Walford in her book *Recollections of a Scottish Novelist* (London, 1910). Recalling her girlhood in Edinburgh in about 1860, she wrote of the family dancing-master, Mr Thomas M'Glashen, who was also summoned each year to Windsor Castle to teach the young princes and princesses:

> One winter M'Glashen instituted a series of small and select gatherings for the purpose of practising reels and strathspeys. We went in for various recondite forms of these, and there were experts among us. One, a very young and pretty one, was a favourite pupil, and to the surprise of her master, he saw her one evening standing motionless, while the 'Hoolichan' [the Reel of Tulloch] was in full swing.
> 'Miss Ina, what is the matter? Why are you not dancing?'
> She replied that she could not think of a step.
> *A* step? and she knew twenty!

The diversity of the various versions of the Highland Fling may come as a surprise to those who only know the modern standardised dance. However, no traditional dance is fixed and static, but it grows and changes with time. Each performer contributes something, possibly a small change in step or perhaps some small idiosyncrasy of style. Those to whom he or she teaches the dance at first try to copy that style and preserve those steps, but, in time, make their own changes and develop their own style. Undoubtedly some of these changes are unconscious, for no two people perform a dance exactly alike; some may even be due to faulty memory, but many will be conscious 'improvements'. If the dance is one which is taught by a professional dancing-teacher, then the greater the number of teachers the greater will be the number of different versions of the dance in current use at any one time. If the dance is widely known and there are few opportunities, because of lack of communications, for one district's version to be compared with another's, then local variations will arise in increasing numbers.

What is unusual, in the case of the Highland Fling, is not the number of different versions which existed in the second half of the nineteenth century, but the fact that since then all these versions have virtually disappeared to be replaced by a single standardised version. The tendency towards standardisation began with the present century and increased considerably after the First World War. There were two principal reasons for this. First was the great reduction in the number of teachers of Highland dancing which took place after the War. If country people wished to learn to dance it was no longer necessary for them to wait like the innkeeper in Inverary who, in 1784, 'was in easy circumstances, ... and a dancing master came every year from a distance to spend some months at his house, exclusively occupied in giving [his children] lessons' [35]. Sometimes communities would wait as long as two years for a visit from an itinerant teacher, but once transport facilities in the rural areas had improved, families could go by bus or train to the nearest town to attend classes. This led in an obvious way to a reduction in the number of versions of dances in current use.

In the towns, too, there was a reduction in the number of teachers of Highland dancing. The virtual disappearance of the Reel from the ballroom with the introduction of jazz and the more modern couple dances meant that teachers of ballroom dancing no longer had to teach the steps of the Highland Fling. Thus the teaching of Highland dancing was left more and more to a few specialists who taught nothing but Highland dancing. This was in marked contrast to the state of affairs in the late nineteenth century. David Anderson, for example, who taught in Dundee from about 1870 until about 1905, was one of the most successful competitors of his time at the Highland Games, yet was just as much a teacher of ballroom dancing as of Highland dancing and he taught all the ballroom dances then in vogue.

The second reason for the standardisation of the dance was the same as that for the Sword Dance. Namely, the emulation of successful competitors at the Games. If a competitor was consistently successful there was an obvious temptation to copy his or her steps. In the old days this had no great effect, for competitors at the Games were drawn from a few well-known urban teachers and their pupils. The itinerant teachers and their pupils did not, in general, compete and were thus free from this influence towards standardisation. In more recent times, however, when the number of versions in current use had become smaller than ever before, this influence has been decisive. With the increasing ease of communications it became customary for most teachers of Highland dancing to compete personally and to enter their pupils. Competitors now travel long distances, even from overseas, to attend the Games and the same dancers compete at Games all over Scotland. All can thus see and imitate the steps or style of the most successful dancers. The result has been that all but a handful of steps have disappeared, the same steps being performed by all competitors. Writing in 1952 D G MacLennan, himself a famous teacher and competitor who used to dance ten steps in his version of the Highland Fling, said, 'The set-steps now described for this dance have been accepted as standard for over fifty years'. In his book *Highland and Traditional Scottish Dances*, he gives six steps plus two 'extra or alternative steps'. Standardisation was completed by the publication of *Highland Dancing* by the Scottish Official Board in 1955 where eight steps are given.

We have rescued over sixty steps once used in the Highland Fling and, in Chapter 10, we give a selection of the more interesting ones. A dancer would not normally dance more than ten and usually only six or eight in a performance. Just as an interesting sidelight to conclude this Chapter, we noted that in Logan's *The Scottish Gael* he refers to two brothers 'who were good violin players, exhibit feats of great agility. Part of their performance consisted of dancing the Highland Fling, in that style called the Marquis of Huntley's, Strathspeys over a rope, and Gille-Callum over a fiddle bow'. On experimenting we found that it is quite possible to dance some steps of the Fling whilst skipping in an ordinary skipping rope!

5

The 'Games' Dances:
Shan Trews, The Sailor's Hornpipe
and The Irish Jig

The dance Shan Trews, or *Seann Triubhas* in Gaelic, can be traced back to about 1790. A 'Scottish Gentleman' using the *nom de plume* of Philo Scotus, recalling a visit to Musselburgh Town Hall, Midlothian in 1793 to see a play, noted that he and his school friends were surprised to see 'Davy Tamson (to whose fiddle we danced "The Blackamoors Jig" and "Shant Trews", under the tuition of Mr Salmon) take his place in front of the pit' [36]. In the *Scots Magazine,* vol. 60, 1798, a contributor gives various hypothetical suggestions for the names of various dances. He writes, '*Shan Trews*' or rather '*Sans Trews*',… its significance is probably the same as that of the modern phrase of sans cullottes. These dances… are now common throughout Scotland'.

At this time it was not regarded as essentially a Highland dance. It was performed to a fiddle tune called 'Sheann Triubhas Uillichan', Willie's old trousers. This tune was previously called 'The Deil Stick the Minister' and is said to have had a scurrilous set of words. Certainly the tune was regarded as insulting enough to a minister for a piper in Stirling, in 1690, to be fined for playing the tune in the churchyard. The insulting nature of the tune may also have had some relation to the term 'Stickit Minister' which is defined by Charles MacKay in *A Dictionary of Lowland Scotch* (London, 1888) as 'A term of obliquay in Scotland for a candidate for holy orders who has failed to pass the necessary examination or to give satisfaction to the congregation before whom he preached the probationary sermon. The phrase is equal to the vulgar English – "old stick in the mud".'

The first occurrence we found of the tune is in one of the collections of Scottish tunes published in London in 1700 [37]. The song, known as 'Seann Triubhas Uilleim' was written to the tune after the 1745 rising, by the Gaelic poet Duncan Ban MacIntyre who gave it the additional title 'Oran do 'n bhri-ogais' (Song to the Breeches) [38]. The words are a protest against the fact that the law which banned the wearing of Highland dress did not distinguish between the rebel Highlanders and those, like Duncan himself, who had fought for the

Government. 'Uilleim' (William or Willie) was, of course, the Duke of Cumberland who had beaten the rebel Highlanders at the battle of Culloden in 1746. As a tune normally took the name of the latest song set to it, 'Deil Stick the Minister' became 'Willie's old trousers'. The dance may well have been composed to the first tune and when the tune changed name the dance did like-wise just as in the case of social dances which, in former times, took the name of the tune to which they were danced. Frequently the same set of instructions would appear under the name of different tunes even in the same volume.

In the *Museum Illustrations* (additional notes) written *c.* 1820 for *The Scots Musical Museum*, the editor, William Stenhouse, notes:

> This is no mine ain house: This song was written by Ramsay... In the Museum, Ramsay's verses are not set to the original tune... but to a very old air, called *Deil stick the Minister*, from an old, but rather licentious song,
>
>> If ye kiss my wife,
>> I'll tell the minister, etc., etc.,
>
> The tune is printed in Oswald's Caledonian Pocket Companion, book vii printed about the year 1743... There is a set of the tune of 'Deil stick the minister', inserted in Fraser's Gaelic airs, under the title of 'Sean Truid's Uillachan', printed in 1816... Of course we must believe it to be of Gaelic Extraction; but the Gaelic title will not do: it is evidently a barbarous translation of Willie's Shantrews. The word *shan*, is a common Scottish adjective, signifying poor or shabby, and *shantrews*, in the same dialect, literally means shabby or poor looking trowsers, a name by which the tune has been always been known in common with its still more objectionable title, at all our dancing schools for many generations.

Elizabeth Grant, in her *Memoirs*, records that in 1804, 'We were often over at Kinrara, the Duchess [of Gordon] having perpetual dances, either in the drawing-room or the servants' hall, and my father returning these entertainments in the same style... We children sometimes displayed our accomplishments on these occasions in a very prominent manner, to the delight, at any rate, of our dancing-master. Lady Jane[1] was really clever in the Gillie Callum and the Shean Trews'. The Duchess's favourite footman 'played the violin remarkably well, and as every tenth Highlander at least plays on the same instrument tolerably, there was no difficulty in getting up a highly satisfactory band on any evening that the guests were disposed for dancing'. In 1805, at Tennochside in Lanarkshire, Elizabeth, not to be out-done by Lady Jane, 'danced my Shean Trews... in a new pair of *yellow* (!) slippers bought at Perth'.

Knowledge of the dance was not confined to Scotland. We have already noted in Chapter 1 that the dance was being taught in London in 1800 by Mr D'Egville and in 1815 in Winchester and Salisbury. In 1806 it appeared several times in the programme of Messrs. Ogden, Winder and R Ogden's Pupils' Ball in Halifax. In 1816, Thomas Wilson, in his *Companion to the Ballroom* (London, 1816) gives

---

[1] Lady Jane Montague, grand-daughter of the Duchess of Gordon, with whom Elizabeth shared a dancing-master.

Messrs. OGDEN, WINDER, & R. OGDEN's

PUPIL'S BALL,

ON WEDNESDAY, THE 29th DAY OF JANUARY, 1806,

IN THE

THEATRE, HALIFAX,

PART FIRST.

The First Part to conclude with a NEW BALLET DANCE, by TWENTY-FOUR LADIES and GENTLEMEN,

MISS WILD;	SCOTCH SOLO.
Masters Bates, and S. Nicholl, Misses Ward and Bates,	STRATHSPEY.
WALTZE by six Ladies.	
Masters Brown, Mason, Frobisher, and Collington,	LORD COLLINGWOOD's HORNPIPE.
Misses Smith, Hemingway, Tasker, and Frobisher,	SHANTRUCE.
Masters Stocks, Abbott, and Haigh,	SAILOR's HORNPIPE:
Masters Pollard and Ward, Misses S. Wooller and Mallinson,	STRATHSPEY.
COTILLION LA CHASE.	
Miss Tasker,	HORNPIPE.
Masters Nicholl, T. Milnes, G. Brown, and Walker,	HORNPIPE.
Masters Stocks and Oates, Misses Emmett and Nelson,	MINUET et STRATHSPEY.
Masters Frobisher and Collington, Misses Robertson and Gill,	IRISH REEL.
Masters Bagnold and J. Gregory, Misses Lister and M. Frobisher,	MINUET et STRATHSPEY.
Misses Boothroyd and Jenkinson,	IRISH JIGG.
Masters Firth, Fletcher, and Staveley, Misses Fletcher, Hall, Ormerrod, Taylor, Speight, Spencer, E. Smith, Nicholl, and Freeman,	SCOTCH REEL.
Misses S. and M. Woollers, Aked, and Shuttleworth,	SCOTCH SOLO.
Masters Ashworth and Gill, Misses Spencer and Speight,	IRISH REEL.
COTILLION LA ASSEMBLY HARMONIOUS.	
Masters Haigh and Abbott, Misses Stocks and Haigh,	MINUET et STRATHSPEY.
Masters Gill, M. Oates, Alexander, Smith, Hemingway, and Lister, Misses Ross, H. Hemingway, Boothroyd, Gill, Milner, and E. Nelson,	SCOTCH REEL.
Masters Hemingway, Lister, Alexander, and Smith,	COLLINGWOOD's HORNPIPE.
Misses Smith and Hemingway,	IRISH JIGG.
Masters Thompson and W. Haigh, Misses R. Frobisher and J. Stocks,	MINUET et STRATHSPEY.
Masters H. Staveley, Wooller, Abbott, Haigh, and Turner, Misses Jenkinson, Haigh, A. Nelson, Bortoft, Oates, Stocks, and Robertson,	SCOTCH REEL.
Misses Jenkinson, Ross, Ormerrod, and Boothroyd,	SHANTRUCE.
Masters Lister and Hemingway, Misses J. Stocks and Haigh,	IRISH REEL.
Masters R. Haigh and Adams, Misses Illingworth and Bagnold,	MINUET et STRATHSPEY.
Master Collington, Miss Ross,	IRISH JIGO.
Misses Milner, Haigh, Gill, and J. Stocks,	SHANTRUCE.
COTILLION LES VENDANGEURS.	
Misses Smith and Tasker,	DEBERBALL MINUET et GAVOTT.
Masters Ashworth, Gregory,	SAILOR's HORNPIPE.
Masters Brown, Mason, Frobisher, and Collington,	NELSON's HORNPIPE.
Masters Milnes, Naylor, H. Staveley, and S. Milnes,	HORNPIPE.
Misses Boothroyd and Smith,	MINUET DE LA COURE et GAVOTT.
SECOND COTILLION LA ASSEMBLY HARMONIOUS.	
Misses Hall, E. Smith, Wooller, and Fletcher,	SCOTCH SOLO.
Misses Spencer, Speight, and Taylor,	SHANTRUCE.
Masters Staveley and Ashworth, Misses Brown and Naylor,	SCOTCH REEL.
Misses Brown, Nicholl, Freeman, and Taylor,	STRATHSPEY.
Masters Haigh and M. Oates, Misses Ormerrod and Haigh,	IRISH REEL.
Masters Milnes and S. Milnes, Pollard, Gregory, Naylor, and Ward, Misses Hirst, Bland, Farrer, Dodsou, Mallinson, and Walker,	SCOTCH REEL.
Misses Jenkinson, Ormerrod, Frobisher, and R. Frobisher,	MINUET et STRATHSPEY.
Masters Oates, Gill, and Oates,	SAILOR's HORNPIPE.
Master Wooller, Misses Bortoft, Pollard, and Hirst,	STRATHSPEY.
Misses Dodson, Bland, Walker, and A. Nelson,	STRATHSPEY.
Misses Oates, Farrer, Naylor, and Stocks,	SCOTCH SOLO.
FIRST COUNTRY DANCE,	TRIP to KILKENNY.
QUADRILLE for Sixteen.	

PART SECOND.

MISS WILD,	SCOTCH SOLO.
Masters Alexander and Smith, Misses Milner and E. Nelson,	MINUET et STRATHSPEY;
Masters R. and W. Haigh, Bagnold, Thompson, J. Gregory, and Adams, Misses Illingworth, Bagnold, Lister, M. Frobisher, J. Stocks, and R. Frobisher,	SCOTCH REEL.
FIRST MEDLEY COTILLION.	
Masters Bates, S. Nicholl, Pollard, and Ward,	HORNPIPE.
Master Lister,	HORNPIPE---DUSTY-MILLER.
Masters Brown and Mason, Misses Hemingway and Taylor,	IRISH REEL.
Master Nicholl, Misses Aked, Shuttleworth, and Farrer,	STRATHSPEY.
Misses Nelson and Tasker,	IRISH JIGG.
Misses Ward, Bates, Mallinson, and A. Nelson,	SCOTCH SOLO.
Masters Firth, Staveley and Fletcher,	LORD COLLINGWOOD's HORNPIPE.
LES TROIS BUTTONEE COTILLION.	
Master Frobisher, Misses Ormerrod, Frobisher, and Tasker,	YORK MINUET.
Masters Thompson, Bagnold, and J. Gregory,	SAILOR's HORNPIPE.
Masters Hemingway and Lister, Misses Boothroyd and Ross,	MINUET et STRATHSPEY.
Masters Adam, and R. and W. Haigh,	SAILOR's HORNPIPE.
Masters Frobisher, Collington, Brown, Mason, Oates, and Stocks, Misses Tasker, Frobisher, Smith, Nelson, Emmett, and Hemingway,	SCOTCH REEL.
Masters Firth and Oates, Misses Fletcher and Wooller,	STRATHSPEY.
Misses Wild, A. Nelson, S. Wooller, and Mallinson,	SCOTCH REEL.
Misses Illingworth, Bagnold, Lister, and M. Frobisher,	HIGH DANCE.
VOUS L'ORDONNEZ COTILLION.	
Masters Ashworth and Gregory, Misses Ormerrod and Frobisher,	MINUET et STRATHSPEY.
Masters Brown and Mason, Misses Smith and Hemingway,	MINUET et STRATHSPEY.
Misses Nicholl, Freeman, Brown, and Speight,	SCOTCH SOLO.
Misses Frobisher, and R. Frobisher, Abbott,	IRISH JIGG.
Masters Haigh, Patchett, Stocks, and Wooller,	LORD COLLINGWOOD's HORNPIPE.
Misses Smith and Tasker,	YORK MINUET.
Masters G. Brown and Walker, Misses S. and M. Wooller,	STRATHSPEY.
Misses Emmett, Stocks, Robertson, and H. Hemingway,	SHANTRUCE.
SECOND MEDLEY COTILLION.	
Masters Milnes, H. Staveley, Turner, and S. Milnes,	HORNPIPE.
Misses Nelson, Spencer, R. Frobisher, and J. Stocks,	HIGH DANCE.
Masters Gill, Oates, Smith, and Alexander,	LORD COLLINGWOOD's HORNPIPE.
Misses Spencer, Speight, Taylor, and Robertson,	MINUET et STRATHSPEY.
Masters Nicholl, S. Nicholl, Bates, G. Brown, T. Milnes, and Walker, Misses Aked, Shuttleworth, Wooller, M. Wooller, Bates, and Ward,	SCOTCH REEL.
Misses Hirst, Farrer, Bland, and Oates,	SCOTCH SOLO.
Masters Hemingway, Alexander, Smith and Patchett,	SAILOR's HORNPIPE.
Masters Fletcher and Staveley, Misses Hall, and E. Smith,	STRATHSPEY.
Misses Bortoft, Pollard, Dodson, and Walker,	SCOTCH SOLO.
Masters Stocks and Oates, Misses Emmett and Stocks,	IRISH REEL.
Masters Naylor and Wooller,	HORNPIPE.
Masters Frobisher and Collington, Misses Tasker and Frobisher,	MINUET et STRATHSPEY.
COTILLION LA TEMPLE DE PAIX.	
Masters Turner, Wooller, and T. and S. Milnes,	HORNPIPE.
Masters Gill and M. Oates, Misses H. Hemingway and Gill,	MINUET et STRATHSPEY.
SECOND COUNTRY DANCE,	L. NELSON's VICTORY.

The whole to conclude with

A BALLET DANCE,

BY TWENTY-FOUR LADIES AND GENTLEMEN.

GOD SAVE THE KING   AND RULE BRITANNIA.

Doors to be opened at Half past Three o'Clock, and the Ball to begin precisely at Four.
Tickets to be had of Messrs. A. and R. OGDEN, at the Talbot, and of Messrs. HOLDEN and DOWSON, Printers.
Boxes and Pitt 4s 3s. each—Upper Boxes 2s. 6d.—Gallery 2s.

Messrs. Ogden, Winder, and R Ogden's Pupils' Ball, Theatre Royal, Halifax, 1806

the instructions for a country dance set to the tune 'Shan Truish Willichan' and notes that the solo dance 'consists of a number of steps necessary to be taught by a master'.

We do not know when or where the dance was first introduced at Highland Games. Apart from the years 1832 and 1835, when an ordinary instrumental orchestra provided the music for all the dances at the Edinburgh competitions, the music had always been provided by a piper. So, when the dance was accepted at the Games the tune used was changed from 'Sheann Triubhas Uillichan', the fiddle tune to which it had always been danced, to one which could be played on the pipes. For many years now the usual tune has been 'Whistle o'er the Lave o't'. The change of tune and the use of the pipes may well have altered the style and the tempo of the dance. The Scottish Official Board gives eighteen steps plus a 'finish' but states that the dance 'consists normally of not more than eight or ten steps'. As an example of steps which are very different to those known today we give just two steps in Chapter 11 which were taught by James Neill of Forfar.

Two other dances sometimes performed at Highland Games deserve mention. Tne Sailor's Hornpipe and the Irish Jig have been included in some Games although they have no connection with the Highlands. We do not know when or where they were first introduced but certainly they were both performed at the Games held at Luss in Dunbartonshire in 1893 [39]. A version of the Irish Jig is described in David Anderson's *Ballroom Guide* (3rd edition, Dundee, *c.* 1894) and this is very similar to that performed at modern Games. This Scottish Irish Jig is performed in the manner, costume and burlesque style of the music hall stage and bears no resemblance to the true Irish Jig. D G MacLennan wrote, 'I much regret to say that I have a very poor opinion of the Irish Jig, which passes under that name in Scotland'.

The Sailor's Hornpipe was certainly popular on the Edinburgh stage early in the nineteenth century, as recorded at the Theatre Royal in January 1819 when a 'Naval Hornpipe' was introduced between the main item and a farce which followed. Similarly, a 'sailor's hornpipe' was performed at the Pantheon in March of the same year. Both were reported in the *Caledonian Mercury* for that year. By 1848 it was included in the repertoire of dancing-masters. Mr Lowe, a teacher in Inverness, put on an exhibition at his annual ball that year of a 'boat's crew of jolly tars, arrayed in appropriate costume… performing their hornpipe in gallant style' [40]. In 1900 Graham MacNeilage 'Gold Medallist' advertised private tuition in the Sailor's Hornpipe and Irish Jig in addition to his public classes [41].

Most of the itinerant teachers of whom we have records taught the Sailor's Hornpipe to their pupils, often under the alternative name of Jacky Tar. Like the Irish Jig, it was usually danced in the appropriate costume. By 1900 the Sailor's Hornpipe was as widely known throughout Scotland as the Highland Fling. J Scott Skinner, in *The People's Ballroom Guide* (Dundee, *c.* 1905), gives a version of the Sailor's Hornpipe and remarks 'no exhibition dance is more popular than the Sailor's Hornpipe, or Jacky Tar, as it is sometimes called'. He also notes

'Exhibitions of the Irish Jig, however, are occasionally given at Highland games and there are two or three of our professional dancers who excel at it'.

We have never made any attempt to collect versions of these two dances and do not know to what extent they altered over the years. We have, however, noted that nearly all the teachers of whom we have knowledge in England also taught versions of these dances. They were popular all over the north of England where they were often taught, along with other 'character' dances and 'fancy' dances, together with older country dances and the ballroom dances then in vogue. In our first reference in this Chapter we noted 'The Blackamoors Jig' and it is of interest that several dancing-masters in the north west counties of England taught a dance called 'The Jolly Nigger Dance' in which the children blacked their faces and wore a simulation of the costume of the music hall 'minstrel show' once so popular.

6

Clog-Dancing

Clog-dancing, involving the beating out of a musical rhythm with the toes and heels, was popular throughout England and the Lowlands of Scotland within living memory and has undergone a popular revival within recent years. The clogs referred to were those with wooden soles and heels and leather uppers worn by working people in town and country. To prolong the life of the soles they often had a narrow band of iron or rubber nailed under the sole and heel round the outer edge – caulkers.

There were two forms of clog-dancing. The first was extempore dancing in which the dancers fitted such steps or beats as they wished to the music, rarely repeating the same sequence of steps each time they danced. This form of dancing was popular on the street corner where young men would make the sparks fly with iron-shod clogs on cobbled streets. It was also popular in the crowded pub where dancers would compete for a pint of beer or a pair of clogs given by the landlord for the dancer executing the greatest number of steps. It was generally the noise made by the dancer's feet beating out the rhythm which was the attraction, not the look of the dancing. Regular dancers often kept a pair with fancy tooled leather uppers for dancing rather than wearing their iron-shod clogs.

In the second form of clog-dancing, set sequences of movements were used and were usually repeated in the same order by a dancer each time they danced although the order might vary from one dancer to another. The ordered sequence was sometimes known as a complete dance with its own name. With this more exact form two separate styles can be distinguished. In one, the movements are very close and compact and the whole emphasis is on the virtuoso beating of the feet to the music. In the other, the dancer performs wider movements from side to side and makes full use of the floor space available and the steps are obviously designed to be seen by an audience. This second, more formalised style possibly originated, along with other solo dances, on the eighteenth century stage. There, an evening's entertainment consisted of a long play, a short comedy and one or two song or dance acts interspersed throughout the programme. There are numerous reports of such solo dances in Edinburgh and Glasgow newspapers including a 'Clog Hornpipe' danced by a Mr Bristow at the Theatre Royal, Edinburgh, in 1819. In the north of England clog hornpipes were danced at the Theatre Royal in Ripon in 1854.

Over the years the different styles of performance mingled and, in the late nineteenth century, clog-dancing became popular on the music hall stage where many of the well-known stars such as Dan Leno and Charlie Chaplin included it in their acts. At this time the dancing became more competitive and formal competitions were organised, both in the provinces and in London and Glasgow. Every few years 'World Championships' were held and Dan Leno won a magnificent belt as the World Champion in 1880. He subsequently lost the title and the belt was stolen from the winner but Dan won a new belt at Oldham in 1883. In Glasgow, 'Championships' were held in the Britannia Music Hall in Trongate in the 1880s. It is of interest that, at some of these competitions, the judges sat *under* the stage to judge the dancers by the beat of their feet to the music. There were claimants to the title 'World Champion' up until at least 1900 but whether these claims were as a result of competitions or individual challenges is not known. For example, at least one dancer, Robert Doran of Maryport, Cumbria, issued a challenge half a dozen times in the local newspapers. When the challenge was not accepted he declared himself 'Champion of Cumberland'.

Our first encounter with clog-dancing was in Dalbeattie in Kirkcudbrightshire (now joined with Wigtownshire and Dumfriesshire to form Dumfries and Galloway) where we found that it had been quite common up until about 1920. The only named clog dances mentioned to us were the Liverpool Hornpipe and the Lancashire Hornpipe. These had been taught at classes around about 1900 but, in general, the steps seemed to have depended on the taste and inventive ability of the dancers. At one time the young men of the district used to vie with each other to see who could create the best steps. Clog-dancing had been equally popular in Kirkcudbright itself but it died out earlier than in Dalbeattie. The clog-dancing of the style of the music hall was popular only amongst young men. It is probable that it was taught to young girls but did not remain popular with them as they grew up. In the north west of England we learnt that as girls developed a more mature figure they found the bouncy action of clog-dancing uncomfortable before the advent of the brassiere in 1912. There was also the fact that the popular venue for much of the dancing was in the public houses and few girls would frequent them.

Another of our informants, Mr William Lawson of Lanark, who was seventy-eight years old when we met him in 1958, learnt his dancing firstly from 'Professor' Blackley. The old style teachers often adopted the title of 'Professor' and Mr Blackley was widely known by that title all over Lanarkshire and Dumfriesshire. Mr Blackley had been taught by an equally well-known teacher, John Muir, and he began teaching himself in about 1880. Mr Lawson later took lessons from Mr Willy Service who was an all-round dancer who taught ballroom dancing as well as specialising in step-dancing. Mr Lawson's solos included the Highland Fling, Sword Dance, Shan Trews, Jacky Tar and the Irish Jig as well as clog-dancing. In addition, he knew and taught 'big-boot' dancing. This was 'tap' type dancing in which boots two feet or so in length were worn!

The clog dances which Mr Lawson knew were the Liverpool Hornpipe,

Lancashire Hornpipe and the Mathieson Hornpipe. We know nothing of the last one and have not met it again. It was possibly made up locally by, or for, some-one of that name. He had at least twenty-one steps for the dances and, like other dancers, he used to have small bells attached to the laces of his clogs, or on the sides, but later had 'jinglers' in the heels of the clogs. These consisted of lead balls or 'chuckie-stanes' placed in a groove in the base of the heel and then cov-ered with a brass plate. Mr D G MacLennan also told us that he performed the Liverpool Hornpipe wearing clogs with 'jinglers'.

In Wigtownshire, another teacher, Mr Thomas Shanks, learnt his ballroom dancing in about 1900 from 'Professor' McQuiston who held classes all over Ayrshire and Wigtownshire. When Mr Shanks was about sixteen he learnt step-dancing from Mr Peter Marshall, and, after attending his classes for a year or two, worked in partnership with him for a while. By 1914 Mr Shanks was working on his own and his repertoire included the Highland Fling, Sword Dance, Shan Trews, Sailor's Hornpipe, Irish Jig, Liverpool Hornpipe and a Clog Dance. As we recorded in our book on social dancing [42], most of the dancing-masters could both dance and play the fiddle at the same time and would play for their own classes, often using the fiddle bow to administer a corrective tap to un-ruly pupils. Mr Shanks was no exception and, in addition, he was a piper. He performed his clog-dancing in special clogs (not his working clogs) with bells on the front and 'jinglers' in the heels, but for the Liverpool Hornpipe he wore Highland dancing pumps. His pupils would have worn their best shoes or boots and many would have worn clogs as their every day footwear at that period.

Other informants in this area confirmed that, in their young days around 1900, clog-dancing was widespread. It was performed at concerts, done in the kitchens and often on the plates at the bottom of the coal pits. These plates were sheets of steel, roughly four feet by two feet and half an inch thick, nailed to wooden planks, on which the hutches of coal could be slewed round to change direction. Many people did not have formal tuition but 'picked it up'. Girls danced as well, as clog-dancing was not considered unfeminine, but it was not popular with them.

On the other side of the country clog-dancing was equally popular. Mr William Adamson, whom we mentioned in Chapter 1 as teaching throughout East Fife, learnt a Liverpool Hornpipe and Lancashire Hornpipe from his father, together with a distinct Clog Hornpipe. We visited Mr Adamson at his home in Kingskettle, Fife, several times from 1956 until 1960 and we are indebted to him for his great contribution to our knowledge of social dancing as well as solo dances. He died in 1966 at the age of eighty-six. Mr Adamson danced the first two dances in Highland dancing pumps which had heels made of several layers of leather added to them, but he used clogs with bells under the instep for the Clog Hornpipe. The occurrence of clog-dancing in Fife is not an isolated in-stance in that part of the country; we learnt from other sources that a Clog Hornpipe was also included in the repertoires of teachers in Arbroath and Perth. Mr James Neill, had the music for a Clog Dance amongst the collection of music used for his finishing balls. Like most teachers, Mr Adamson and Mr Neill played the fiddle for their classes and for their own dancing. When teaching solo dances Mr Adamson held his fiddle under his right arm, the bow in his right hand pointing forward. He strummed the strings with his right hand whilst fingering the strings with his left hand.

These dances are not, of course, strictly Scottish in origin, although local version and variations obviously arose. They are an example of the spread of a popular form of entertainment from the music hall stage just as earlier styles of dancing spread from the more formal stage. Their spread was made easier by the increased facilities for travel and communication in the late nineteenth century. One Scottish writer commenting on the style of performance of other dances when the music was played too fast, wrote in 1887, 'the thing degenerates into the railway speed performance of a clog dance in a pantomime' [43]. The dances Liverpool Hornpipe and Lancashire Hornpipe, which had such widespread popularity, may possibly have originated in Lancashire where this form of dancing was particularly popular and, because the sequences were actually named, they endured where other local sequences would have been ephemeral. We feel that those dances that we have recorded are part of the history of solo dancing in Scotland and we give instructions for several dances in Chapter 12.

7

The Dirk Dance

Throughout the literature there are frequent references to a Dirk Dance. As in the case of the Sword Dance there is nearly always some confusion about the form of the dance. It is often not clear whether it is a dance for two men simulating a fight or a dance for one. The references are often to a dance called 'Macinorsair'.

For instance, in 1806, Sir John Sinclair, a member of the committee arranging the Edinburgh piping competition for the Highland Society of London, wrote to Mr Palliser, Factor to the Duke of Atholl, that 'slow Highland dances, emblematical of war or courtship' should be exhibited at the Edinburgh Theatre. He noted that there were one or two persons at Dunkeld who knew the dances and that 'Neil Gow [the well-known musician] knows who they are and the tune that ought to be played'. At that time music for some of the dances at the competitions was played by an orchestra. The letter is endorsed in pencil, 'Alex^r. Gow – Peter Robertson "The Battle", "Mc an Fhorsair" – played by Donald Dewar'. The Duke of Atholl's descendent, writing in 1908, remarked, 'Mc an Fhorsair (the Forester's Son) was the ancient Sword-dance, quite different from "Gille Callum"' [44]. In the MS records of the Edinburgh competitions for 1841 it is noted that, amongst the prizes was 'Two Guineas for Dirk Dance. J MacBeth, John Thompson'.

In 1822 General Stewart, writing about the story of the Earl of Crawford dancing in Hungary, which we noted in the chapter on the Sword Dance, adds as a footnote, 'This dance was called "Makinorsair". I have seen it performed by old men, but it has now disappeared. As arms were not in use in later times, an oaken staff supplied the place of the sword' [45]. Thus, the report of the piping competition seems to imply that two men danced together, as the dance was called 'The Battle' but it could equally apply to individual performances as was the case with the Earl of Crawford.

In *The Scottish Gael*, James Logan wrote:

> The dirk dance is a curious remain of the ancient amusements of the Gael, but from the change of manners, few of the Highlanders have now the least knowledge of it. … This performance has been represented in London, where two brothers, of the name of MacLennan, were almost the only individuals who could execute it, but the species of dance which is now known does not appear to be the same as the

ancient. One James MacPherson, aged 106, several years since, saw the two persons execute this dance, and declared it was not, by any means, in the old national way.

This was definitely a dance for two and the two brothers MacLennan were great-uncles of D G MacLennan from whom his eldest brother, William, also a famous dancer, learnt the dance. Mr MacLennan noted in his book *(op. cit.)* that in the revised edition of *The Scottish Gael*, 1876, the date of the last performance of the dance in London, is given as 1850. In a letter Mr MacLennan stated that he and his brother danced the Dirk Dance together and used the tune 'Biodag air MacThomais' or 'Biodag air MacAlasdair' both of which are given by K N MacDonald in *Puirt-a-Beul* (Glasgow, 1901) who translates the titles as 'Thomas' son wears a dirk' and 'MacAlister wears a dirk'. Again these are simply nonsense rhymes set to the music as in 'Gille Callum da' pheigin' used for the Sword Dance, as described in Chapter 3.

In bringing the story of the Dirk Dance up to the present day one of the most interesting descriptions of the 'ancient' dance is given by Sir John Graham Dalyell in his *Musical Memoirs of Scotland* (Edinburgh, 1849). He is also writing of the piping competitions in Edinburgh but he gives a long, vivid description of the Dirk Dance:

> A sort of tragi-comic *savage dance*, called the Dirk Dance, was exhibited as of native origin, for the first time, at the competition of 1841. Whether it has been transmitted from earlier times or is merely of modern – very recent contrivance, as some assert – may be questioned. Here a dancer appears brandishing a dirk or poniard, lays it on the stage and dances round it. While he is describing a wide circuit another coming forth snatches up the weapon. The owner having a second in reserve they fight: one is stabbed, and falls; the victor, dragging him to a suitable place, dances round his body in a very savage style, then slaps one foot which begins to quiver, next a hand, which quivers also, after this the other hand, which quivers – and as all three members quiver a further slap on the other foot produces symptoms of animation. Whiskey is now offered to the resuscitant, who proving incapable of the draught, most of it is swallowed by the victor himself. He raises the wounded man, then able to share the proffered beverage, restoration follows, and both dance together.

This description is of great interest for two reasons. It will be seen later that parts of the description could apply to a dance taught in Canada early this century but, in addition, it bears a great resemblance to an old miming dance, Cailleach an Dùdain (The Old Woman of the Mill-dust). Dalyell seems to accept that the dance may well have been of 'recent contrivance' and it is just possible that some dancers, hearing that formerly there had been a Dirk Dance, evolved a fighting dance from the old miming dance. As far as we know the earliest reference to Cailleach an Dùdain is in Alexander Campbell's *The Grampians Desolate (op. cit.)* as one of the dance-songs to which Dannsa na Cailleach (The Old Woman's Dance) was performed. The account probably refers to the Perthshire Highlands *c.* 1780. The dance was known in the Hebrides and we collected a version in Benbecula in 1953. The best description of the dance is in an unpublished MS which was in the possession of the Right Reverend Kenneth Grant, Bishop of Argyll and the Isles, in the 1950s who gave us permission to reproduce it [46, 47].

The description was written by Father Allan MacDonald and probably refers to Eriskay in the late nineteenth century:

> There is a dance called 'Cailleach an durdain' – 'The Carlin of the dust'. It is a Punch and Judy dance and has a special pipe tune for itself called 'Cailleach an Durdain'. Two take part in the dance – an old man and an old trembling shivering hag (a man dressed in punch attire does her part). The old hag comes in trembling and quivering with a stick in her hand and her husband similarly armed. They fight with the sticks – dancing all the time. Finally the old man thrusts his stick into her body and she falls down dead. The old man beats his hands and howls most atrociously as it occurs to him that he has murdered the old woman. The sudden change from anger and animosity to broken-heartedness for the loss of his partner in life is ridiculous. He bends over her only to find out more surely that she is dead. The lamentation is heart-rending. Again and again he bends over her and again his sorrow is only intensified. He bends down and touches her boot and the foot rises a little and quivers away most singularly. The old man regains a little confidence. He bends down again and touches the other foot, and it too begins to shake incessantly. At these signs of returning life he bursts out into hysterical laughter. He touches the hands one by one. They too begin to quiver. The old carlin stretched out on the floor with her two feet and two hands quivering looks ridiculous to a degree and the spectators nearly drown the piper with their uproar. The old man then bends down and touches her hair and up she springs with renewed life and they both rush into each other's arms gleefully.

There is a ritual element in this dance that makes it of extreme interest. The man-woman, and the death and resurrection, are features of many ritual performances elsewhere in the world. The reference to mill-dust is an indication that, at one time, the old woman may have been disguised by blacking her face. The mill-dust or *dùdain*, is the dark dust from a small variety of oats which were grown in the Isles. When the oats were threshed with a flail the dust made the thresher's face quite black.

In the version we collected in Benbecula we were told 'it is not a dance really, but a sort of play', the death and resurrection having been forgotten. Two men dance it, the one playing the old woman wearing a coat and skirt with a shawl over his head. The old woman is supposed to be fond of whisky and the husband often comes home from work to find her out drinking. The dance begins with the husband coming in, stick in hand, and dancing round looking for his wife. The old woman then enters, leaning on a stick and 'shaking all over with fear and the effects of drink'. Her husband dances round her beating her with his stick. She makes no attempt to defend herself and, finally, he kicks her on her backside and she falls over. She lies on the floor, quivering all over, while her husband dances round her, kicking her and brandishing his stick. Finally he kicks her to her feet and chases her from the room. The performance took 15 to 20 minutes. The words of the first verse of the song which we also collected in Benbecula can be translated as:

Carlin of the mill-dust (thrice) keep thy rear to me!
Carlin of the mill-dust (twice) keep thy back to me, keep thy quarter to me!
Carlin of the mill-dust (twice) over with it! back with it! keep thy quarter to me!
Carlin of the mill-dust (twice) down with it! up with it! let it not be brought down (?) !
  Keep thy back to me! Keep thy quarter to me!

A more mystic version of the dance is given by Alexander Carmichael in *Carmina Gadelica* (Edinburgh, 1900) in which he refers to the stick as a 'druidic wand'. When the old woman is lying on the floor he lifts up each hand and foot in turn, breathes on them and touches them with the stick and they come to life. Finally he breathes into her mouth and touches her heart with the stick and she comes to life.

We mentioned earlier a Dirk Dance taught in Canada at the beginning of this century. This is fascinating dance and we feel it should be included in this account. It was taught to us by Mrs Mary Isdale MacNab of Vancouver. In 1948 Mrs MacNab, a well-known teacher for many, many years, came over to the Royal Scottish Country Dance Society Summer School at St. Andrews. At this time she also taught in London and, as pupils of Jack McConachie, we attended these sessions. We became friends and, on subsequent visits to this country, she stayed with us at our home on Merseyside. Mrs MacNab died in 1966 shortly after we had visited her at her home in Vancouver.

Mrs MacNab had the custom of 'selling' dances to favoured pupils and friends with the stipulation that the particular dance should be their personal dance, not to be taught to anyone else. In 1952 she offered us the Dirk Dance for a nominal sum. It bears a striking resemblance to Logan's description of a dancer brandishing the dirk, laying it on the floor and dancing round it in a wide circuit.

Mrs MacNab was born in Glasgow but her family emigrated to Canada in 1907 when she about ten years old. She had already had dancing lessons from Mr E E Henderson in Glasgow, and, shortly after going to Vancouver, she took lessons from Mr D C Mather. She and her sister had individual lessons from him and either her mother, or Mr Mather himself, insisted that they write down all the instructions for the dances in their exercise books. Mrs MacNab knew little of Mr Mather except that he came from Lochcarron in Ross-shire where he had been piper to 'a lady'. This was Lady Ann Murray, at Courthill.

Mrs MacNab had the impression that Mr Mather's forbears came from Perthshire but we know only that he was an orphan and was brought up at the Royal Caledonian School at Bushey, Hertfordshire where he would have been taught to dance and pipe. The school was founded in 1815 for orphans of Scottish parentage and families of the Scottish regiments. We well remember the exhibitions of dancing by the children from there at the Wembley Scottish Society in the 1940s. When he left school in 1887 Mr Mather entered the service of Lieutenant Colonel Stewart MacDougall of Lunga in the Treshnish Isles, near Mull. He was later piper to various other land owners. He was a well-known competitor at piping competitions and several of his own compositions have been published. He also took prizes for dancing at various Games including those at Stornoway on Lewis in 1893, the first time that professionals took part. He returned to Stornoway in the winter of 1893–4 and held classes in piping and dancing. We are indebted to Mr J C MacLean, who was Secretary of the Gourock Highland Association, for much of the information about Mr Mather.

In 1899 Mr Mather emigrated to Canada and, sometime after 1914, went to America where he died in a car accident in 1941. At the time of his death he was living in Montana. His medals for piping were returned to Scotland, to the Castle Wynd Museum in Inverness. Some time between 1907 and 1914 he taught Mrs MacNab and her sister the Dirk Dance. This had about fifteen steps of which we have six. As we said earlier it bears some resemblance to the dance noted by Dalyell in that the dancer brandishes the dirk, lays it on the floor, dances round it, and there is the miming of savage striking with the dirk. At one point the dirk is held in the teeth. Were it not for that one movement the dance would seem to portray much more nearly the use of a sword, for in combat a dirk is held point downwards in the fist, not held aloft to flourish. If that were indeed the case the dance would resemble the Sword Dance performed by the Earl of Crawford who flourished 'a naked broadsword to the evolutions of the body'.

We have already noted that Mr D G MacLennan and his brother danced a Dirk Dance which had been learnt from their great-uncle. Mr MacLennan knew Mr Mather well and when we consulted him about the dance from Canada he wrote, 'I can recollect Mather being in our house about 1892, when I was trying the Dirk Dance (dual) with W^m, and W^m was arranging a Dirk solo out of it, though *it* was not danced anywhere. So, Mather *may* have worked up a dance from that'. It is of interest to note that, in the 1950s, Dr Frank Rhodes found memories of a Dirk Dance in Cape Breton Island, Nova Scotia, amongst very old people who had come originally from Moidart and from Barra [48] (see appendix).

We know that teachers all over Scotland made up dances or altered them and perhaps that was the case with the Dirk Dance; we shall never know. The dance we give is a vigorous, exciting one, quite unlike any other solo dance. Tom was reluctant to teach the dance because of Mrs MacNab's stipulation about ownership and only taught it to one other person in his lifetime to ensure its preservation. However, we feel it should now be recorded here or it will be lost forever.

Contents of Dance Instructions

8

Instructions for the Dances

W e should again emphasise that there can be no *correct* version of a dance which has been in existence for many years. Many factors will have influenced its development. Some dancers will forget or misinterpret instructions, some will alter a dance to 'improve' it. Above all, no dancer can copy quite exactly the dancing of another although the reproduction may be very close. Physical attributes, age, etc and practical considerations such as footwear, will all influence a performance. We noted before that, prior to 1914, the light dancing pumps were worn only by professional dancers.

We have collected from many sources and we pay tribute to all the people who gave so freely and happily of their time and knowledge. Details of each informant will be given with the dances. Inevitably, in order to trace the dances back as far as possible, we interviewed elderly people. However, one has only to think of the great ballet teachers giving lessons well after they had retired from active dancing to realise that age is no barrier to teaching.

In the following pages we give the version of a dance which we collected in its most clear and complete form. Where there were really significant differences in versions of steps we note that difference with the name of the source. Other versions of some of the dances have, of course, appeared in other publications but the versions here all make a contribution to the picture of step-dancing in Scotland and our instructions are as accurate as we can make them to reproduce the dances as performed by our informants. In most cases they were checked by repeated visits and by cross-checking with other informants.

Firstly, in order to describe the dances we give details of the basic positions used in the steps and our method of relating the movements of the dancer's feet to the various beats of the music.

The Basic Positions

Before instructions can be given for individual dances it is necessary to give general instructions for basic positions of the feet used throughout the dances. Many professional dancing-masters in Scotland made use of the five basic positions of the feet used in classical ballet, even if they did not explicitly mention them by name, and those classical positions enable us to give a reasonable description of many of the steps which were in common use. These classical positions are given in Diagram 1 in the case in which the *working* foot is the right foot. These positions were first defined by a French dancing-master, Rameau, in 1725 *(op. cit.)*.

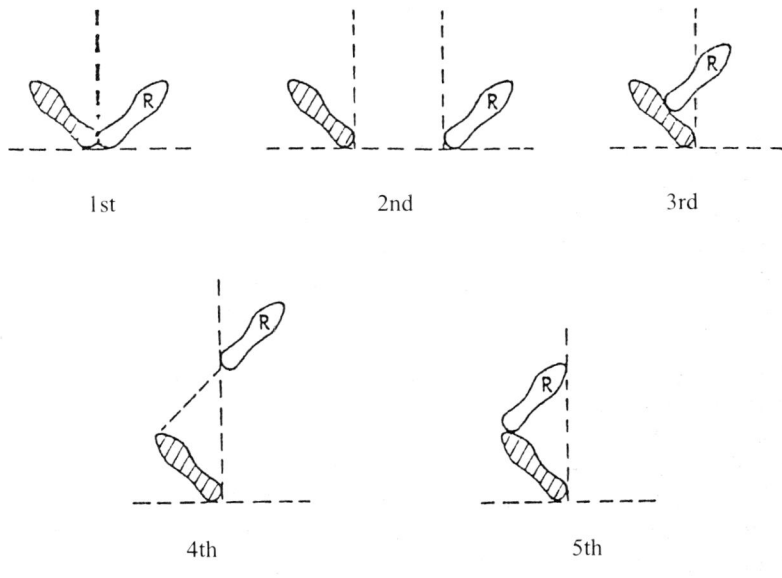

Diagram 1

There are also rear positions corresponding to 3rd, 4th and 5th positions, in which the working foot is placed to the rear of the supporting foot as shown in Diagram 2.

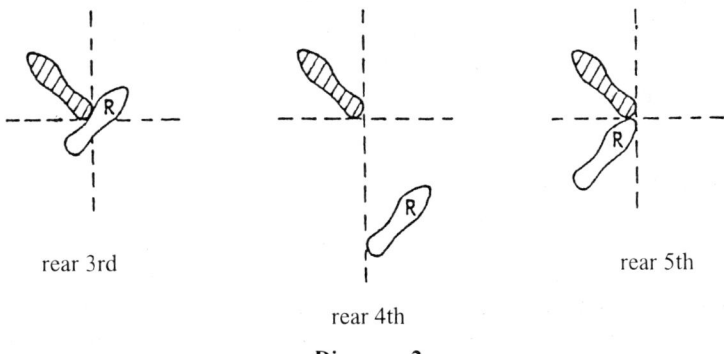

Diagram 2

Although adequate for many steps these positions are not sufficient to be able to give exact descriptions of all the steps used in the solo dances and we therefore need to define further basic positions. For those additional positions we have simply added a qualifying word such as 'semi' or 'intermediate' to the name of the nearest classical position. This is the method also used by the Scottish Official Board of Highland Dancing. In our descriptions of steps the positions given will be precisely those given by our informant in the majority of cases. In the few cases where the position used by the informant is not one of the basic positions we will use the basic position nearest to our informant's actual position. We use R for 'right' and L for 'left' when these words are used as adjectives and RF for 'right foot' and LF for 'left foot' respectively.

In the illustrations of the various positions the *line of direction* is an imaginary line on the ground at right angles to the plane of the dancer's body and is indicated by an arrow. The *supporting* foot is inclined at an angle of 45° to the line of direction. This was the position taught by dancing-masters.

A *ground* position is one in which both feet are in contact with the floor. In the classical 1st, 3rd and 5th positions in Scottish dancing the working foot is placed with the toes and ball of the foot on the floor and with the heel fairly close to the floor. In addition the working foot can also be *pointed* in a *ground* position on the toe, when only the tip of the big toe touches the floor, and it can be placed on the *half-point*, when the pads of the first two or three toes are on the floor but the ball of the foot is not touching the floor, and on the *ball of the foot*, with the pads of the toes and the ball of the foot on the floor.

In the various *aerial* positions the working foot is off the floor. In a *very low aerial* position the toe of the working foot is about one inch off the floor, in a *low aerial* position it is in a horizontal line with the ankle, and in a normal *aerial* position it is in a horizontal line with the centre of the calf of the supporting leg.

The closed positions

A *closed position* is one in which the working foot is in contact with either the supporting leg or foot. As a matter of convenience we include under this heading the various 5th aerial positions, although these are not strictly 'closed' in the sense defined above. The closed positions are thus 1st position, the various 3rd and 5th, and the front and rear leg positions. In these positions, except where stated to the contrary, the feet are at right angles to each other and each is inclined to the line of direction at an angle of 45°. The heel of the supporting foot is fairly close to the ground. The actual height of the heel of the supporting foot from the ground varied considerably from dancer to dancer. It altered, too, according to the dancer's footwear.

1st position

The two feet are placed with heels together with the toes and the balls of the feet on the ground. The heels are just off the floor, both at the same level.

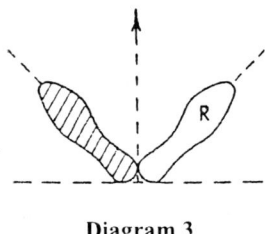

Diagram 3
1st position

3rd position

The working foot is placed with the pads of the toes and the ball of the foot on the floor with the heel just touching the inner edge of the instep of the working foot (the instep being defined as the *upper* surface of the foot between the toe joint and the ankle).

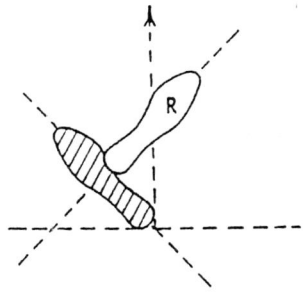

Diagram 4
RF in 3rd position

3rd very low aerial position

The ball of the working foot rests against the inner edge of the instep of the sup-porting foot. The toe of the working foot is about one inch from the floor and the sole of the working foot is at an angle of about 60° to the floor.

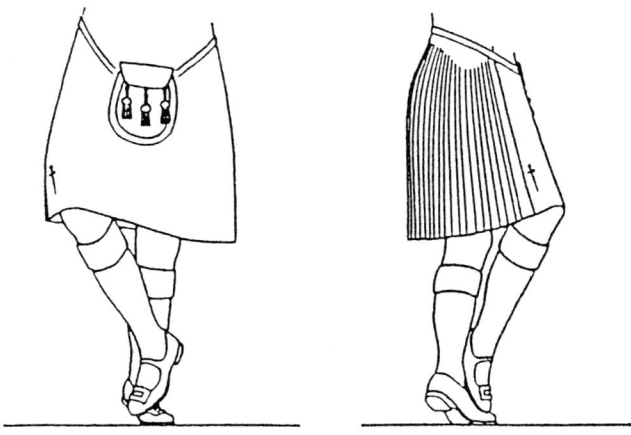

Diagram 5
RF in 3rd very low aerial position

Rear 3rd position

The working foot is placed with the inner edge of the instep touching the heel of the supporting foot. The pads of the toes and the ball of the working foot are on the floor and the heel raised just off the ground.

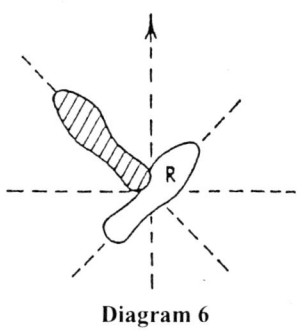

Diagram 6
RF in rear 3rd position

5th position

There are three methods of placing the working foot in 5th position where the working foot touches the big toe joint of the supporting foot.
a. *RF in 5th position.* The RF is placed with the pads of the toes and the ball of the foot on the floor with the heel just touching the top of the big toe of the LF.
b. *Ball of RF in 5th position.* The R heel is raised high off the floor and crossed right over the L toe.

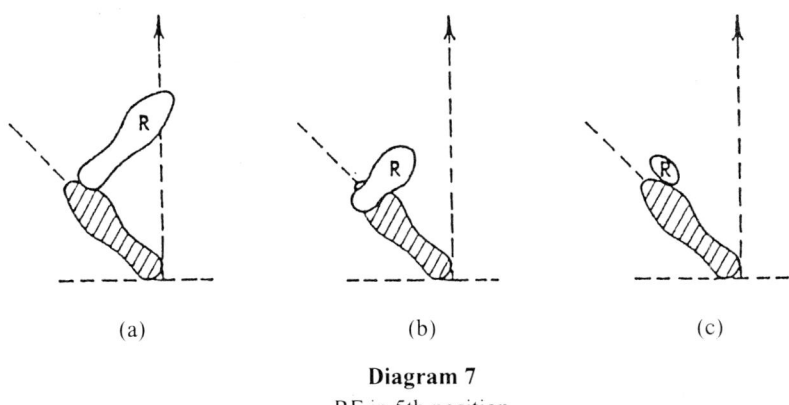

(a)   (b)   (c)

Diagram 7
RF in 5th position

c. *RF on the half-point, or R toe pointed, in 5th position.* The RF is as nearly vertical as possible (this will depend on the stiffness of both the dancer's shoes and ankle-joints), and the R knee points to the side.

5th aerial positions

When the RF is in a 5th aerial position the LF is inclined at $45°$ to the line of direction and the R toe is placed at the appropriate height vertically above the position in Diagram 7(c), with the RF as nearly vertical as possible with the R knee pointed to the side.

Rear 5th position

The big toe of the working foot touches the supporting foot. We use three different methods of placing the working foot in the rear 5th position.

a. *RF in rear 5th position.* The RF is placed with the pads of the toes and the ball of the foot on the floor with the heel just off the floor and the top of the big toe just touching the edge of the L heel.

b. *R toe closed under L instep in rear 5th position.* Both heels are well off the floor and the R toe is right under the L instep.

c. *R toe pointed in rear 5th position.* The RF is as nearly vertical as possible and the R knee points to the side.

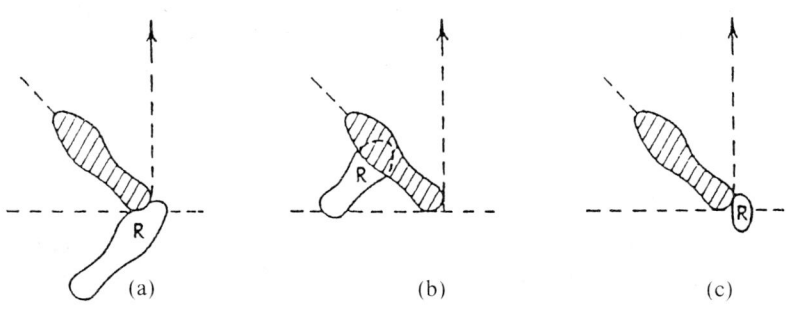

Diagram 8
RF in rear 5th position

Front and rear leg positions

In the front leg position the working foot is placed with the outer edge of the sole against the shin of the supporting leg, with the sole of the foot vertical, and the back of the heel just touching the bottom of the kneecap of the supporting leg. In the rear leg position the working foot is placed with the inner edge of the sole against the back of the calf of the supporting leg, again with the foot vertical and the heel at the same height from the floor as in the front leg position. In both positions the supporting foot is inclined at 45° to the line of direction, with the heel off the floor and the knee of the working foot pointed to the side (Diagram 9).

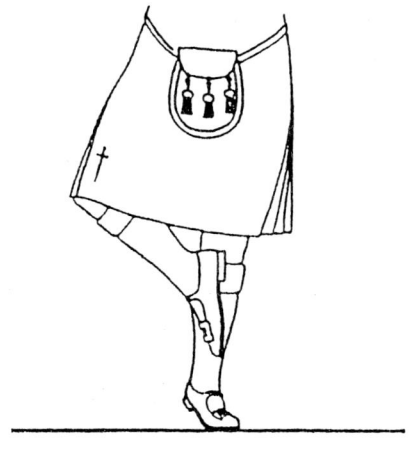

Diagram 9
RF in front leg position

We will also use the terms *low rear leg position* and *very low rear leg position*. In these the working foot is placed against the back of the supporting leg as in the ordinary rear leg position but with the toe of the working foot at the height indicated by the term.

The open positions

An *open position* is one in which the working foot is not in contact with the supporting leg or foot. These positions are the various 2nd and 4th positions and the crossed position.

In an open position, the supporting foot is inclined at an angle of 45° to the line of direction, with the heel off the floor. When the toe of the working foot is pointed in an open position, the knee of the working leg should be straight. When a step or spring is made on to the working foot in an open position, the knee of the working leg should be slightly relaxed.

2nd and 4th positions

The classical 2nd and 4th positions only enable us to describe movements of the working foot to the side, front and rear. We require further positions to enable us to describe movements of the working foot in other directions. To these we give the names '2nd intermediate', '4th intermediate' and 'rear 4th intermediate' and they are shown in Diagram 10, where the working foot is the RF.

The classical positions remained standard throughout the years with the exception of the 4th position. Some teachers, and not only of Scottish dancing, used two variations. Instead of the working foot being taken out at an angle from the *heel,* as in Diagram 10, it was taken out either from the *instep* or from the *toe.* In the very few cases where our informant used the latter position we have used the phrase '4th in front of 5th'.

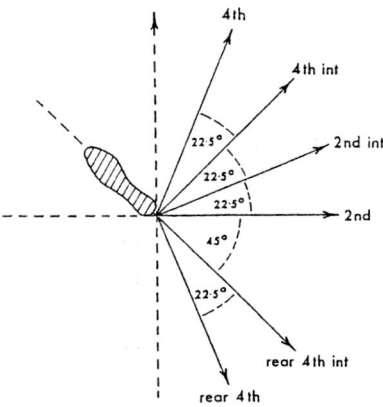

Diagram 10

Notes

i. When the toe of the working foot is pointed in an open position, the working foot is, as far as possible, pointed in the appropriate direction shown in Diagram 10. An exception is the 4th position, where the working foot is inclined at 45° to the *line of direction*. The positions of the working foot in 2nd, 4th int. and 4th positions are shown in Diagram 11.

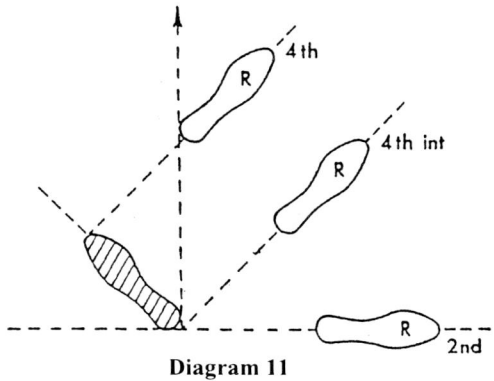

Diagram 11

ii. When a step or spring is made on the working foot in an open position, the working foot is inclined at an angle of 45° to the line of direction. The positions of the RF when a step or spring is made on to it in 2nd, 4th int., 4th and rear 4th positions are shown in Diagram 12. The distance between the heels of the supporting foot and the working foot is approximately one foot's length.

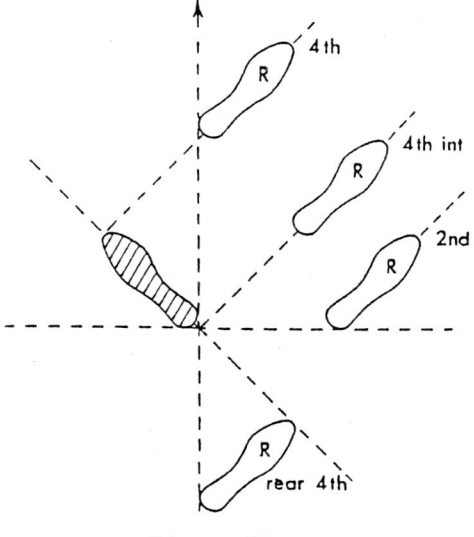

Diagram 12

iii. We also require *semi-open positions*, in which the working foot is placed midway between 1st position and the corresponding full open position. Diagram 13 shows the positions of the feet when a step or spring is made on the RF in semi 2nd and semi 4th positions. In each case the distance between the heels is approximately one half foot's-length.

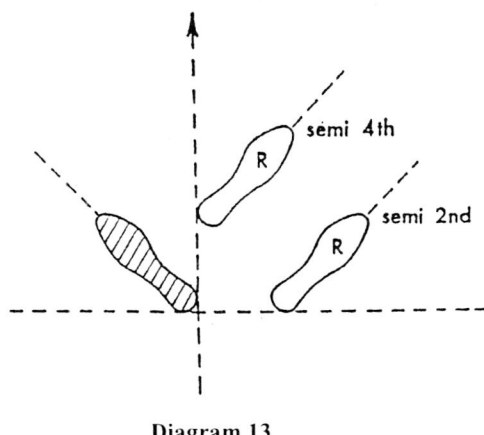

Diagram 13

iv. In the various 2nd and 4th *aerial positions*, the working foot is extended, at the appropriate height, in the directions shown in Diagram 10, the knee of the working leg being kept straight. In the 2nd, 2nd int. and 4th int. aerial positions, the working foot actually points in the directions shown in Diagram 10. In the 4th aerial position, the working foot is inclined at 45° to the *line of direction*, while in the rear 4th and rear 4th int. aerial positions, the toe of the working foot is turned out as far as possible (Diagram 14).

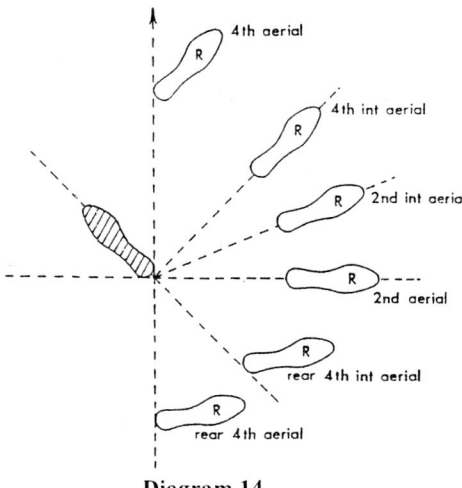

Diagram 14

v. We also require a semi 4th very low aerial position in which the working foot is about one inch vertically above the semi 4th ground position (Diagram 13).

Crossed position

Diagram 15 shows the RF placed in crossed position. The feet are at right angles to each other and equally inclined to the line of direction, and both heels are close to the floor.

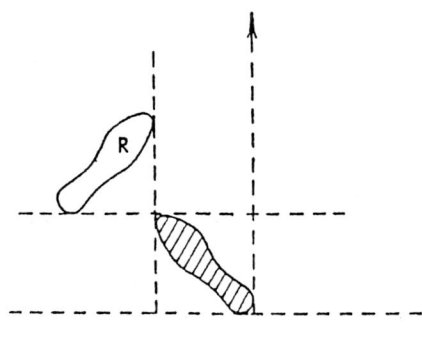

Diagram 15

Hand Positions

We have not generally given hand positions for the dances collected unless the informant had special movements. In these cases they are put under the relevant count of music in bold type within square brackets. Standard 'Games' hands can be used if preferred, i.e. opposite hand to foot or both hands raised.

Counting of the Steps to Music

In our descriptions of steps we describe the movements of the dancer's feet corresponding to the various beats of the music, the musical beats themselves being indicated by a system of counting. This counting of the beats is an important aid in the teaching of steps – beginners tend to find it easier to perform movements to numbers than to perform them to the beats of a particular tune – so that the counting must correspond not only to the beats of the music, but must also be easy to say.

The type of tune used for a dance indicates the counting rhythm. In the dances given here the tunes are either strathspeys, Scotch measures, reels, jigs or hornpipes.

Strathspeys are slow tunes in 4/4 time with the four beats in the bar almost evenly accented although there is, of course, a slightly stronger accent on the first beat of each bar. Many of the beats are made of a semi-quaver and a dotted quaver. The following example shows the form of two typical bars of a strathspey and a good example is 'The Marquis of Huntly's Highland Fling'.

Variations in the counting of steps, similar to those given for hornpipes, can be used.

Scotch measures and **reels** are both quick tunes in Common time and nowadays, are usually written in 4/4 time. A reel is a very smoothly flowing tune, eg, 'The De'il Among the Tailors' and the essential rhythm is a quaver one and the four beats in the bar are almost evenly accented (again with a slightly stronger accent on the first beat). The rhythmic skeleton of a typical bar is thus shown below with the four beats marked 1, 2, 3, 4.

This method of counting the beats, however, is not particularly well suited to the fairly numerous steps performed to reel tunes in which the movements fall only on the first and third beats of the bar. In our descriptions we use the more convenient counts 1 & 2 & as shown below.

A **Scotch measure,** such as 'Flowers of Edinburgh' or 'Petronella', is a much more bouncy tune than a reel. It has a crotchet rhythm with two main beats and two weaker beats in each bar. The rhythmic skeleton of a typical bar is shown below. Here the four beats are most naturally represented by the counts 1 & 2 &, as indicated; the beats are of equal duration but there is a strong accent on the beat 1, a medium one on beat 2, and weak accents on the two beats &.

A *jig* is a quick tune in 6/8 time in which the melodic units are either a crotchet and a quaver or a triplet of quavers. Jigs are further divided into *single* or *double* jigs as the first or the second of these melodic units predominates. Thus a single jig has the essential rhythm:

while a double jig is:

Typical examples of single jigs are 'Scottish Reform' and 'The New Rigged Ship', while 'The Irish Washerwoman' and 'Over the Water to Charlie' are good examples of double jigs.

The other tune type we use is ***hornpipe***. Up until about 1780 the term *hornpipe* appears to have meant a tune in 3/2 rhythm. After 1780, single, double and treble hornpipes appear. In about 1800 the term 'treble hornpipe' was used for horn-pipes in common time. Tunes of this type were used for clog-dancing in both Scotland and England and typical examples are 'Soldier's Joy', 'The White Cockade', 'The Clog Hornpipe' (Navvie on the Line), and 'The Manchester Hornpipe' (Rickett's Hornpipe).

The rhythmic skeleton of a hornpipe is basically eight quavers in a bar and the simplest form of counting would be 1 & 2 & 3 & 4 &. If additional movements are used in dancing a step these can be indicated by counting 1 and a 2 or 1 an & a 2. These can easily be said aloud whilst teaching and written as follows.

1 & 2 & 3 & 4 &

1 & a 2 & a 3 & a 4 & a

Throughout all the instructions for steps, numbers in bold face type indicate the numbers of the bars of music, ie, **1, 2,** etc. and those in ordinary type face are the beats within the bar, e.g. 1 & a. Count **1**.2 refers to the second count in the first bar. Where no instruction is given against the beat of the bar then the dancer pauses for that count.

The timing of the music is the other important factor in recreating these dances. For each of the dances we have recorded the approximate timing as used by the informant when performing the dance for us. Most steps take eight bars of music to perform starting with one foot which is then repeated off the other foot, giving 16 bars in total. We generally give the speed in terms of the number of seconds taken to perform the full 16 bars of music.

9

Dances from the Hebrides

In the following pages we give instructions for those dances from the Hebrides for which we have a reasonable number of steps. We do not give the instructions for Flowers of Edinburgh, Over the Hills and Far Away and Lads with the Kilt although we collected a few steps of each of these which had survived from the teaching of Ewen MacLachlan.

Between 1953 and 1956 we collected information from very many people on South Uist and Benbecula with the help of Dr Frank Rhodes, who also collected on his own. Several of our informants were old enough to remember Ewen MacLachlan and their personal memories included the fact that Ewen's young men pupils usually wore their working boots for the classes and the girls wore ordinary shoes made to measure on the island. Sometimes they would dance in stockinged feet. Ewen himself wore ordinary boots, even when giving an exhibition at a dance. This would mean that the foot positions and, in particular, the pointing of the toes would not be as precise as those of a modern dancer. We are as precise as we can be in our instructions in order to reproduce the way the dances were shown to us by our informants. The descriptions of a particular dance from various informants did, in fact, correspond very closely.

Our informants had, mainly, derived their knowledge from two sources, namely Donald MacDonald and Archie MacPherson, who had danced for D G MacLennan in 1925. Archie MacPherson had only been eleven years old when Ewen was holding his last classes and was too young to attend the classes which were for 'young men and women'; Ewen did not teach anyone under fifteen or sixteen years old. However, Archie watched the older pupils and practised the dances and, at the end of the session when Ewen held his 'dancing-master's ball', he insisted that Archie perform some of the dances. Archie was judged the winner at the competitions in 1925. We were told that Donald MacDonald was a 'comedian' who had concocted the dances from fragments. His versions of some of the dances were certainly different from those derived from Archie MacPherson, thus enforcing our statement about the variations in versions of dances and the reasons for them. According to D G MacLennan, Donald MacDonald himself admitted that some of his versions were not authentic and D G MacLennan 'arranged' the dances to some extent when he published them.

We obtained verification of steps and dances from many people but our main sources of actual steps are given below with their ages when they were interviewed. On South Uist these were:

a. Mrs Annie MacDonald, 89, and her daughter Harriet, *c.* 45, of Daliburgh. Mrs MacDonald's husband, Donald, had learnt his dancing from Ronald Morrison, who was known as Ronald the Dancer and had been a pupil of Ewen. They both knew the dances and were able to show the steps.
b. Donald Walker, *c.* 35, of Daliburgh, who had learnt from Donald MacDonald.
c. Roderick MacLean, *c.* 67, of Kilaulay, Eochar.
d. Angus O'Henley, *c.* 75, of Loch Boisdale. He had learnt his dancing from a visiting teacher and had 'picked up' the local dances.

On Benbecula they were:

e. Angus John MacLennan, *c.* 75, Hacklett. He had learnt from his father who had been a pupil of Ewen.
f. Roderick MacPherson, *c.* 75, of Liniclett Muir. He had also learnt from his own father who was a pupil of John MacMillan, another of Ewen's pupils.

We also collected information from Cissie MacDonald of Arisaig, Inverness. She was a former Highland Games dancer and had learnt her 'Hebridean' dances from Donald MacDonald of Daliburgh. We were also given confirmation of steps by Farquhar MacNeil of Jedburgh. Our most detailed information came from John MacLeod, aged 46, whom we first met in Glasgow in 1953. He was a native of Eochar, South Uist, and had been taught by Archie MacPherson, who was also of Eochar. He had, himself, taught the dances on Barra in the 1930s and was still a very active dancer and was able to teach us virtually complete versions of five of the following dances.

In our descriptions we give our main source and note variations given by other people by their initials. Where possible we give an idea of the speed at which our informants felt the dances should be performed. We do not usually give arm movements as these were not often clearly remembered – indeed, they may not have been standard – and they varied from dancer to dancer. As an indication of suitable movements for a modern dancer, John MacLeod used the Highland Games convention of raising the opposite arm to the working foot. The elbow was approximately at eye level with the lower arm and hand curved slightly in over the head. The fingers were held loosely curved with the thumb and middle finger almost touching, a position derived from the snapping of thumb and middle finger which was always a feature of dancing in Highland Reels. When both feet were moving in rapid succession both arms were raised except for movements such as the 'shuffles' used to complete a step. Then the arms would be placed akimbo on the waist with fingers and thumbs turned back. Where there was a variation from this convention we note it with the description of the dance.

Over the Water to Charlie

We collected two main versions of this dance. The first five steps which we give came from John MacLeod. The last one of these also came from pupils of Donald MacDonald together with the next five. Two variations from pupils of Donald MacDonald are noted. The steps which D G MacLennan obtained from Archie MacPherson are similar to those taught by Donald MacDonald which suggests that a union of all the steps collected by us is a fairly close approximation to the dance as taught by Ewen MacLachlan.

The music used was the jig 'Over the Water to Charlie', although John MacLeod danced to a version of 'Gillean an fheilidh' (The Lads wi' the Kilt) at a speed of 17 seconds per step (16 bars).

The following named movements are used in the description of the dance:

Toe Beat

We describe 'toe beat RF'.

Count	I	Hop on LF taking RF out to 4th int low aerial position
	&	Brush RF in towards 5th position
	a	Beat RF in 5th position
	2	Beat LF in rear 5th position.

The dancer keeps this position for the next two beats, counts & a, and this is to be understood in future where no specific instructions are given for the rest of a bar. When the RF has to be in an *open* position for the beginning of the next bar, it is put there as soon as the weight has been taken on the LF.

D W used a slightly different rhythm in which the first two beats were closer together and the RF was not extended fully on the first beat, with the brush in nearer to 5th position. A McD and H McD had no brush in but gave two beats with the RF near to 5th position.

Heel Beat

We describe 'heel beat RF'.

Count	I	Hop on LF and bring RF to 5th low aerial position
	&	Beat R heel in 5th position
	a	Beat R heel in 5th position
	2	Beat LF in rear 5th position.

Sometimes the R Heel moved in a little or out a little between the two beats. There were the same variations in this as we noted in 'toe beat'.

Ronde

We describe 'ronde RF'. Start with RF in 4th int aerial position.

Count	1	Hop on LF and shake RF (by bending and straightening the knee) back to 2nd int aerial position
	&	Hop on LF and shake RF back to 2nd aerial position
	2	Drop on to RF in rear 5th position.

Shuffles

We describe 'shuffle RF and LF'.

Count	1	Drop on to LF and take RF out to 4th int aerial position
	&	Brush RF in to 5th position and out again
	a	Hold this position
	2	Drop on to RF and take LF out to 4th int low aerial position
	&	Brush LF in to 5th position and out again
	a	Hold this position.

1st step

1	1	Hop on LF placing RF in 2nd position
	2	Hop on LF lifting RF to back leg position
2		Toe beat RF finishing with RF in 5th low aerial position
3, 4		Perform bars 1, 2 contrariwise
5, 6		Repeat bars 1, 2 finishing with RF in 4th int low aerial position
7, 8		Shuffle LF, RF, LF, RF
		Perform bars 1 to 8 contrariwise.

2nd step

1	1	Hop on LF closing R toe to L toe (LF pointing straight to the front and RF turned in)
	2	Hop on LF closing R heel to 1st position
	&	Carry RF out to 4th int aerial position
2		Ronde RF moving to the left on the hops and end with LF in a (2nd?) low aerial position ready for the next bar
3, 4		Perform bars **1, 2** contrariwise
5, 6		Repeat bars **1, 2** finishing with LF in 4th int low aerial position
7, 8		Shuffle RF, LF, RF, LF
		Perform bars **1** to **8** contrariwise.

3rd step

1		Toe beat RF
2	1	Jump forward on to RF swinging LF round to the front
	2	Jump forward on to LF swinging RF round to the front
3		Toe beat RF
4	1	Hop back on LF with RF in low front leg position
	&	Hop back on LF carrying RF round to low back leg position
	2	Drop on to RF cutting LF away to 4th int aerial position
5–8		Perform bars **1** to **4** contrariwise
		Repeat bars **1** to **8**.

4th step

1		Toe beat RF finishing with RF in 4th int aerial position
2	1	Hop on LF and shake RF in to front leg position and out again
	2	Hop on LF and shake RF in to back leg position and out again
3		Toe beat RF finishing with RF in low front leg position
4	1	Hop on LF with RF in low front leg position
	&	Hop on LF taking RF to low back leg position
	2	Hop on to RF cutting LF to 4th int aerial position
5–8		Perform bars **1** to **4** contrariwise
		Repeat bars **1** to **8**.

5th step

1, 2	Toe beat RF and RF again
3, 4	Toe beat LF and LF again
5, 6	Toe beat RF and LF
7, 8	Shuffle RF, LF, RF, LF
	Perform bars **1** to **8** contrariwise.

6th step

1	1	Hop on LF placing RF in semi 2nd position
	2	Hop on LF closing ball of RF to 5th position
2		Perform bar **1** contrariwise
3, 4		Toe beat RF and LF
5, 6		Perform bars **1, 2** contrariwise
7, 8		Shuffle RF, LF, RF, LF
		Perform bars **1** to **8** contrariwise.

7th step

1	1	Step forward on to RF with LF hanging loosely behind
	2	Step back on to LF with RF hanging loosely in front
2		Ronde RF finishing with LF held loosely in front
3, 4		Perform bars **1, 2** contrariwise
5, 6		Toe beat RF and LF
7, 8		Shuffle RF, LF, RF, LF
		Perform bars **1** to **8** contrariwise.

8th step

I	I	Step on to R heel in semi 2nd int position
	&	Close LF to RF (instep to heel)
	2	Step on to R toe in semi 2nd int position
	&	Close LF to RF
2	I	Step on to R heel in semi 2nd int position
	&	Close LF to RF
	2	Step on to R toe in semi 2nd int position
3, 4		Perform bars 1, 2 contrariwise
5, 6		Toe beat RF and LF
7, 8		Shuffle RF, LF, RF, LF
		Perform bars 1 to 8 contrariwise.

There is a lift or slight hop on the LF before bar 1 and on the RF before bar 3.

9th step

I	I	Hop on LF placing RF in 2nd position
	2	Hop on LF lifting RF to back leg position
2		Heel beat RF finishing with RF in 4th int aerial position
3		Ronde RF, landing on RF slightly to the left of 5th rear position
	&	Step on to L heel in semi 2nd position
4	I	Close RF to LF (instep to heel)
	&	Step on to L toe in semi 2nd position
	2	Close RF to LF
5–8		Perform bars 1 to 4 contrariwise
		Repeat bars 1 to 8.

This step is also performed with toe beat R in bar 1.

10th step

I		Toe beat RF finishing with RF in low front leg position
	&	Hop on LF moving RF round to low back leg position
2	I	Drop on to RF and lift LF to low front leg position
	&	Hop on RF moving LF round to low back leg position
	2	Drop on to LF and carry RF out to 4th int low aerial position
3, 4		Toe beat RF and LF
5, 6		Perform bars **I, 2** contrariwise
7, 8		Shuffle RF, LF, RF, LF
		Perform bars **I** to **8** contrariwise.

The dancer should make a full turn to the R in bar **2** and a full turn to the L in bar **6**.

This step is also performed with ronde RF in bar **I**.

Highland Laddie

Of all the 'Hebridean' dances this was the best preserved. Roderick MacPherson danced ten steps which were confirmed in outline by Angus John MacLellan, who had all but the ninth step, and by Donald Walker and John MacLeod who had seven and eight steps, respectively. Farquhar MacNeil also knew the first six steps. We give Roderick MacPherson's version and note variations.

The music used was the reel, 'Highland Laddie' played at a speed of 16 seconds per step.

The following named movements are used in the description of the dance:

Toe beat

We describe 'toe beat RF'.

Count   I   Hop on LF and beat RF in semi 4th int position
        &   Beat RF in 5th position
        2   Beat LF in rear 5th position.

When the RF has to be in some *open* position for the beginning of the next bar, it is put there as soon as the weight has been taken on the LF.

Heel beat

We describe 'heel beat RF'

Count   I   Hop on LF and beat R heel in 5th position
        &   Beat R heel in 5th position
        2   Beat LF in rear 5th position.

Spring, step, close

We use this name to describe a movement which is danced in many traditional styles. Where to step and how to close depends on individual dancers. 'Spring, step, close to the R' as danced by R MacP is as follows:

Count   I   Spring on to both feet with RF in 5th position
        &   Step on to RF in semi 2nd int position
        2   Close LF to RF (instep to heel).

A J MacL closed instep to heel while J MacL closed with ball of LF in rear 5th position. The movement is also done diagonally forward with a step to semi 4th int position.

Hop, step, close

We describe 'hop, step, close to the R'.

Count   I   Hop on LF and take RF out to 2nd int low aerial position
         &   Step on to RF in 2nd int position
         2   Close LF to RF (instep to heel).

Again, exact positions varied from dancer to dancer.

Ronde

We describe 'ronde RF'.

Count   I   When starting with RF in 4th int aerial position: Hop on LF and shake RF (by bending and straightening the knee) back to 2nd int aerial position.
               If starting with the weight on the RF: Drop on to LF and take RF out to 2nd int aerial position
         &   Hop on LF and shake RF back to 2nd aerial position
         2   Drop on to RF in rear 5th position.

The LF is put in the appropriate position for the next movement as soon as the weight has been taken on the RF.

Points

We describe 'four points starting with the RF'. This is used to finish all steps on bars **7, 8**.

Count   I   Spring on to LF with RF in semi 4th int position
         2   Spring on to RF with LF in semi 4th int position
               Repeat bar I.

There is one variation which must be mentioned here. R MacP and D W used four points to finish a step but A J MacL and J MacL finished with four shuffles as in Over the Water.

1st step

I	I	Spring on to LF with RF in 2nd int position
	2	Hop on LF and make a full turn to the L with RF in back leg position
2		Spring, step, close to the R
3, 4		Spring, step, close to the L and to the R
5, 6		Perform bars **I, 2** contrariwise
7, 8		Four points starting with RF
		Perform bars **I** to **8** contrariwise.

D W used 4th int position in bar **I** and toe beat in bars **2, 3** and **4**.

2nd step

I, 2	Toe beat RF and LF
3, 4	Ronde RF and LF
5, 6	Toe beat RF and LF
7, 8	Four points starting with RF
	Perform bars **I** to **8** contrariwise.

Other dancers gave ronde with LF and RF in bars **3, 4**.

3rd step

I, 2	Toe beat RF and LF
3, 4	Hop, step, close diagonally forward with RF and LF
5, 6	Toe beat RF and LF
7, 8	Four points starting with RF moving back to original position
	Perform bars **I** to **8** contrariwise.

The other three dancers with this step gave spring, step, close to the side instead of hop, step, close diagonally forward.

4th step

I	I	Step on to R heel in semi 2nd int position
	&	Close LF to RF (instep to heel)
	2	Step on to R toe to semi 2nd int position
	&	Close RF to LF
2	I	Step on to R heel in semi 2nd int position
	&	Close LF to RF
	2	Step on to R toe to 2nd int position
3, 4		Perform bars I, 2 contrariwise
5, 6		Toe beat RF and LF
7, 8		Four points starting with RF
		Perform bars I to 8 contrariwise.

This step should be danced with a slight syncopation on bars I to **4**.

A J MacL and D W gave this step exactly while J MacL started with a hop on the LF with RF in 3rd aerial position followed by a step on to the R heel in 3rd position, close LF, step on to R toe in 2nd position, close LF, step on to R heel in 2nd position, close LF.

5th step

I, 2		Toe beat RF and LF
2	I	Spring forward on to LF swinging RF through a semicircle to the front
	2	Spring forward on to RF swinging LF through a semicircle to the front
4	I	Hop back on RF
	2	and hop back again on RF swinging LF back through a semicircle to rear semi 4th int aerial position
5, 6		Toe beat RF and LF
7, 8		Four points starting RF
		Perform bars I to 8 contrariwise.

There were the following variations:

In bar **3** A L MacL swung the loose foot round to the front, the others left it hanging loosely behind. J MacL took the foot straight through to the front to drop on it but D W swung it forward in a semicircle before dropping on it.

In bar **4** J MacL and A L MacL came back with three beats, viz, 1 Hop back on RF, & Hop back on RF, 2 Drop back on to LF, ending with RF in 4th int aerial position or a loose front aerial position. D W came back with two beats in bar **4**, but followed them with toe beat LF and RF (instead of RF and LF).

6th step

I	I	Spring on to RF and take (shake?) LF out to 2nd int aerial position
	&	Hop on RF and shake LF back to 2nd aerial position
	2	Drop on to LF and lift RF to low front leg position
	&	Hop on LF moving RF round to low back leg position
2	I	Drop on to RF and lift LF to low front leg position
	&	Hop on RF moving LF round to low back leg position
	2	Drop on to LF and lift RF to low front leg position
3, 4		Repeat bars I, **2**
5, 6		Toe beat RF and LF
7, 8		Four points starting with RF
		Perform bars I to **8** contrariwise.

D W danced the following variant:

I	I	Spring on to both feet with RF in 5th position
	&	Carry RF out to 2nd int aerial position
	2	Hop on LF and shake RF back to 2nd aerial position
2	I	Step on to RF slightly to L of rear 5th position
	&	Step on to LF in semi 2nd position
	2	Step on to RF slightly to L of 5th position
3, 4		Perform bars I, **2** contrariwise
5, 6		Toe beat LF and RF
7, 8		Four shuffles starting with LF.

Blue Bonnets

Versions of this dance were collected from many people. We give seven steps from John MacLeod and then three other steps, one from Farquhar MacNeil, one from Annie and Harriet MacDonald and Cissie MacDonald and one from Angus O'Henley. It was danced to the tune of the same name and John MacLeod danced at a speed of 18 seconds for a step.

The following named movements are used in the description of the dance:

Hop-backstep

The movement begins with a hop on the last beat of a bar.

Count	&	Hop on LF moving RF to low back leg position
	I	Drop on to RF and lift LF to low front leg position
	&	Hop on RF moving LF round to low back leg position
	2	Drop on to LF and lift RF to low front leg position (or take RF out to any 'open' position required for the next bar).

In the instructions we give this as:

	&	Hop on LF and,
I		hop-backstep RF and LF.

Blue Bonnets (B.B.) step

All the steps include a 'Blue Bonnets' step (B.B.) and a close.
We describe first the version danced by J MacL with the RF.

		Begin with RF in 4th int aerial position
3	I	Drop on to RF pointing LF in rear 5th position
	&	Hop on RF and take LF to 4th int aerial position
	2	Hop on RF pointing LF in 5th position
	&	Hop on RF and take LF to 4th int aerial position
4	I	Drop on to LF pointing RF in rear 5th position
	&	Hop on LF and take RF to 4th int aerial position
	2	Hop on LF pointing RF in 5th position.

Blue Bonnets (B.B.) step

As danced by D W, A MacD, H MacD, C MacD and A O'H

		Begin with RF in 4th int aerial position
3	I	Hop on LF with RF in 4th int aerial position
	&	Beat RF in towards 5th position
	a	Drop on to RF in 5th position with LF in low back leg position
	2	Hop on RF pointing LF in 5th position
	&	Hop on RF and take LF to 4th int aerial position
4		Perform bar **I** contrariwise.

D W and A O'H performed this step very 'tightly' with a double beat in 5th position instead of a beat in.

Close

We describe first 'close with RF' as danced by J MacL.

7	I	Hop on LF and place ball of RF in 5th position, pivot R foot to swing R heel over LF and out again
	&	Swing R heel over LF and out again
	2	Swing R heel over LF and out again, this time taking the RF out to the side
8	I	Spring on to RF with LF in semi 4th int position
	2	Spring on to LF with RF in semi 4th int position.

F McN kept the R heel over the LF on beat **I.2.**

'Close with RF' as danced by the others:

7	I	Hop on LF brushing RF in from 4th int low aerial position to 5th position and,
	&	out again
	2	Hop on LF and brush RF in and,
	&	out again
8	I	Spring on to RF with LF in semi 4th int position
	2	Spring on to LF with RF in semi 4th int position.

D W and A O'H had smaller movements in bar **I** than described here, while C MacD had full shuffles in bar **2**.

1st step

I	I	Step on to RF in 2nd int position
	&	Close LF to RF (instep to heel)
	2	Step on to RF in semi 2nd int position
2		Perform bar **I** contrariwise
3, 4		B.B. step with RF
5, 6		Repeat bars **I, 2**
7, 8		Close with RF
		Perform bars **I** to **8** contrariwise.

The dancers moved forward on bars **I, 2, 5, 6** rather than to the side and moved back either by moving back on the other bars or by turning and returning back on the second half of the step. For the way in which F McN danced the first bar of this step, see the instructions for bar **I** of the 1st step of Scotch Measure.

2nd step

I	I	Step on to RF in 4th int position
	&	Close LF to RF
	2	Step on to RF in semi 4th int position
	&	Hop on RF and,
2		hop-backstep LF and RF
3, 4		B.B. step with LF
5, 6		Perform bars **I** and **2** contrariwise
7, 8		Close with RF
		Perform bars **I** to **8** contrariwise.

C MacD and A O'H moved forward on the first two bars.

3rd step

I	I	Spring on to both feet with RF in 5th position
	&	Step back on to RF in semi rear 4th int position, taking it over L ankle
	2	Step on to LF slightly to right of 5th position
	&	Hop on LF and,
2		hop-backstep RF and LF
3, 4		B.B. step with RF
5, 6		Repeat bars I and 2
7, 8		Close with RF
		Perform bars I to 8 contrariwise.

There was some variation in the performance of bar I of the 3rd step. A MacD, H MacD and C MacD stepped forward on to the RF and then carried LF in front of that. D W simply beat the RF in 5th position and then beat the LF in rear 5th position.

4th step

This step is essentially the same as **Step 3**, except that a complete turn to the R is made in the first two bars. J MacL insisted that the whole turn be made on bar **2** while D W started the turn with the toe beat described in Over the Water.

5th step

	&	Hop on LF and take RF to 4th low aerial position
I	I	Brush RF back to just behind 1st position
	&	Brush RF forward to just in front of 1st position
	a	Brush RF back to just behind 1st position
	2	Brush RF forward to 4th low aerial position
	&	Drop on to RF and take LF to 4th low aerial position
2		Perform bar I contrariwise
3, 4		B.B. step with LF
5, 6		Perform bars I, 2 contrariwise
7, 8		Close with RF
		Repeat bars I to 8 contrariwise.

For the first two bars D W gave Hop four times on LF and each time brush RF from back and to front again.

6th step

1	1	Spring on to LF with RF in semi 4th int position
	2	Spring into true 2nd position (i.e., both feet in 2nd position)
2	1	Spring on to RF with LF in semi 4th int position
	&	Spring on to LF with RF in semi 4th int position
	2	Spring on to RF with LF in semi 4th int position
3, 4		B.B. step with LF
5, 6		Perform bars **1, 2** contrariwise
7, 8		Close with RF
		Perform bars **1** to **8** contrariwise.

7th step

1	1	Spring on to LF and point R toe in 5th position
	&	Hop on LF and place R heel in 5th position
	2	Hop on LF and point R toe in 5th position
2		Perform bar **1** contrariwise
3, 4		B.B. step with RF
5, 6		Repeat bars **1, 2**
7, 8		Close with RF
		Perform bars **1** to **8** contrariwise.

8th step

1	1	Slide on to RF in 4th int position
	&	Hop on RF there with LF in low back leg position, and face half R
	2	Step on to LF in semi 4th position (relative to the new direction)
	&	Hop on LF and,
2		hop-backstep RF and LF moving back and ending facing front in original position
3, 4		B.B. step with RF
5, 6		Repeat bars **1, 2**
7, 8		Close with RF
		Perform bars **1** to **8** contrariwise.

F McN also performed this step with a full turn to the R on bar **2**.

9th step

I	I	Hop on LF and take RF to 2nd int position
	&	Hop on LF and bring RF in to 5th position
	2	Spring on to RF and take LF to 2nd int position
	&	Hop on to RF and bring LF in to 5th position
2	I	Spring on to LF and take RF to 2nd int position
	&	Hop on LF and bring RF in to 5th position
	2	Spring into true 2nd position (i.e. both feet in 2nd position)
3, 4		B.B. step with RF
5, 6		Repeat bars I, 2
7, 8		Close with RF

Perform bars I to **8** contrariwise.

10th step

	&	Hop on RF and,
1, 2		hop-backstep LF, RF, LF, RF, moving backwards through a small clockwise circle to end facing the front
3, 4		B.B. step with RF
	&	Hop on LF and,
5, 6		hop-backstep RF, LF, RF, LF, moving backwards through a small anti-clockwise circle to end facing the front
7, 8		Close with RF

Perform bars I to **8** contrariwise.

Tullochgorm

John MacLeod had eight of the original ten steps and we give these as Steps 1 to 7 and Step 10. Farquhar MacNeil confirmed six of these and gave Step 8 whilst Annie MacDonald could remember just one step (her first) which we give as Step 9.

The dance was performed to the strathspey tune of the same name at a speed of 12 seconds for a step (8 bars of music). A description of the term 'shuffle' is given with the dance, Over the Water to Charlie.

1st step

1	1	Spring on to LF and take RF out to 2nd position
	2	Hop on LF and lift RF to front leg position
	3	Hop on LF and shake RF out to 4th int aerial position and back
	4	Hop on LF and shake RF out and back again
2		Perform bar 1 contrariwise
3		Repeat bar 1
4		Four shuffles starting with the RF
		Perform bars 1 to 4 contrariwise.

2nd step

1	1	Spring on to LF and lift RF to front leg position
	2	Hop on LF moving RF round to back leg position
	3	Spring on to both feet with LF in 5th position
	&	Step on to LF in semi 2nd int position
	4	Close RF to LF (rear 5th position)
2		Perform bar 1 contrariwise
3		Repeat bar 1
4		Four shuffles starting with RF
		Perform bars 1 to 4 contrariwise.

3rd step

I	I	Spring on to LF and lift RF to front leg position
	2	Hop on LF moving RF round to back leg position
	3	Spring on to both feet with RF in 5th position
	&	Step on to RF in semi 2nd int position
	4	Close LF to RF (rear 5th position)
2		Perform bar I contrariwise
3		Repeat bar I
4		Four shuffles starting with RF

Perform bars I to 4 contrariwise.

4th step

I	I	Spring on to LF and take RF out to 2nd position
	2	Hop on LF and lift RF to front leg position
	3	Spring on to RF and take LF out to 2nd position
	4	Hop on RF and lift LF to front leg position
2	I	Spring on to LF and take RF out to 2nd position
	2	Hop on LF and lift RF to back leg position, turning L
	3	While facing in the opposite direction, hop on LF and take RF out to 2nd position
	4	Hop on LF and lift RF to front leg position, completing the turn to L to face the original direction
3, 4		Perform bars I and 2 contrariwise

Repeat bars I to 4.

5th step

I	I	Spring on to LF and point R toe in 5th position
	2	Hop on LF and beat R heel in 5th position
	3	Spring on to RF and point L toe in 5th position
	4	Hop on RF and beat L heel in 5th position
2		Four shuffles starting with RF
3, 4		Perform bars I and 2 contrariwise

Repeat bars I to 4.

6th step

As the 5th step but with 'heel, toe' instead of 'toe, heel'.

7th step

As the 3rd step, but with 'back leg position' and then 'front leg position' instead of *vice versa.*

8th step (F McN)

1	1	Drop on to RF and point L toe in rear 5th position
	2	Drop on to LF and point R toe in 5th position
	3	Drop on to RF and point L toe in rear 5th position
	4	Drop on to LF and point R toe in 5th position
2	1	Drop on to RF and beat LF in back leg position
	2	Hop on RF and beat LF again in back leg position
	3	Hop on RF moving LF round to front leg position
	4	Hop on RF and shake LF in 4th int aerial position
3, 4		Perform bars 1 and 2 contrariwise
		Repeat bars 1 to 4.

9th step (A MacD, her 1st step for the dance)

1	Hop four times on LF placing R heel, ball of RF, R heel, ball of RF in 5th position
2	Perform bar 1 contrariwise
3	Repeat bar 1
4	Four shuffles starting with LF
	Perform bars 1 to 4 contrariwise.

10th step

As the 1st step, but with a full turn to the L on the first bar, and with full turns to the R and to the L on bars 2 and 3.

Miss Forbes

We describe the seven steps remembered by Cissie MacDonald and note the variants known by Annie MacDonald. The tune used is the reel of the same name sometimes noted as 'Miss Forbes' Farewell to Banff'. We do not have any record of the speed danced by the informants.

The following two movements are used in the description of the dance.

Miss Forbes (M.F.) step

We describe 'M.F. step with RF'

3	I	Spring on to both feet with RF in 5th position
	2	Hop on RF with LF in low back leg position
	&	Swing LF out to 4th int low aerial position
4		Perform bar I contrariwise.

Close

We describe 'close with RF'

7	I	Hop on LF brushing RF in from 4th int low aerial position to 5th position and,
	&	out again
	2	Hop on LF and brush RF in and,
	&	out again
8	I	Spring on to RF in 1st position, take LF out to 4th int low aerial position and brush it in to 5th position
	&	Brush LF out again to 4th int low aerial position
	2	Spring on to LF in 1st position, take RF out and brush it in and,
	&	out again.

1st step

	&	Hop on LF and take RF to 4th low aerial position
I	I	Step on to RF in 4th position
	&	Close LF to RF (toe under instep)
	2	Step on to RF in semi 4th position
	&	Hop on RF and take LF to 4th low aerial position
2	I	Step on to LF in 4th position
	&	Close RF to LF (toe under instep)
	2	Step on to LF in semi 4th position
3, 4		M.F. step with RF
	&	Hop on LF and,
5, 6		repeat bars I and 2
7		Close with RF
		Perform bars **I** to **8** contrariwise.

Dancing in a small room C MacD turned on bars 5 and 6 and returned to the original position in the final eight bars ending facing front. A MacD interchanged bars **3** and **4** with bars **5** and **6**.

2nd step

I	I	Hop on LF pointing RF to 4th in front of 5th position *
	&	Keeping LF on floor, place RF in 4th in front of 5th position
	2	Keeping RF on floor, beat LF in its own position
	&	Pause with both feet on floor
2	I	Step on to RF slightly to L of rear 5th position
	&	Step on to LF in semi 2nd int position
	2	Step on to RF slightly to L of 5th position
	&	Pause with both feet on floor
3, 4		Perform bars I and 2 contrariwise
5, 6		M.F. step with RF
7, 8		Close with RF
		Perform bars **I** to **8** contrariwise.

* See note about different versions of 4th position in section on Basic Steps.

A MacD gave a different version of bar **1**, namely:

1	**1**	Step forward on to RF crossing slightly over to the L
	&	Hop on RF with LF in low back leg position
	2	Step back on to LF in original position
	&	Hop on LF with RF in low back leg position.

3rd step

1	**1**	Step on to R heel in semi 4th int position
	&	Close LF to RF (toe to heel)
	2	Step on to R toe in semi 4th int position
	&	Close LF to RF (toe under foot)
2		Repeat bar **1**
3, 4		Perform bars **1** and **2** contrariwise
5, 6		M.F. step with RF
7, 8		Close with RF
		Perform bars **1** to **8** contrariwise.

4th step

1	**1**	Hop on LF with RF in rear 5th position
	2	Hop on LF with RF in 5th position
	&	Carry RF round to back leg position
2	**1**	Drop on to RF in rear 5th position, carrying LF up to front leg position and round to back leg position
	&	Drop on to LF in rear 5th position, lifting RF to front leg position
	2	Keep weight on LF and take RF through back leg position down to rear 5th position (R toe under L foot)
3, 4		Perform bars **1** and **2** contrariwise
5, 6		M.F. step with RF
7, 8		Close with RF
		Perform bars **1** to **8** contrariwise.

5th step

I	I	Drop on to LF and take RF out to 4th aerial position
	&	Brush RF back to just behind 1st position and forward to 4th aerial position again
	2	Hop on LF
	&	Brush RF back and forward again
2		Perform bar **I** contrariwise
3, 4		M.F. step with LF
5, 6		Perform bars **I** and **2** contrariwise
7, 8		Close with RF
		Perform bars **I** to **8** contrariwise.

6th step

Note: For bars **I, 2, 5** and **6** count 1 an & 2 an & as shown below.

1 an   2 an   &   3 an   &   4 an   &

I	I	Drop on to LF and lift RF just clear of the floor above 5th position with the knee forward
	an	Beat RF out towards 4th position and back again
	&	Drop on to RF in 1st position and lift L knee well up in front with lower leg hanging loosely
	2	Hop on RF with LF in this position
	an	Beat LF out towards 4th position and back again
	&	Drop on to LF in 1st position and lift R knee up in front
2		Repeat bar **I**
3, 4		M.F. step with RF
5, 6		Repeat bars **I** and **2**
7, 8		Close with RF
		Perform bars **I** to **8** contrariwise.

7th step

I	I	Moving RF forward and to the R in a semi-circle, spring on to RF in 2nd position
	&	Step on to LF in semi 4th position in front of 5th position
	2	Keeping LF on the floor, beat RF in 2nd position
	&	Hop on RF and point LF to 4th in front of 5th position
2	I	Step on to LF in 4th in front of 5th position
	&	Hop on LF with RF in low back leg position
	2	Step back on to RF in previous position
	&	Pause with both feet on the floor
3, 4		Perform bars I and 2 contrariwise
5, 6		M.F. step with RF
7, 8		Close with RF
		Perform bars I and 8 contrariwise.

Scotch Measure

This dance was remembered by Farquhar MacNeil, Donald Walker and Annie MacDonald. We give six steps from Farquhar MacNeil, the first of which was remembered by Annie MacDonald, together with three steps from Donald Walker. The tune used was 'Dornoch Links' and Farquhar MacNeil danced at a speed of 22 seconds per step.

The following three named movements are used in the description of the dance.

Spring, step, close

We describe 'Spring, step close to the R'

Count | 1 | Spring on to both feet with RF in 5th position
| & | Step on to RF in 2nd position
| 2 | Close LF to RF in rear 5th position.

Scotch Measure (S.M.) step

The movement starts with hop LF, step RF, step LF on counts & 1 & 2, with double beats inserted before each change of supporting foot.

	&	Hop on LF and lift RF just clear of the floor above 5th position with the knee forward
	a	Beat RF out towards 4th position and back again
5	1	Drop on to RF in 1st position and lift L knee well up in front with the lower leg hanging loosely
	&	Hop on RF in this position
	a	Beat LF out towards 4th position and back again
	2	Drop on to LF in 1st position and lift R knee up in front
6		Repeat these movements.

We print this as:

	&	Hop on LF and,
5, 6		S.M. step.

A MacD finished with RF in 4th int low aerial position, F McN with RF above semi 2nd position with the toe pointing in towards LF, both ready for 'close'. D W used a backstep with a hop instead of the above.

Close

We describe first 'close with RF' as danced by F McN.

7	I	Hop on LF and place ball of RF in 5th position, pivot RF to swing R heel over LF and out again
	&	Swing R heel over LF and out again
	2	Swing R heel over LF and hold this position
8	I	Spring on to RF with LF in semi 4th int position
	2	Spring on to LF with RF in semi 4th int position.

We now describe 'close with RF' as danced by D W and A MacD.

7	I	Hop on LF brushing RF in from 4th int low aerial position to 5th position and,
	&	out again
	2	Hop on LF and brush RF in and,
	&	out again
8	I	Spring on to RF with LF in semi 4th int position
	2	Spring on to LF with RF in semi 4th int position.

1st step

	a	Hop on LF and,
I	I	step on to RF in 2nd int position with the body turned slightly to the R
	&	Close LF to RF (instep to heel)
	2	Swivel on both feet to the L to end with L heel over R instep
	a	Hop on RF
2		Perform bar I contrariwise
3, 4		Repeat bars I and **2**
	&	Hop on LF and,
5, 6		S.M. step
7, 8		Close with RF
		Perform bars I to **8** contrariwise.

D W danced the first four bars forward with no hop.

2nd step

I	I	Hop on LF and lift RF to front leg position
	2	Hop on LF moving RF round to back leg position
2		Spring, step, close to the R
3, 4		Perform bars I and 2 contrariwise
	&	Hop on RF and,
5, 6		S.M. step
7, 8		Close with LF
		Perform bars I to 8 contrariwise.

3rd step

I		Spring, step close to the R
2	I	Spring on to RF with LF in semi 4th int position
	&	Spring on to LF with RF in semi 4th int position
	2	Spring on to RF with LF in semi 4th int position
3, 4		Perform bars I and 2 contrariwise
	&	Hop on LF and,
5, 6		S.M. step
7, 8		Close with RF
		Perform bars I to 8 contrariwise.

4th step

I	I	Spring on to both feet with RF in 5th position
	2	Spring on to both feet, both in 2nd position
2	I	Spring on to both feet with RF in 5th position
	&	Spring on to both feet with LF in 5th position
	2	Spring on to both feet with RF in 5th position
3, 4		Perform bars I and 2 contrariwise
	&	Hop on RF and,
5, 6		S.M. step
7, 8		Close with LF
		Repeat bars I to 8 contrariwise.

5th step

I		Spring, step close to the R
	&	Carry RF up through front leg position and round to back leg position
2	I	Drop on to RF in rear 5th position, carrying LF up to front leg position and round to back leg position
	&	Drop on to LF in rear 5th position, lifting RF to front leg position
	2	Keep weight on LF and take RF through back leg position down to rear 5th position (R toe under L foot)
3, 4		Perform bars I and 2 contrariwise
	&	Hop on LF and,
5, 6		S.M. step
7, 8		Close with RF
		Perform bars I to 8 contrariwise.

6th step

As 5th step but with a full turn to the R in bar **2**.

7th step

I	I	Step on to R heel in semi 2nd int position
	&	Close LF to RF (instep to heel)
	2	Step on to R toe in semi 2nd int position
	&	Close LF to RF
2	I	Step on to R heel in semi 2nd int position
	&	Close LF to RF
	2	Step on to R toe in semi 2nd int position
	&	Hop on RF with LF in 3rd low aerial position
3, 4		Perform bars I and 2 contrariwise
	&	Hop on LF and,
5, 6		S.M. step
7, 8		Close with RF
		Perform bars I to 8 contrariwise.

8th step

1	1	Step on to RF in semi 4th position
	&	Hop on RF leaving LF hanging loosely behind
	2	Step back on LF in original position
2	1	Beat RF in 1st position
	&	Beat LF in 1st position
	2	Beat RF in 1st position
3, 4		Perform bars **1** and **2** contrariwise
	&	Hop on LF and,
5, 6		S.M. step
7, 8		Close with RF
		Perform bars **1** to **8** contrariwise.

9th step

1	1	Spring on to both feet, both in 2nd position
	&	Spring on to LF with RF in semi 4th int position
	2	Spring on to both feet, both in 2nd position
	&	Spring on to RF with LF in semi 4th int position
2		Repeat bar **1**
3	1	Step on to RF in 4th position
	&	Close LF to RF (instep to heel)
	2	Step on to LF in semi 4th position
4		Perform bar **3** contrariwise
	&	Hop on LF and,
5, 6		S.M. step
7, 8		Close with RF
		Perform bars **1** to **8** contrariwise.

Aberdonian Lassie

This version was collected from Farquhar MacNeil in 1953 when he was living in Jedburgh. In 1989 a young Swedish dancer and researcher, Mats Melin of Stockholm, learnt a version of the dance from Mrs Katie-Anne MacKinnon of Barra. Mrs MacKinnon had learnt the dance from Mr MacNeil who has been back in Barra and involved with dancing for a number of years. It is only to be expected that, after a passage of nearly forty years, there will be some variations in present-day versions. Our notes of the version which we collected were in rather a rough form and I am indebted to Mats Melin for editing them for me.

This was one of the earliest dances which we collected and it was not until later that we collected the many Reel steps which are now used in the Highland Fling (see Chapter 4). The steps in this dance bear many similarities and with hindsight it may be that Aberdonian Lassie is also simply a collection of Reel steps.

Music – we did not note any particular tune for the dance but today it is danced to the jig, 'The Quaker's Wife'. Farquhar MacNeil danced at a speed of 16 seconds per step.

Hand movements are given bold italic in square brackets.

1st step

1	1	Spring on to LF and point R toe in 2nd position
	2	Hop on LF and place RF in rear leg position
2	1	Spring forward on to RF and point L toe in 2nd position
	2	Hop on RF and place LF in rear leg position
		[L hand raised in bar 1, R hand raised in bar 2]
3	1	Hop on RF and place L toe in 5th position moving forward
	2	Hop on RF and place L heel in 5th position continuing forward
4		Repeat bar **3** contrariwise moving forward
		[Arms akimbo]
5,6		Repeat bars **1** and **2** contrariwise, still moving forward
		[R hand raised in bar 5 and L hand raised in bar 6]
7	1	Spring on to RF and point L toe in 2nd position
	2	Making a half turn to the right, hop on RF plaacing LF in rear leg position. The dancer is now facing in the opposite direction to that in which he began.
8	1	Hop on RF and point L toe in 2nd position
	2	Hop on RF and place LF in front leg position
		[R hand raised]
		Repeat bars **1** to **8** contrariwise.

NB: Bars **7** and **8** will be referred to as 'Close'.

2nd step

1	1	Hop on LF and place R toe in 2nd position
	2	Hop on LF and place RF in rear leg position
	and	Place R heel about 6" to the right of L instep
	a	Rock the RF to place the ball of the foot on the ground transferring weight to it; the heel should be kept low off the ground
2	1	Close LF to flat 5th rear position
	and	Place R heel about 6" to the right of L instep
	a	Rock the RF to place the ball of the foot on the ground transferring weight to it; the heel should be kept low off the ground
	2	Close LF to flat 5th rear position
	and	Place R heel about 6" to the right of L instep
	a	Rock the RF to place the ball of the foot on the ground transferring weight to it; the heel should be kept low off the ground
		[L hand raised]
3, 4		Repeat bars **1** and **2** contrariwise
5, 6		Repeat bars **1** and **2**
7, 8		'Close'
		Repeat bars **1** to **8** contrariwise.

3rd step

1	1	Hop on LF and point R toe in 2nd position
	2	Hop on LF and bring RF to rear leg position
2	1	Hop on LF and bring RF to front leg position
	2	Hop on LF and shake RF in 4th int aerial position and leave it in this position
		[L hand raised]
3	1	Spring on to both feet with LF in 5th position
	2	Hop on RF and shake LF in 4th int aerial position
4	1	Bring ball of LF to rear 5th position, crossed behind RF
	and	Step on RF to 2nd position
	2	Bring ball of LF to 5th position, crossed in front of RF
		[Both arms circle up in front of the body, out and down the sides to meet low in front of the body again]
5, 6		Repeat bars **3** and **4** contrariwise
7, 8		'Close'
		Repeat bars **1** to **8** contrariwise.

NB: On bars **4** and **6** the feet are sliding along the floor in a flattish way during the sideways movement.

4th step

I	I	Hop on LF and point R toe in 2nd position
	2	Hop on LF and bring RF to rear leg position
		[L hand raised]
	and	Hop on LF again and
2	I	Drop on RF in 5th rear position, at the same time raising LF to low front leg position
	and	Hop on RF again and
	2	Drop on LF in 5th rear position, at the same time raising RF to low front leg position
		[This is a backstep with a hop and both arms are raised]
3	I	Drop on RF in 5th rear position
	and	Place L heel in 5th position
	a	Rock the LF to place the ball of the foot on the ground, transferring weight to it; the heel should be kept low off the ground and the position is a flat 5th
	2	Beat on RF in 5th rear position
	and	Place L heel in 5th position
	a	Rock the LF to place the ball of the foot on the ground, transferring weight to it; the heel should be kept low off the ground and the position is a flat 5th
		[Arms akimbo]
4		Repeat bar **3** contrariwise
5, 6		Repeat bars **I** and **2** contrariwise
7, 8		'Close'
		Repeat bars **I** to **8** contrariwise.

5th step

I	I	Hop on LF and point R toe in 2nd position
	2	Hop on LF and bring RF to rear leg position
2	I	Hop on LF and bring RF to front leg position
	2	Hop on LF and shake RF in 4th int aerial position and leave it in this position
		[L hand raised]
3	I	Spring on to both feet with RF in 5th position
	and	Make a short step on to RF in half rear intermediate position, carrying RF past L ankle with the sole of the foot as nearly as possible flat against the L leg and with the R knee turned out
	2	Step on LF crossed in front of RF
	and	Hop on LF bringing RF up to rear leg position
4	I	Backstep with RF bringing LF to low front leg position
	and	Hop on RF and
	2	Backstep with LF bringing RF to low front leg position
		[Both arms raised]
5, 6		Repeat bars **3** and **4** contrariwise
7, 8		'Close'
		Repeat bars I to **8** contrariwise.

6th step

I	I	Hop on LF and place R toe in 2nd position
	2	Hop on LF and place RF in rear leg position
		[L arm raised]
2		Repeat bar I contrariwise
3, 4		Hopping on L foot make a complete turn to the left (as in the Fling)
		[Arms akimbo]
5	I	Drop on RF pointing L toe in 5th position
	2	Spring on to LF pointing R toe in 5th rear position
6		Repeat bar **5**
		[Both arms raised]
7, 8		'Close'
		Repeat bars I to **8** contrariwise.

Bars **5** and **6** are the same as the 'rocking' movement in the modern Fling.

First of August

We give ten steps performed by John MacLeod who danced to the tune 'White Cockade' at a speed of 20 seconds per step (16 bars). Roderick MacLean danced Steps 1, 2, 4 and 7 and Donald Walker also had a version of the dance. The eleventh step comes from Mary Isdale MacNab which she learnt from a Glasgow man, William MacPherson.

Arms were held akimbo with the backs of the fingers against the waist.

This is a 'tap' style dance and so the movement given as Brush LF/RF must be made to give a distinct tap sound.

The special movements used in the dance are given below. Note, the 'Single Treble', 'Double Treble' and 'Break' all start with a 'Catch in'. This runs across the end of one bar (last two beats) and the beginning of the next. For example, where bar 3 gives 'Single Treble RF', this actually starts on the last two beats of the previous bar.

Catch in RF

Count	4	Hop on LF and take RF out to 4th int low aerial position
	&	Brush RF in towards 5th position
	I	Beat RF in 5th position and transfer weight on to it.

Treble LF

Count	&	Brush LF out towards 4th int position
	2	Brush LF in towards 5th position
	&	Beat LF in 5th position and transfer weight on to it
	3	Beat RF in rear 5th position.

Single Treble RF (Catch in RF and Treble LF)

Count	4	Hop on LF and take RF out to 4th int low aerial position
	&	Brush RF in towards 5th position
	I	Beat RF in 5th position and transfer weight to it
	&	Brush LF out towards 4th int position
	2	Brush LF in towards 5th position
	&	Beat LF in 5th position and transfer weight on to it
	3	Beat RF in rear 5th position.

Double Treble RF

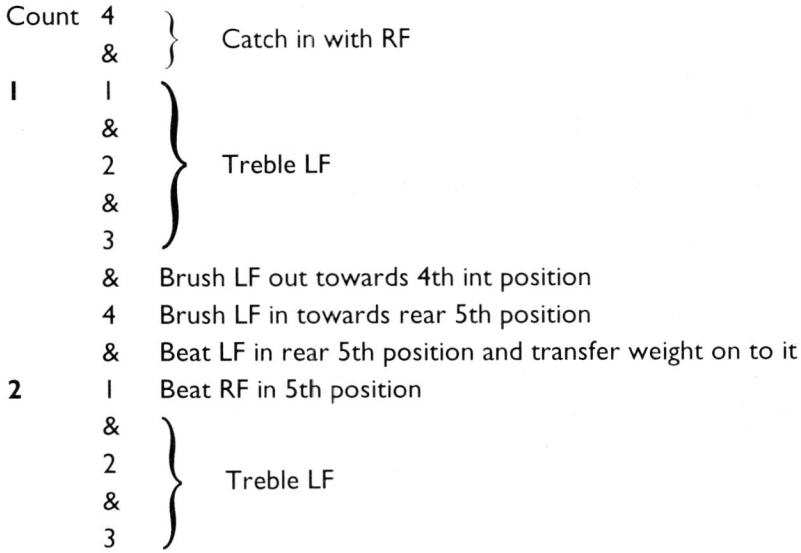

Count	4	}	Catch in with RF
	&	}	
I	I	}	
	&	}	
	2	}	Treble LF
	&	}	
	3	}	
	&		Brush LF out towards 4th int position
	4		Brush LF in towards rear 5th position
	&		Beat LF in rear 5th position and transfer weight on to it
2	I		Beat RF in 5th position
	&	}	
	2	}	Treble LF
	&	}	
	3	}	

Break RF *(always on bars **7, 8** starting on count **6**.4)*

7		Single treble RF
	&	Brush LF out towards 4th position
	4	Brush LF in towards 1st position
	&	Hop on RF
8	I	Step on LF in rear 5th position

Then EITHER:

| | 2 | Step back on RF in rear 4th position |
| | 3 | Spring forward on to LF, bringing RF to rear 5th low aerial position |

OR:

	&	Double beat with RF in 4th position, ending with,
	2	R toe on ground and weight on LF
	3	Drop on R heel.

(The first is from John MacLeod, the second from Mrs MacNab, who collected it in Glasgow in 1952 from William MacPherson.)

1st Step

On bars **1–8** describe a clockwise circle to place, the reverse on **9–16**.

1	1	Hop on LF and shake RF out to 4th int aerial position and back to 5th low aerial position
	2	Repeat count 1
	3	Spring on to RF and bring LF to 5th low aerial position
2		Perform bar **1** contrariwise
3, 4		Single treble RF, LF
5, 6		Repeat bars **1, 2**
7, 8		Break RF

Perform bars **1–8** contrariwise.

2nd Step

1, 2	Double treble RF
3, 4	Single treble LF, RF
5, 6	Double treble LF
7, 8	Break RF

Perform bars **1–8** contrariwise.

3rd Step

1	1	Hop on LF, point R toe in 5th position
	2	Hop on LF, place R heel in 5th position
	3	Spring on to RF, point L toe in 5th position
2		Perform bar **1** contrariwise
3, 4		Single treble RF, LF
5, 6		Repeat bars **1, 2**
7, 8		Break RF

Perform bars **1–8** contrariwise.

4th Step

| Figure a | Figure b | Figure c |

1	1	Jump forward to land on toes with feet together (Fig. a)
	2	Pivot on toes to move heels apart and take weight on heels (Fig. b)
	3	Pivot on heels to turn toes out and take weight on toes (Fig. c)
2	1	Slide both feet together to bring LF into 5th position
	2	Slide on toes back into position in Fig. c
	3	Slide both feet together to bring RF into 5th position
3, 4		Single treble RF, LF
5, 6		Repeat bars 1, 2
7, 8		Break RF
		Perform bars 1–8 contrariwise.

5th Step

As 3rd step but interchange counts 1 and 2 in bar 1.

6th Step (Crabwalk)

On bars **1–8** describe a half circle clockwise to R (facing out from centre of circle).

Complete the circle on bars **9–16**.

1	1	Jump forward to land on flat of feet with toes together and heels apart
	2	Pivot on R heel and L toe to end in 1st position, feet flat on ground, having moved to R
	3	Pivot on R toe and L heel to end as in 1.1 having moved to right
2	1	Repeat count 1.2
	2	Repeat count 1.3
	3	Repeat count 1.2
3, 4		Single treble RF, LF
5, 6		Repeat bars 1, 2
7, 8		Break RF
		Perform bars 1–8 contrariwise.

7th Step

1	1	Step forward on R heel in 4th position with toe pointing out
	2	Step forward on L heel next RF in 1st position, weight on both heels
	3	Step back on R toe in rear 5th position
	4	
	&	Spring, bringing L toe back to starting place,
2	1	and placing R heel in 4th position
	2	Repeat count 1.2
	3	Repeat count 1.3
3, 4		Single treble LF, RF
5, 6		Perform bars 1, 2 contrariwise
7, 8		Break RF
		Perform bars 1–8 contrariwise.

8th Step (Charleston – our name)

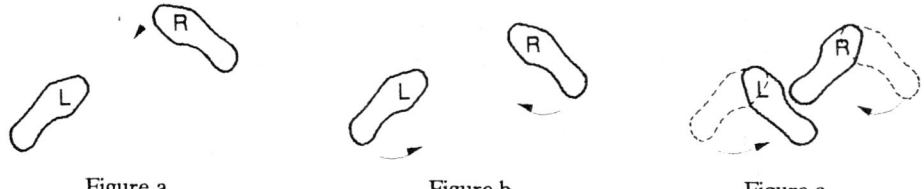

Figure a   Figure b   Figure c

Start with weight on LF, RF in 2nd int low aerial position (Fig. a) toes turned in, 12" apart.

I	I	Put R toe down as in Fig. b and pivot on toes to 3rd position (Fig. c) R heel over LF
	2	Pivot on R toe, taking LF to 2nd low aerial position, toes turned in, 12" apart
	3	Perform beat 1.I contrariwise
	4	
	&	Pivot on L toe, moving RF to 2nd low aerial position as at beginning
2	I	Compress counts 1.I, 2 into I count
	2	Compress counts 1.3, & into I count
	3	Repeat 2.I
3, 4		Single treble RF, LF
5, 6		Repeat bars 1, 2
7, 8		Break RF
		Perform bars 1–8 contrariwise.

9th Step

I	I	Hop on LF and lift RF in front leg position
	2	Step on to RF in 2nd position
	3	Close LF to rear 5th position
2	I	Three backsteps, begin by taking RF to front leg position and,
	2	carry it round behind LF to rear leg position drop on RF in rear,
	3	5th position and repeat with LF, RF while turning once round to R,
3, 4		Single treble LF, RF
5, 6		Perform bars 1, 2 contrariwise
7, 8		Break RF
		Perform bars 1–8 contrariwise.

10th Step

1	1	Spring on to both feet into 5th position, RF in front
	3	Spring on to 5th position, LF in front
2	1	Spring into 5th position, RF in front
	2	Spring with feet apart
	3	Spring into 5th position, LF in front
3, 4		Single treble LF, RF
5, 6		Repeat bars **1, 2** contrariwise
7, 8		Break RF
		Perform bars **1–8** contrariwise.

11th Step

Move to R on **1, 2** and to L on **5, 6**. Feet should be about 6" apart in **1** and **2** (and when repeated) except on the two stamps.

	4	Hop on LF, RF in 2nd low aerial position, toe turned in
	&	Tap with R toe
	a	Beat R heel just in front of 1st position and transfer some weight to it
1	1	Beat with L heel on spot
	&	Step on R toe slightly to R of 1st position
	2	Step on L toe beside RF
	&	Step on R heel slightly to right of 1st position
	3	Step on L heel beside RF
	&	⎫
	4	⎬ Repeat counts 1. & 2 & 3
	&	
2	1	⎭
	2	Stamp on flat of RF
	3	Stamp on flat of LF
3, 4		Single treble RF, LF
5, 6		Perform bars **1, 2** contrariwise
7, 8		Break RF
		Perform bars **1–8** contrariwise.

(TMF noted this in 1975 as move to R on **1–8**, back on **9–16** ie bars **5, 6** are: Repeat bars **1, 2**.)

10

The Highland Fling

Today the Highland Fling consists of six or eight steps but prior to 1900 a dancer usually performed ten steps. The steps used were primarily a selection taken arbitrarily from the steps used in the part of the Highland Reel danced to strathspey rhythm. We know of at least sixty possible steps and, in the following pages we give the most interesting of those. The order in which we give the steps has no particular significance except for Step 1. This was almost invariably used as the first step whatever selection was danced.

We note first those steps collected from oral tradition and then those from literary sources. We list our sources at the end of the chapter and indicate them by letters in brackets at the beginning of each step.

The tune 'The Marquis of Huntly's Highland Fling' or any strathspey can be used at a speed of 40–42 bars per minute. McIntyre North in his *Book of the Club of True Highlanders*, written in 1880, suggests 38–48 bars per minute.

The following named movements are used in the description of the dance:

Fling[1]

This occupies one bar of music. We give the movement performed with RF.

Count	1	Hop on LF and place RF in 2nd position
	2	Hop on LF and raise RF to rear leg position
	3	Hop on LF and carry RF round to front leg position
	4	Hop on LF and bring RF to rear leg position

When the working foot moves round the leg from back to front or vice versa, it should be kept as close to the supporting leg as possible.

The movement is also performed while turning. For instance, in 'Fling RF, turning to the L', a full turn to the L is made on counts 2–4. About half the turn is made on count 2 and the remainder more or less equally on counts 3 and 4. In

---

[1] The Official Board calls this step 'Shedding'; McIntyre North calls it 'Round the leg', Scott Skinner 'Round the knee' and D Anderson refers to it as 'Spread and swing three'.

this way the dancer is slowing down towards the end of the turn so that his balance is well under control. Care should be taken to avoid beginning the turn too early, i.e. on count 1.

Backstep

This occupies one count of the music, but several backsteps are usually combined to fill one bar. 'Backstep RF' is normally performed starting with the RF in front leg position, and is as follows:

Count 1   Carry RF round to rear leg position and, without pausing, slide it
            down behind the L leg and drop on it, at the same time raising
            LF quickly to front leg position.

The movement is effectively that of sliding the RF down behind the L leg *and ankle* and under the L foot, so that the R toe takes the place formerly occupied by the L toe. It is essential here to have the toes and knees turned well outwards, and care should be taken to ensure that the RF does pass through rear leg position (and not a slightly lower position) before sliding down the L leg. The movement can also be performed starting with the working foot in rear leg position. In either case the finishing position is the same.

It is very probable that this step is the one described by Logan in *The Scottish Gael*, written in 1831 [34]: 'the backstep, in which the feet are alternately slipped behind, and reach the ground on, or close to, the spot occupied by the one just removed, is of difficult requirement, and severely exerts the muscles of the calves of the legs. So much dexterity can some persons display in this, that they will go through the setting tune of the music without moving beyond the space marked by the circumference of their bonnet'.

It is worth noting here that according to D G MacLennan, the notion that the whole of the Highland Fling should be danced on one spot dated from the 1890s. He averred that the originator of the idea was the MacIntosh of MacIntosh who, when judging at Inverness, became irritated by the dancers moving about and gave each one a chalked square in which to dance. Scott Skinner was supposed to be responsible for perpetuating the saying about the bonnet – rather as a joke.

Frontstep

This is simply the reversal of a backstep, and again occupies one count. Frontstep RF is usually performed starting with RF in rear leg position, and is as follows:

Count I   Carry RF round to front leg position and, without pausing, slide it
               down in front of the L leg and drop on it, at the same time
               raising LF quickly to rear leg position.

It can also be performed starting from front leg position. In either case the finishing position is the same.

Shuffles

We describe first a shuffle performed with the LF. This is begun with the weight on the LF and with the RF in 4th int low aerial position.

Count I   Spring off the LF and bring the RF back and drop on it, at the same
               time extending LF to 4th int low aerial position
       &   Brush LF in to 3rd position and immediately out again to 4th int
               low aerial position (so that it arrives in the latter position on the
               actual count &)

On the count 1, the LF reaches 4th int low aerial position at exactly the same time as the RF meets the floor. Immediately following the count 1, the LF begins to move in towards 3rd position, meeting the floor on the way in at approximately semi 4th position. It then brushes along the floor until the sole of the foot meets the R instep, then brushes out again to 4th int low aerial position, leaving the floor on the way out at approximately semi 4th position.

The use of hands in the Highland Fling is rather arbitrary. They can either be held on the waist or raised. The general convention is 'opposite hand to foot', ie, the hand opposite to the working foot is raised. In movements where there is a rapid change of the working foot (e.g. Backstep RF, LF, RF, LF) it is normal, but by no means invariable, to raise both hands together. On turning movements such as 'fling, turning to the R or L', some teachers kept to the 'opposite hand to foot' rule, whilst others kept both hands on the waist.

David Anderson, *Universal Ball-room and Solo-Dance Guide* (Dundee, *c.* 1899), states that 'In all the steps, Gentlemen should hold up the hand opposite to the leading foot, the arm bent, and the hand right above the head (about 4 inches). Vary the steps by putting hands on sides at intervals'. North *(op. cit.)* says, 'the arms should be raised when necessary so as to balance the body in an unostentatious manner, and not in a jerky or windmill fashion'.

1st step

This step, consisting entirely of 'fling' movements, is common to all of our collected versions. In all but one version, source (b) it was the first step. It is also the first step in all the printed versions, subject to slight differences in the location of 2nd position.[2] In view of this we are tempted to suggest that this was the original Highland Fling step referred to so frequently in the Reel.

1–4	Fling RF, LF, RF, then fling LF turning to the R
5–8	Perform bars **1** to **4** contrariwise.

There are a number of steps consisting only of 'fling' movements and we give just two other examples.

2nd step (c, j)

1–4	Fling RF three times, then fling LF turning to the R
5–8	Perform bars **1** to **4** contrariwise.

3rd step (c)

1–4	Fling RF, fling LF, turning to the R, fling LF, then fling RF, turning to the L
5–8	Repeat bars **1** to **4**.

4th step (a, b, i)

1	1	Hop on LF and place RF in 2nd position
	2	Hop on LF, raising RF to rear leg position
	3	Hop on LF, placing RF in 2nd position
	4	Hop on LF, raising RF to front leg position
2, 3		Perform bar **1** contrariwise, then repeat bar **1**
4		Fling LF turning to the R
5–8		Perform bars **1** to **4** contrariwise.

It is possible to combine the movement of bar **1** above with the 'fling' movement in a number of ways. The following example is of this type but there is a slight variation in bar **2**.

---

[2] See notes about printed sources.

5th step *(h)*

1		Fling RF
2	1	Hop on LF, and place RF in 2nd position
	2	Hop on LF, raising RF to rear leg position
	3	Hop on LF, placing RF in semi 4th int position
	4	Hop on LF and beat twice with RF in front leg position
3, 4		Fling RF, then fling LF turning to the R
5–8		Perform bars **1** to **4** contrariwise.

The use of toe and heel movements provides a number of steps which are both interesting and easy. The following step has a number of variants, but we give the one which we found most pleasing.

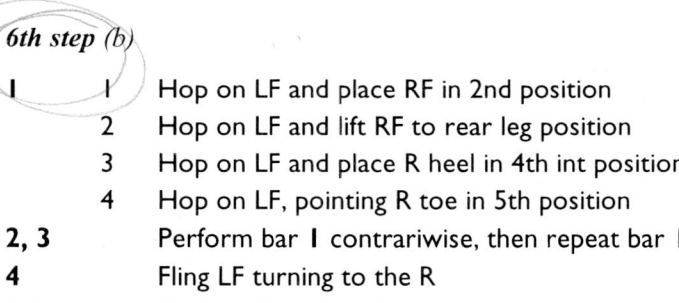

6th step *(b)*

1	1	Hop on LF and place RF in 2nd position
	2	Hop on LF and lift RF to rear leg position
	3	Hop on LF and place R heel in 4th int position
	4	Hop on LF, pointing R toe in 5th position
2, 3		Perform bar **1** contrariwise, then repeat bar **1**
4		Fling LF turning to the R
5-8		Perform bars **1** to **4** contrariwise.

Another simple toe and heel movement is the following:

7th step *(g)*

1		Fling RF
2	1	Hop on LF and place R heel in 5th position
	2	Hop on LF, pointing R toe in 5th position
	3	Hop on RF and place L heel in 5th position
	4	Hop on RF and point L toe in 5th position
3, 4		Fling RF, then fling LF turning to the R
5–8		Perform bars **1** to **4** contrariwise.

Among the toe and heel steps there are a few in which the toe is turned in. The following is a typical example.

8th step *(a)*

I	I	Hop on LF and place R toe in semi 4th int position, the toe being turned inwards
	2	Hop on LF and place R heel in semi 4th int position
	3	Hop on LF and point R toe in semi 4th int position
	4	Hop on LF, lifting RF to front leg position
2, 3		Perform bar **I** contrariwise, then repeat bar **I**
4		Fling LF turning to the R
5–8		Perform bars **I** to **4** contrariwise.

Another heel and toe step contains shuffles rather than the Fling in bars **4** and **8**.

9th step *(f)*

I	I	Hop on LF and place R heel in semi 4th int position
	2	Hop on LF and point R toe in semi 4th int position
	3	Hop on LF and place R heel in semi 4th int position
	4	Hop on LF, lifting RF to front leg position
2, 3		Perform bar **I** contrariwise, then repeat bar **I**
4		Shuffle LF, RF, LF, RF
5–8		Perform bars **I** to **4** contrariwise.

In the following step the heel and toe movement is combined with the 'cross', ie, a spring, landing 5th position. The term 'cross' is mentioned in various written sources.

10th step *(f)*

I	I	Spring into true 2nd position (both feet in 2nd position, weight equally on both feet)
	2	Spring on to both feet, with RF in 5th position
	3	Spring again into true 2nd position
	4	Spring on to both feet, with LF in 5th position
2	I	Hop on LF and place RF in 2nd position
	2	Hop on LF and lift RF to rear leg position
	3	Hop on LF and place R heel in 4th int position
	4	Hop on LF, pointing R toe in 5th position
3, 4		Perform bars **I** and **2** contrariwise
5–8		Repeat bars **I** to **4**.

The next two steps and their variants are usually termed 'backsteps'.

11th step *(b, e)*

1, 2	Fling RF, backstep RF, LF, RF, LF
3, 4	Perform bars **1** and **2** contrariwise
5–8	Repeat bars **1** to **4**.

12th step *(c)*

1	1	Hop on LF and place RF in 4th position
	2	Hop on LF, raising RF to front leg position
	3	Backstep RF
	4	Backstep LF
2, 3		Perform bar **1** contrariwise, then repeat bar **1**
4		Fling LF turning to the R
5–8		Perform bars **1** to **4** contrariwise.

The next two steps incorporate the 'frontstep'.

13th step *(d, g)*

1, 2	Fling RF, backstep RF, LF, frontstep RF, LF
3, 4	Fling RF, then fling LF turning to the R
5–8	Perform bars **1** to **4** contrariwise.

14th step *(i)*

1	1	Hop on LF and place RF in 2nd position
	2	Hop on LF, raising RF to rear leg position
	3	Hop on LF, placing RF in 2nd position
	4	Hop on LF, raising RF to front leg position
2	1	Frontstep RF (ending with LF in rear leg position)
	2	Hop on RF, retaining LF in rear leg position
	3	frontstep LF (ending with RF in rear leg position
	4	Hop on LF, retaining RF in rear leg position
3, 4		Fling RF, then fling RF turning to the R
5–8		Perform bars **1** to **4** contrariwise.

The next two steps incorporate a 'change-over', i.e. a change of the working foot occurs on the last or last but one beat of the bar. The usual step of this type, which is given by the Official Board, is rather dull, but it has a number of interesting variations. The following 'hesitation' step is very attractive.

15th step (k)

I		Fling RF
2	I	Hop on LF and place RF in 2nd position and
	2	hold this position for the whole of count 2
	3	Spring on LF and, passing RF through rear leg position, drop on RF, bringing LF to rear leg position
	4	Hop on RF and point L toe in 5th position
3, 4		Perform bars I and 2 contrariwise
5–8		Repeat bars I to 4.

16th step (l)

I	I	Hop on LF, placing RF in 2nd position
	2	Hop on LF, raising RF to rear leg position
	3	Hop on LF, carrying RF round to front leg position
	4	Backstep RF
2, 3		Perform bar I contrariwise, then repeat bar I
4		Fling LF turning to the R
5–8		Perform bars I to 4 contrariwise.

We have collected a number of variants of this type of step and we give just two. In each case they have the same basic pattern as Step 16 so we simply give the description of the first bar in each case. In the first (d, g) this is:

I	I	Hop on LF, placing RF in 2nd position
	2	Hop on LF, raising RF to back leg position
	3	Hop on LF, raising RF to front leg position
	4	Carry RF round to rear leg position, and then drop on it, at the same time carrying LF out to 2nd low aerial position.

The second variant (j) is:

I	I	Hop on LF and point R toe in 5th position
	2	Hop on LF and place R heel in 5th position
	3	Hop on LF raising RF to front leg position
	4	Backstep RF.

Another step of rather similar type is the following:

17th step (e)

I	I	Hop on LF and place RF in 2nd position
	2	Hop on LF, raising RF to rear leg position
	3	Hop on LF, placing RF in 4th int position
	4	Hop on LF, raising RF to front leg position
2		Perform bar I contrariwise
3	I	Hop on LF and place RF in 4th int position
	2	Hop on LF, raising RF to front leg position
	3	Drop on to RF and raise LF to rear leg position
	4	Drop on to LF and raise RF to front leg position
4		Backstep RF, LF, RF, LF
5–8		Perform bars I to 4 contrariwise.

The next two steps use a movement known as 'cover the buckle' which has now completely disappeared from the dance. In former times women's shoes were often fastened with a buckle and men's sometimes had an ornamental buckle across the front.

Cover the Buckle

As performed with the right foot the step is as follows:

Count	I	Cross R leg over in front of L leg and put R toe down beside and to the L of the L toe, toes touching and ankles close together. Then rock over to the L so that the weight falls on the RF and the R heel nearly touches the floor, but keeping the L toe firmly on the floor (the L ankle must bend a little)
	2	Rock back to the R in the same manner so that the L heel nearly touches the floor
		Rock back to the L, and then again to the R, in the same way on counts 3, 4.

It is possible that this is the original form of the 'rocking step' used in the modern standardised version. As performed with the right foot, this is:

Count   I   Drop on to RF (with foot rather flat, heel nearly touching the floor) and point L toe in rear 5th position
         2   Spring on to LF, pointing R toe in 5th position
          Repeat counts I and 2.

18th step *(h)*

I	I	Hop on LF and place RF in 2nd position
	2	Hop on LF, raising RF to rear leg position
	3	Hop on LF, placing RF in semi 4th int position
	4	Hop on LF and beat twice with RF in front leg position
2		Cover the buckle with RF
3, 4		Perform bars I and **2** contrariwise
5–8		Repeat bars I to **4**.

19th step *(a, i)*

I	I–3	Carry RF round to the L of the LF, moving RF in a semi-circle and keeping it close to the floor, and rock to the L, to the R and to the L, as in 'cover the buckle'
	4	Hop on RF and take LF out to 2nd low aerial position
2, 3		Perform bar I contrariwise and then repeat bar I
4		Fling LF turning to the R
5–8		Perform bars I to **4** contrariwise.

We conclude this selection of traditional steps with three containing turns made at half the speed of the usual Fling turn. They are strikingly similar to a Reel step described by the Aberdeenshire teacher Francis Peacock in 1805. When Peacock wrote his book, *Sketches relative to the history and theory but more especially to the practice and art of dancing*, he was an old man of eighty-two and had been teaching in Aberdeen since 1744. His descriptions of steps therefore probably refer to that early period. It is of interest that he had a wide knowledge of the different steps used throughout the Highlands and the Islands. He noted that, 'Our Colleges draw thither, every year, a number of students from the Western Isles, as well as from the Highlands, and the greater part of them excel in [Reels]..., some of them, indeed, in so superior degree that I, myself, have thought them worthy of imitation'. Of all the steps known to us we feel that we can ascribe the greatest antiquity to the following.

20th step *(i)*

I	I	Hop on LF, placing RF in semi 2nd position
	2	Hop on LF and raise RF to rear leg position, making a quarter turn to the L
	3	Hop on LF, placing RF in semi 2nd position
	4	Hop on LF and raise RF to rear leg position, making a further quarter turn to the L
2–4		Repeat bar I, three times, making two full turns in all
5–8		Perform bars I to 4 contrariwise.

21st step *(h)*

I, 2		Perform bars I and 2 as above but using 2nd position, not semi 2nd
3	I	Hop on LF, placing RF in 2nd position
	2	Hop on LF, raising RF to rear leg position
	3	Hop on RF, placing LF in 2nd position
	4	Hop on RF, raising LF to rear leg position
4		Backstep LF, RF, LF, RF
5–8		Perform bars I to 4 contrariwise.

22nd step *(i)*

I		Fling RF, making a half turn to the L on counts 2–4
2	I	Hop on LF, raising RF to semi 2nd position
	2	Hop on LF and raise RF to rear leg position, making a further quarter turn to the L
	3	Hop on LF and place RF in semi 2nd position
	4	Hop on LF and raise RF to rear leg position, making a further quarter turn to the L
3, 4		Repeat bars I and 2
5–8		Perform bars I to 4 contrariwise.

* * * * *

We turn now to versions of the Highland Fling found in the four printed sources noted at the end of the chapter.

A good deal of care is required in the interpretations of the descriptions of steps given in these books because of changes which have occurred in the style of performance since about 1890. Before 1890 there seem to have been two styles in use which differed from each other in one minor respect, both, however, being quite different from that in use in the present day.

The difference between the two pre-1890 styles lay only in the manner in which the first beat of the 'fling' movement was performed. In one style, true 2nd position was used, ie, the dancer would spring into true 2nd position (both feet in 2nd position) with the weight evenly distributed. Mozart Allan uses this form and two of his steps using this are as follows:

23rd step *(m)*

1–4	Fling RF, LF, then fling RF turning to the L, then fling LF turning to the R
5–8	Perform bars 1 to 4 contrariwise.

24th step *(m)*

1, 2	Fling RF turning to the L, then fling LF turning to the R
3–8	Repeat bars 1 and 2 three times.

In the other pre-1890 style, the first beat of the fling movement was performed in *semi* 2nd position, ie, the dancer would hop on LF and place RF in semi 2nd position. This form was used by Anderson in his version for gentlemen and by McIntyre North.

The real difference between the pre-1890 versions and the style used today lies in the *open* positions used throughout the dance. Before 1890, the open positions used were those which we have termed *semi* open. Thus, when the dancer pointed a toe, either to the side or to the front, the knee was bent and the lower leg and foot were in an almost vertical line. The fully extended leg with straight knee seen in the modern style was introduced by William MacLennan, brother of D G MacLennan. D G MacLennan records that his brother's principal teacher for Highland dancing (he also studied ballet) was the famous John McNeill, Senior, of Edinburgh.

In a letter D G MacLennan told a nice story of John McNeill's teaching, 'The "spread" as taught by John McNeill for the first beat in any Highland Fling step was simply "jump into true 2nd position, heels about 15" apart"'. McNeill used to put a penny between the dancer's toes when in 1st position – 'no his own penny, mind you' – and it had to be 'equi-distant' from their toes when they had made the 'spread'. There was no violent spring on the movement. Other dancers admired William's version and it was copied to replace the older 'spread'. The term 'spread' was used by other teachers.

Amongst our traditional sources it is of interest that the two people (h, i) who preserved the older style of position also preserved the steps which we deemed to be of the greatest antiquity.

There are considerable differences in style between Anderson's versions for ladies and for gentlemen; the ladies' leg positions being more decorous. For example, the 'fling' is performed low round the ankle. There is also a special turn to be used by ladies in place of 'fling turning to the R (or L)'. The instructions given by Anderson for the turn to the right are 'hold up Left Foot, Hop 2 on Right, going full round – cross with left in front [i.e. spring on to both feet with LF in 5th position], then cross with Right in front'. We give just one step from the ladies' Highland Fling as an example of the style.

25th step (n)

I	I	Hop on LF and place RF in semi 2nd position
	2	Hop on LF and bring RF to low rear aerial position
	3	Spring on to both feet with RF in 5th position
	4	Spring on to both feet with LF in 5th position
2, 3		Perform bar I contrariwise, then repeat bar I
4		Ladies turn to the R as described above
5–8		Perform bars I to **4** contrariwise.

Anderson's steps achieved wide popularity. We have found eight out of his ten steps given for gentlemen amongst our traditional sources and his 8th and 10th steps appear in the Official Board's version as the 6th and the 3rd step. It is of interest that he says, 'The Highland Fling, or any of the Highland Fling steps, must be danced on one spot, and the dancer must not go forward and backward as in a Hornpipe, as sometimes taught'. This was not an opinion shared by all teachers and Scott Skinner's version contains one step which breaks this rule. We cannot give precise descriptions of Scott Skinner's steps as they are too brief to permit an accurate interpretation. We can say, however, that several of them are similar to ones collected from traditional sources.

There remains the version given by McIntyre North (o). His descriptions are given with sufficient clarity for us to be virtually certain of reconstructing the steps as they were performed by McIntyre himself. The steps are very attractive and we give the following examples. 'Round the leg' is an old term for the 'fling' and starts by placing the working foot in semi 2nd position (see Illustration 9). Numbers in brackets indicate McIntyre North's numbering.

26th step *(M.N's 3rd step)*

1	1	Spring on LF and place RF in 2nd position
	2	Hop on LF, sliding RF along floor to 5th position
	3 4	Repeat counts 1 and 2 contrariwise
2		As bar 1, but sliding RF and LF to 5th rear position on counts 2 and 4
3	1	Draw up LF to low back leg position, and drop on it, at the same time raising RF to front leg position
	2 3 4	} Three backsteps RF, LF, RF
4		Round the leg with LF turning to the R
5–8		Repeat bars 1 to 4 contrariwise.

27th step *(M.N's 4th step)*

1		Round the leg with RF
2	1	Hop on LF and place RF in 2nd position
	2	Hop on LF, raising RF to back leg position
	3	Spring on to RF in close 4th int position, bringing LF to low back leg position
	4	Drop back on LF in original spot, bringing RF to 5th position
3, 4		Perform bars 1 and 2 contrariwise
5, 6		Repeat bars 1 and 2
7	1	Draw up LF to low back leg position, and drop on it, at the same time raising RF to front leg position
	2 3 4	} Three backsteps RF, LF, RF
8		Round the leg with LF turning to the R.

28th step *(M.N's 8th step)*

1	1	Hop on LF and place RF in 4th int position
	2	Hop on LF and lift RF to back leg position
	3	Hop on LF and place RF in 4th int position
	4	Hop on LF and lift RF to back leg position
2	1	Hop on LF and place R heel in 2nd position
	2	Hop on LF and place R toe in 2nd position, the toe turned inwards
	3	Hop on LF and place R heel in 4th int position
	4	Hop on LF and point R toe in 5th position
3–6		Perform bars **1** and **2** contrariwise, then repeat bars **1** and **2**
7		Round the leg with LF turning to the R
8		Four backsteps LF, RF, LF, RF.

29th step *(M.N's 9th step) – This is a syncopated step*

1	1 ⎫	
	2 ⎬	First three beats of round the leg RF
	3 ⎭	
	4a	Hop on LF and place RF in back leg position and immediately
	b	carry RF out to a 2nd low aerial close position
2	1	Drop on RF in 5th position, raising LF to back leg position
	2a	Drop on LF, raising RF to 5th low aerial position
	b	Drop on RF, raising LF to 5th low aerial position
	3	Drop on LF, leaving RF in 5th position
	4	Hop on LF, shaking RF out twice in 4th int position
3, 4		Perform bars **1** and **2** contrariwise
5, 6		Repeat bars **1** and **2**
7		Round the leg with LF turning to the R
8		Four backsteps LF, RF, LF, RF.

McIntyre North remarks 'In this, the dancer should keep as near as possible in one spot, and should avoid raising the foot of one leg higher than the under side of the kneecap of the other, and each foot as a rule marks time for the other'. The diagram below is taken from a tracing of McIntyre North's illustration of which he notes: 'In the detail (plate) each column represents the various positions in which the limbs are placed in each step, the commencement of the step being shown at the bottom'. There are only nine columns for ten steps as he used column E twice in different steps. They illustrate very clearly the pre-1890 open position in which the knee was bent and the lower leg and foot were almost in a vertical line.

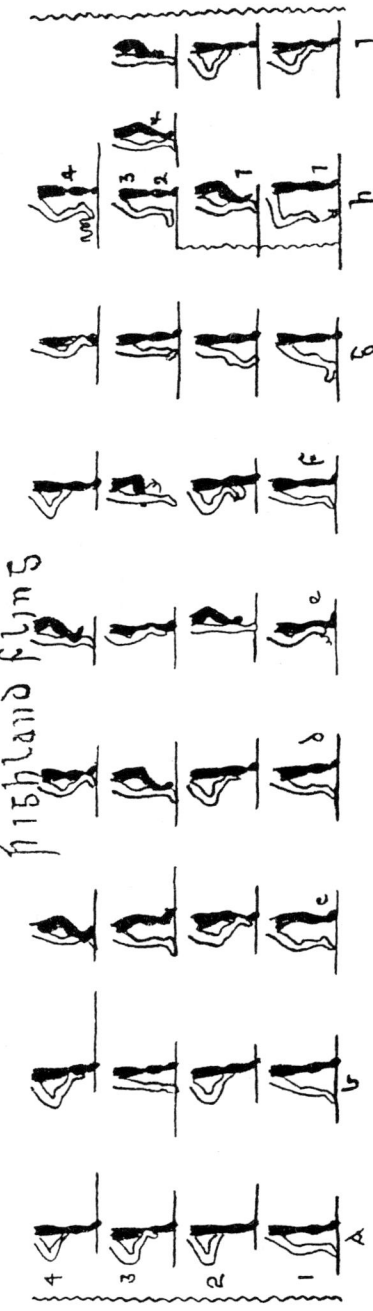

Illustration from *Book of the Club of True Highlanders*, C N MacIntyre North
(London, 1880)

Our collected versions of these steps were learnt from the following people:

a. Mr Buie of Lamlash, Arran, then living in Birkenhead, Merseyside. He was taught to dance in 1900 by Mr McKelvie in Lamlash.
b. Mr Forbes, Keig, Aberdeenshire, who learnt from other dancers *c.* 1885.
c. Mr Lachlan Gillies, Morroch, Arisaig, Inverness. He learnt one version of the dance *c.* 1902 from Mr MacDougall, an itinerant teacher from Argyllshire who had as many as twenty-four steps in his repertoire and taught different versions of the dance in different places. Another version he learnt *c.* 1906 from Mr MacLeod, a carpenter and itinerant teacher from Glasgow. Mr Gillies, himself, was a judge at the Arisaig and Glenfinnan Games for a number of years.
d. Mr Sandy Gillies, Glen Uig, Moidart, who was taught there by Mr MacDougall. He was 77 in 1955.
e. Mr Alex MacIntosh, Daliburgh, South Uist, who also learnt from Mr McLeod in Benbecula *c.* 1905.
f. Mr Peter MacKay, Kilaulay, South Uist, a pupil of John MacMillan mentioned in Chapter 2. He learnt the dance *c.* 1890.
g. Mr John MacLean, Glen Uig, Moidart. His uncles had been taught by Mr MacDougall in Glen Uig and he learnt from them.
h. Miss E B MacNicoll of Port Glasgow, then living in Culcheth, near Warrington, Cheshire. Miss MacNicoll's father was a well-known professional Highland dancer and taught dancing in Arbroath. He learnt the dance *c.* 1880.
i. Mr Roy Scott, of North Ronaldsay, then living at Rendall, Mainland of Orkney. He had learnt from his father who was taught by a Mr MacKenzie in North Ronaldsay, *c.* 1880.
j. Miss Winnie Smith, Castlebay, Barra. She had learnt the dance *c.* 1912 from her grand-uncle, Mr Ewan Clayton, a well-known teacher in the North East of Scotland.
k. Mrs Mary Isdale MacNab, of Vancouver, Canada. She learnt the step noted from a well-known piper and professional Highland dancer, Mr D C Mather. (See Chapter 7 for details of both Mrs MacNab and Mr Mather.)
l. Mr Charles Milne, Dufftown, Banffshire, who had learnt *c.* 1890 from Mr Myron, one of the Banffshire family of teachers mentioned in Chapter 1.

Printed Sources

m. Mozart Allan, *Reference Guide to the Ballroom* (new edition, Glasgow, *c.* 1890).
n. D Anderson, Universal Ballroom and Solo-Dance Guide (Dundee, *c.* 1899). This book contains two versions, one for ladies and one for gentlemen. Both versions also appeared separately in pamphlet form in 1886 or earlier.
o. C N McIntyre North, *Book of the Club of True Highlanders* (London, 1880). This version is derived from Sandy MacIntyre, a teacher in Perth. From the information given it would appear to date from about 1850–60.
p. J Scott Skinner, *The People's Ballroom Guide* (Dundee?, *c.* 1905). The version described by Scott Skinner is that danced by his brother, A F Skinner.

Allan's version of the dance has eight steps, the others have ten steps.

11

Dances Collected in Forfar, Fife and Kilmarnock

For many years one of the best known dancing-masters was James Neill whom we mentioned briefly in Chapter 1. He was born on the Glamis estate in the parish of Kirriemuir and started teaching in 1855 and was well known over a wide area covering a region within a radius of fifteen to twenty miles around Forfar. He only retired on 30 March 1918 at the age of eighty-four. His diary for that day bore the comment 'No more classes'!

'Dancie' Neill was taught to dance by John Lowe, a member of an equally renowned family of dancing-masters, and he was taught to play the fiddle by John Lowe's brother, James, who taught music and dancing in Dundee and Fifeshire. The most famous member of the Lowe family was John's brother Joseph who, as well as teaching regularly in Edinburgh and Inverness, taught Queen Victoria and her children at Balmoral and Windsor Castle.

Mr Neill followed very closely in Joseph Lowe's footsteps. In addition to his public and semi-private classes he had an extensive private practice amongst the landed gentry of Angus and Perthshire. For instance he taught the present Queen Mother and her brother at Glamis Castle and three generations of the Atholl family at Blair Castle, the seat of the Duke of Atholl. When he retired he was presented with a cheque for £100 and an inscribed silver cup as a token of esteem from former pupils at a ceremony at Blair Castle. At his classes Mr Neill wore a black jacket and black striped trousers with black patent leather shoes. The only exception was on his visits to Blair Castle when he was expected to wear a kilt. Neither he nor his pupils wore Highland dancing pumps. The girls wore patent leather shoes with a strap around the ankle and with a heel about one inch high. Boys wore black leather evening shoes of the standard style of the period. It must be remembered that before the First World War only professional dancers wore the now common soft Highland dancing pumps and usually then only at Highland Games and that footwear has an enormous effect on style of performance. We give a full account of Mr Neill's classes in *Traditional Dancing in Scotland*.

Mr Neill's repertoire of solo dances included Highland Fling, Sword Dance (several versions), Shan Trews, Jacky Tar (i.e. Sailor's Hornpipe, one version for

**'Dancie' Neill with Her Majesty the Queen Mother (then Lady Elizabeth Bowes-Lyon)
and her brother David**

girls and another for boys), Highland Laddie, Blue Bonnets and Callum Brougach. In 1959 we were able to collect versions of several of these dances from his daughter, Mrs Griselda MacFarlane of Forfar, aged seventy-four. We include his version of the last three dances together with his version of Shan Trews which is quite different from the now standard one.

It is interesting to note Mrs MacFarlane's comments about the general style of her father's dancing. In contrast to the staccato movements of modern dancers, Highland dancing as she knew it from her father was much more smooth and graceful. In this he was obviously influenced by the Lowe family who taught a smooth, refined style suited to the polite ballroom yet still retaining the spirit and vitality of the dances. Joseph Lowe noted in his diary for 29 September 1852 that Queen Victoria showed him some reel steps which she already knew and asked his opinion of them. He told her that they were 'Truly Scotch steps' but in his opinion too rough for ladies and more suitable for men. The Queen agreed and said that she thought Mr Lowe's steps 'much more elegant and the best for ladies she had ever seen' [49].

Mr Neill was a frequent judge at Highland Games and, like the Lowe family, he taught music as well as dancing. His pupils had a wide repertoire of light classical music in addition to Scottish tunes. His Quadrille band played at public functions and at his 'Finishing Assemblies' where his pupils displayed their dancing skills. A newspaper report of *c.* 1895 gives a vivid picture of the atmosphere at a typical assembly: 'FINISHING ASSEMBLY. Mr Neill's pupils held their finishing assembly at Mains of Airlie on Friday last. A long list of dances and exercises was performed to the delight of a large number of parents and friends. The boys danced the Highland Fling and Reel with great spirit, and in capital time. Four girls were very much admired by their tripping of the "Seann Trubhais", but the principal feature in the programme, we think, was the marching drill exercise, which was most efficiently performed, the various movements being done with great precision. The juveniles finished about eight o'clock when Mr Neill announced that the cake presented by the Dowager-Countess of Airlie in honour of the birth of an heir to the Airlie estates would be distributed amongst them... The youngsters were then served with their refreshments, and after a brief interval dancing was resumed, and joined in by the adult pupils and friends.'

We also include in this chapter the dance Scotch Jig, collected from Mr Adamson of Kingskettle, Fife. Two more of Mr Adamson's dances are given in the chapter on clog-dancing. Following this we give a dance collected in Kilmarnock, Miss Gayton's Hornpipe.

Before giving the descriptions of the dances we give several movements as danced by Mr Neill; we include the pas de Basque as an example of a well-known step which is performed in quite a different style today.

Pas de Basque

Performed with the RF

Count 1   Spring on to the RF, moving about nine inches to the R
        &   Place LF in flat 5th position
        2   Beat with RF on the spot.

The step finishes with *both feet on the floor*. The whole step was quite smooth and there was no extension of the LF on the beat.

Mr Neill's Chassé

Count a   Rise on the ball of LF and
        1   Step forward on RF
        &   Close LF to rear 3rd position
        2   Make a small step forward on RF
      a1   Step forward on LF, with a lilt on the RF as the LF passes it. The lilt takes place on the count 'a' and the step forward is completed on the count '1'. (In the lilt the R instep bends so that the R heel is momentarily raised a little from its normal position and then lowered again, whilst the ball of the foot remains on the floor.)
        &   Close RF to rear 3rd position
        2   Make a small step forward on LF
      a1   Step forward on RF etc.

Mr Neill's Ronde *(our name)*

Performed with the RF

Count 1 & Hop twice on LF, at the same time carrying RF round (without any shakes) in a circle towards rear 5th position (the R knee passes over int 4th and 2nd positions and is raised about six inches off the floor)
        2   Place RF in rear 5th position, so that the movement finishes with both feet on the floor.

Mr Neill's Spring four *(Mr Neill's name)*

1	1	Spring on to both feet with RF in flat 5th position, with weight principally on back foot
	2	Perform count 1 contrariwise
2		Repeat bar 1.

Blue Bonnets

Mr Neill only taught this dance to girls. When they danced in public they wore 'tartan plaids' over their dresses with a knitted 'Scots bonnet' in blue with a red tassel. They danced to the tune of the same name at a speed of 18 seconds for 16 bars.

We give the hand movements used in this dance in square brackets. We noted that Mr Neill had no overall rule for hand movements and they varied from dance to dance. The girls did not hold their skirts.

1st step

Begin with RF in 4th low aerial position

I	**I**	Drop on to RF in 5th position, cutting LF to a very loose low rear leg position with the L knee turned well out and well bent, the L toe being about two inches from the floor
	2	Drop on LF in rear 5th position, cutting RF back to 4th low aerial position
2	**I**	Step forward on ball of RF
	2	Step forward on ball of LF
	&	Bring RF quickly to 4th low aerial position
3		Repeat bar I
4	**I** ⎫	
	& ⎬	Pas de Basque with RF moving about six inches to the R with a very slight spring to begin
	2 ⎭	
	&	Cut the LF out to 4th low aerial position
5–8		Perform bars **I–4** contrariwise
9–12		Ronde RF, LF, RF, LF, moving backwards on the hops
13	**I**	Carry RF closely round the LF and step on it in rear 5th position and,
	& 2	immediately take RF out to 4th int aerial position in a leisurely kick, hopping on RF on count 2
13	**I**	Bring LF back and step on it in rear 5th position and,
	& 2	immediately take RF out to 4th int aerial position in a leisurely kick, hopping on the LF on the count 2
15–16		Spring four, LF, RF, LF, RF
		Perform bars **I** to **8** contrariwise.
		[Hands on waist throughout]

2nd step

I	**I**	Slide the RF along the floor in a gliding motion to 2nd int position with a slight bend of the back knee giving an extra extension of the RF
	2	Draw the LF along the floor to close it behind the RF in rear 5th position, rising slightly on the ball of the RF
2		Pas de Basque with RF making a small step to the R to begin
3, 4		Perform bars **I** and **2** contrariwise
5, 6		Repeat bars **I** and **2**
7, 8		Spring four RF, LF, RF, LF
		Perform bars **I** to **8** contrariwise.

> *[At the start of the step hands are held with arms curved, L out to the side and R to the front away from the body with hand curved in towards the waist. On bar I they swing gracefully into the opposite position. On the pas de Basque in bar 2, one is raised and the other lowered, ready to move back for bar 3, 4 etc.]*

3rd step

I, 2	Chassé forward with RF, LF, putting a real lilt into the movement Close in flat rear 5th position
3	Ronde RF
4	Spring with RF, LF as in Spring four
5, 6	Chassé forward with LF, RF, as in bars **I** and **2**
7	Ronde LF, making a half turn to the L on the hops
8	Spring with LF, RF, as in Spring four (now facing in opposite direction to starting position)
	Perform bars **I** to **8** finishing facing original direction.

4th step

I	I	Hop on LF and carry RF out to 4th int aerial position and in to front leg position
	2	Repeat count I
		(in the 4th int aerial position the knee is well bent and the heel turned very well forward, so that, from the front, the lower part of the R leg appears vertical)
2–4		Pas de Basque with RF, LF, RF making one complete turn on the spot to the R (the turn is virtually complete by the end of bar **3**)
5–8		Perform bars **1** to **4** contrariwise
		Repeat bars **1** to **8**.

5th step

I	I	⎫
	2	⎬ Step forward with RF, LF, RF, LF, stepping on the ball of each foot
2	I	⎪
	2	⎭
3		Ronde with RF
4		Spring with RF, LF, as in Spring four
5, 6		Step forward with LF, RF, LF, RF
7		Ronde with LF making a half turn to the L on the hops (the dancer is now facing in the opposite direction to beginning)
8		Spring with LF, RF, as in Spring four
		Repeat bars **1** to **8**.

6th step

I	Slide and close as in bar I of 2nd step
2–4	Pas de Basque with RF, LF, RF, making a complete turn to the R as in the 4th step
5	Slide and close to L
6	Pas de Basque with LF, turning to the L
7, 8	Spring four, RF, LF, RF, LF, completing the turn on the first two springs
	Perform bars **1** to **8** contrariwise.

7th step

1	1	Spring on to both feet with the RF in 4th position in front of 5th with the knees slightly bent and with almost all the weight on the RF
	2	Hop on RF and take LF out to 4th int aerial position in a leisurely extension
2		Perform bar 1 contrariwise
3–6		Repeat bars 1, 2 twice
7, 8		Spring four, LF, RF, LF, RF (there is some doubt about which foot begins this movement)
9	1	Spring on to both feet with LF in front (as in 1.1)
	2	Hop on the RF and take LF to 4th int aerial position in a leisurely extension
10		Perform bar 9 contrariwise
11–14		Repeat bars 9, 10 twice
15, 16		Spring four, LF, RF, LF, RF (again some doubt about starting foot) Perform bars 1 to 16 contrariwise.

On bars 1 to 6 the dancer advances some six feet and then retires to original place on bars 9 to 14 and similarly on bars 17 to 22 and 25 to 30.

If several girls performed the dance together, they usually joined hands in line on this step and, on the springs on the count 1, nodded to each other, first to the person on one side, then to the person on the other.

Highland Laddie

This dance had about eight steps and, again, was taught by Mr Neill only to the girls. Mrs MacFarlane remembered three steps.

The 'ronde' was the same as in Blue Bonnets.

1st step

1, 2		Chassé forward with RF, LF (with a lilt on the RF as the LF passes it, but not on count 2, unlike Blue Bonnets)
3, 4		Ronde RF, LF, moving backwards to original place
5	I	Step on RF in rear 5th position
	&	Place L heel in semi 2nd int position
	2	Close RF to rear 5th position (R toe to L heel)
	&	Place L toe in semi 2nd position
6	I	Close RF to rear 5th position (R toe under L heel)
	&	Place L heel in semi 2nd int position
	2	Close RF to rear 5th position (R toe to L heel)
7, 8		Ronde LF, RF
		Perform bars **I** to **8** contrariwise.

2nd step

I	I	Beat with ball of LF on the spot	
	&	Place R heel in semi 4th int position	
	2	Beat with ball of LF on the spot	
	&	Point R toe in semi 4th int position	Make one half of
2	I	Beat with ball of LF on the spot	a turn to the R
	&	Place R heel in semi 4th int position	
	2	Beat with ball of LF on the spot	
3	I	Hop on the LF and raise the RF to semi 4th int aerial position, with the ankle bent so that the heel is down and the toe up	
	&	Place the R heel in 4th semi int position	
	2	Beat with the ball of the LF on the spot	
4		Repeat bar **3**	

On bars **3, 4** the turn begun on bars **1, 2** is completed. About one third of the turn is made on bar **3**, the rest on bar **4**. On the counts **3**.1 and **4**.1, the RF is effectively poised over the 4th semi int position with the foot already prepared to place the heel on the floor. The rhythm of the movement in bar **3** is similar to that of the double heel beat in the version of Highland Laddie collected in the Hebrides. In this version the first heel beat is replaced by a distinct lift of the heel and the foot is held in the air longer.

5, 8	As in 1st step
	Perform bars **1** to **8** contrariwise.

3rd step

1	Chassé to the R with RF (facing front)
2	Chassé with the LF, making one complete turn to the R
3–8	As in 1st step
	Perform bars **1** to **8** contrariwise.

The first two steps above were also remembered by one of Mr Neill's pupils, Mrs Jenny Chapman of Kirriemuir. In addition she had the following three steps. TMF noted, 'I feel that these steps cannot be accepted without verification'.

Step A

1	1	Cross the R leg well over the L leg and spring on to RF, raising the LF off the floor
	2	Hop on RF, moving about six inches further to the L at the same time
2	1	Hop on RF, moving a further six inches to the L, and shake LF out to 2nd int aerial position and back to front leg position
	2	Repeat count **2**.1
3, 4		Perform bars **1, 2** contrariwise
5, 6		Repeat bars **1** and **2**
7, 8		Spring four RF, LF, RF, LF
		Perform bars **1** to **8** contrariwise.

Step B

I	I	Spring on to both feet with RF in 5th position
	2	Hop on LF and shake RF in 4th int aerial position
2	I	Step on RF in rear 5th position
	&	Step to the L on LF
	2	Close RF to rear 5th position
3	I	Step to the L on L heel
	&	Close RF to rear 5th position
	2	Step to the L on L toe
	&	Close RF to rear 5th position
4		Repeat bar **3**
5, 6		Perform bars **1, 2** contrariwise
7, 8		Spring four (it was not clear which foot was used to start this).

Step C

This begins with RF in 4th low aerial position

I	I	Hop on LF and brush RF in past 1st position and back to a semi 4th rear low aerial position
	2	Hop on LF, and brush the RF back past 1st position and out to 4th low aerial position
		In this step the RF is kept pointing to the front, and the ball of the foot is brushed along the floor as the RF passes the LF.
2		Ronde RF (close to the leg)
3, 4		Perform bars **1** and **2** contrariwise
5		Cross RF over LF and pirouette on the toes to the L
6		Ronde LF
7, 8		Spring four LF, RF, LF, RF
		Perform bars **1** to **8** contrariwise.

Shan Trews (Seann Triubhas)

Steps for this dance were collected from Mrs MacFarlane (Mr Neill's daughter) on two separate visits five months apart. On the first visit she remembered two steps and on the second, six steps. We often found that a visit would stimulate our informant's memory; they would, perhaps, talk with family or friends, thus stimulating their memory further and, on a second visit, would be able to recall more details of their dancing days. We give the steps collected from Mrs MacFarlane on both visits to illustrate this point.

This was danced to the tune 'Whistle o'er the Lave o't'. We did not record any timing when collecting this dance from Mrs MacFarlane.

In this dance 'Spring four' (see p. 130) is also used but here the counting is 1 2 3 4. In addition we require another movement which we have called 'heel and toe'.

Heel and toe with LF

Count		
I	Spring on to both feet, with RF in rear 5th position
&	Make a small step to the L on L heel
2	Close RF to rear 5th position
&	Make a small step to the L on the half-point of LF
3	Close RF to rear 5th position
&	Make a small step to the L on the L heel
4	Close RF to rear 5th position.

Unnumbered step *(collected April 1959)*

1	1	⎫
	2	⎬ Step towards 4th int position on RF, LF, RF on counts 1, 2, 3
	3	⎭
	4	Close L toe to rear 5th position, with the sole of the foot vertical and against the back of the R leg
2	1	⎫ Hop backwards twice on RF (counts 1 &), taking the LF off in
	&	⎬ a little arc, the foot being just off the floor, and then place LF
	2	⎭ in flat rear 5th position (this is a ronde begun from the back)
	3	⎫
	&	⎬ Ronde RF moving backwards on the hops
	4	⎭ (as in Blue Bonnets) on counts 3 & 4
3	1	Step on LF in rear 5th position
	&	Place R heel in semi 2nd int position
	2	Close LF to rear 5th position (L toe to R heel)
	&	Place R toe in semi 2nd int position
	3	Close LF to rear 5th position (L toe under R arch)
	&	Place R heel in semi 2nd int position
	4	Close LF to rear 5th position (L toe to R heel)
4		Spring four LF, RF, LF, RF
5–8		Perform bars 1 to 4 contrariwise.

1st step *(collected April 1959)*

1	1	Spring on to both feet, with RF in flat 5th position
	&	Step on RF in 2nd int position (the weight is kept on the LF until the RF is in that position, so that the effect is almost that of 'point R toe in 2nd int position and then step on it')
	2	Close LF to flat rear 5th position
	3	⎫
	&	⎬ Perform counts 1 & 2 contrariwise
	4	⎭
2, 3		Repeat bar 1 twice
4		Spring four RF, LF, RF, LF (as in Blue Bonnets)
5–8		Perform bars 1 to 4 contrariwise.

1st step (collected September 1959, together with the following steps)

I	I	Spring on to both feet, with LF in 5th position
	&	Step on LF in 2nd int position (the weight is kept on the RF until the LF is in that position, so that the effect is almost that of 'point L toe in 2nd int position, and then step on it')
	2	Close RF to rear 5th position
	3	Spring on to both feet, with RF in 5th position (i.e. simply interchange the position of the feet. There is very little lateral movement of the feet on the spring.)
2, 3		Repeat bar I twice, but make the initial spring on the count I in a similar manner to that on count 3
4		Spring four LF, RF, LF, RF
5–8		Perform bars I to 4 contrariwise.

2nd step

I–3	Perform Heel and toe with LF, RF, LF
4	Spring four RF, LF, RF, LF
5–8	Perform bars I to 4 contrariwise.

3rd step

I	Chassé forward on counts I & 2, 3 & 4 with RF, LF
2	Ronde RF, LF, on counts I & 2, 3 & 4, moving backwards
3	Heel and toe with LF
4	Spring four RF, LF, RF, LF
5–8	Perform bars I to 4 contrariwise.

4th step

I	I	Hop on LF and raise RF in semi 4th low aerial position, with the heel lowered, ready to place the heel on the floor
	&	Place the R heel on the floor in semi 4th position
	2	Beat with LF on the spot
	&	Place the R toe on the half-point on the floor in semi 4th position
	3	Beat with LF on the spot
	&	Place the R heel on the floor in semi 4th position
	4	Beat with LF on the spot. On this bar the dancer makes a complete turn to the R, keeping the LF always on the same spot.
2		Repeat the counts I.I & 2 twice, facing front throughout
3, 4		Perform bars **I**, **2** contrariwise
5, 6		Heel and toe LF, RF
7		Spring four.

[Note by TMF – This step must be wrong. It is probably:

I, 2	As above
3, 4	As in 3rd step].

5th step

Exactly as in the 7th step of Blue Bonnets except that the counting **I**.I, 2; **2**.I, 2; is replaced by **I**.I, 2, 3, 4.

6th step

I	Hop on RF, LF, on counts &I, &2, &3, &4, moving round to the R in a very tight circle
2	Ronde RF on counts I & 2
	Spring two RF, LF, on counts 3,4
3, 4	Perform bars **I**, **2** contrariwise
5–8	Repeat bars I to **4**.

Callum Brougach

This is one of the dances Mrs MacFarlane learnt from her father. We have not found this dance anywhere else traditionally nor any mention in the literature. Mr Neill always claimed that it was the oldest of all the solo dances which he taught. As far as Mrs MacFarlane knew, he only taught it to girls but she was not sure whether this was for traditional reasons or because of the boys' lack of ability. The dance should be performed 'with dignity'.

The tune 'Callum Brougach' occurs in Neil Gow's collection where it is marked 'very old'. It has three parts but only the first two were used for the dance. Under the name 'Calam Breugach' it occurs in *The Skye Collection* by K N MacDonald which was first published in 1887. It was reprinted in Sydney, Nova Scotia, Canada, in 1980 where it is marked 'Strathspey, very old' and the translation of the title is given as 'Lying Malcolm'. We reproduce a copy of the music as used by Mr Neill, together with his music for the Sword Dance. The music belonged to another of his daughters, Miss Ethel Neill. The collection of music also includes a 'Clog Dance'.

The tempo used for the dance was 14½ seconds for 8 bars. Throughout the dance the hands were held lightly down by the dancer's sides.

Three special movements require separate descriptions.

Beat before

This occupies half a bar, or two counts.

Count I   Hop on LF and point R toe in semi 4th position
Count 2   Hop on LF and raise RF to front leg position (heel touching knee-cap).

Beat behind

This also occupies half a bar.

Count I   Hop on LF and point R toe in 5th position
Count 2   Hop on LF and raise RF to rear leg position.

Callum Brougach

Music from James Neill's collection

Highland Fling step

This occupies one bar, or four counts.

Count 1   Spring into the 2nd position, ie, both feet in 2nd and with the
weight equally distributed on both feet
Count 2   Keeping the body in the same position as in count 1, hop on LF
and raise RF to rear leg position
Count 3   Hop on LF and carry RF closely round the L leg to front leg
position
Count 4   Hop on LF and carry RF closely round the L leg to rear leg
position.

This movement can also be performed with one complete turn on counts 2–4,
turning to the L.

1st step

1   1, 2 Beat before with RF
3, 4 Two steps backwards with RF, LF
2   1, 2 Beat behind with RF
3, 4 Two steps forward with RF, LF
3   1, 2 Beat before with RF
3, 4 Beat behind with RF
4   1   Step to the R on RF
2   Close LF to flat rear 5th position
3   Step to the R on RF
4   Hop on RF and raise LF to front leg position
5–8   Perform bars 1 to 4 contrariwise.

This is effectively Mr Neill's step used for the dance 'Highland Schottische'.

2nd step

1	Beat before, then beat behind with RF
2	Repeat bar 1
3, 4	Repeat bars 1, 2 contrariwise
5, 6	Repeat bars 1, 2
7	Perform bar 1 contrariwise, making a complete turn to the L on counts 2–4
8	Spring four LF, RF, LF, RF (as in Blue Bonnets).

This leaves the RF in flat 5th position ready for 3rd step.

3rd step (*performed to the second measure*)

1	1	Beat with RF in flat 5th position
	&	Place LF in rear semi 2nd position
	2	Momentarily transfer the weight to the LF, close RF to flat 5th position, and immediately transfer the weight back to the RF
	& 3 & 4 &	} Repeat counts & 2 of bar 1
2	1 & 2 & 3 & 4	} six times
		On this movement the dancer moves some six feet to the L and backwards.
		Mr Neill referred to this step as a 'jeté'.
3		Highland Fling step with LF
4		Highland Fling step with RF, turning to the L
5	1	Hop on LF, retaining RF in rear leg position
	& 2 etc	} Perform the corresponding parts of bars
6–8		} 1–4 contrariwise

4th step

1	Highland Fling step with RF, making one complete turn to the L
2	Spring four RF, LF, RF, LF
3, 4	Perform bars 1, 2 contrariwise
5–8	Repeat bars 1 to 4.

5th step

I	I	Hop on LF and raise RF to front leg position
	2	Hop on LF and place RF in rear leg position
	3, 4	⎫
		⎬ Repeat counts I, 2 of bar I three times
2	I, 2, 3, 4	⎭
		On these two bars the dancer moves about six feet to the R
3		Highland Fling step with the RF, making one complete turn to the L
4		Spring four RF, LF, RF, LF
5–8		Perform bars I to 4 contrariwise.

6th step

I	I 2	Beat before with RF
	3 4	Beat behind with RF
2	I	Make a small step on the ball of the RF in semi 2nd position, and begin to turn to the R by swivelling on the RF (Fig. a)
	2	Still turning to the R, step on the ball of the LF as in Fig. b
	3	Continue swivelling on both feet, then step on the ball of the RF as shown in Fig. c. The turn should be completed on this count
	4	Hop on RF and bring LF to rear leg position.

 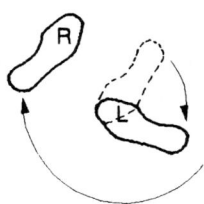

Figure a   Figure b   Figure c

3, 4	Perform bars I, 2 contrariwise
5, 6	Repeat bars I, 2
7	Perform bar I contrariwise
8	Spring four RF, LF, RF, LF

Bars **1, 2** is Mr Neill's Highland Schottische step with a turn.

7th step *(performed to the second measure)*

I	I	Hop on LF and point R toe in 4th position
	2	Hop on LF and extend RF in 4th aerial position (no shake)
	3	Drop on RF in flat 5th position, cutting LF towards rear semi 2nd int position
	& 4 &	Jeté as in
2	I & 2 & 3 & 4	step 3
3	I	Spring into true 2nd position, ie, both feet in 2nd position and with weight equally distributed on both feet
	2	Hop on RF and place LF in rear leg position
	3	Hop on RF and place L heel in 2nd int position
	4	Hop on RF and point L toe in 2nd int position
4		Highland Fling step with RF, making one complete turn to the L
5–8		Perform bars I to 4 contrariwise.

8th step

This is the same as Step 4. This may have been given in error as a 9th step is given when one would expect the dance to finish on the 8th step to fit the music.

9th step

I–3	Highland Fling step three times with RF, making three complete turns to the L
4	Spring four RF, LF, RF, LF
5–8	Perform bars I to 4 contrariwise.

Scotch Jig

We collected this dance from Mr Adamson of Kingskettle, Fife. He had not taught the dance since 1907. It was danced to the tune 'The Laird o'Cockpen' at a speed of approximately 20 seconds per step and Mr Adamson wore his Highland dancing pumps to which a hard heel of several layers of leather had been added.

The following movement is used throughout the dance.

Cast off

We describe 'cast off to the L'.

I	I	A springy step on RF into flat 5th position, at the same time swivelling LF on the toe to point foot out more than usual (the RF goes into what would have been flat 5th position had the LF not swivelled).

 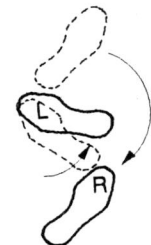

	2	Repeat I contrariwise
2	I	Repeat I.I
	&	Take a small step on LF towards 4th int position
	2	Close RF to flat 5th rear position.

1st step

1	1	Hop on LF and raise RF to front leg position, taking RF out towards 4th int low aerial position before bringing it up (count &1)
	&	Step on RF in semi 4th position
	2	Close LF to flat 5th rear position
2		Repeat bar 1
3, 4		Cast off to the L
5–8		Perform bars 1 to 4 contrariwise
		Repeat bars 1 to 8.

2nd step

1, 2		As Step 1
3	1	Place RF in flat 1st position and transfer weight momentarily on to it
	&	Move LF about 6 inches to the left, transferring weight back to it
	2	Place RF in flat 5th position and transfer weight momentarily on to it
	&	Move LF again about 6 inches to the left, transferring weight back to it
4–6		Repeat bar 3 three times but on the last beat of bar 6 there is no sideways movement, the LF simply beats in 5th rear position
7, 8		Cast off to the L
		Repeat bars 1 to 8 contrariwise.

3rd step

1	1	Cross RF over LF to position shown
	&	Hop on RF bringing LF up to front leg position
	2	Kick LF out (a gentle movement with no shake) to 4th int aerial position
2		Perform bar 1 contrariwise
3–8		As in Step 2.

4th step

1	1	Beat with LF in 5th rear position
	& a	Beat twice with R heel in 5th position, leaving R heel on floor after second beat
	2	Beat with LF in 5th rear position
	& a	Double beat with R toe in flat 5th position
2		Repeat bar **1** contrariwise
3		Repeat bar **1**
4		Repeat bar **2**
5	1	Step on LF in loose 3rd rear position
	& a	Double beat with RF
	2	Step on RF in loose 3rd rear position
	& a	Double beat with LF
6	1	Step on LF in loose 3rd rear position
	& a	Double beat with RF
	2	Step on RF in loose 3rd rear position
7–8		Cast off to the L
		Repeat **1** to **8** contrariwise.

5th step

Cast off to L and then to R four times.

6th step

1	1	Step on LF in loose 1st position
	& a	Double beat with R toe
	2	Step on RF in loose 1st position
	& a	Double beat with L toe
2–6		Repeat bar **1** five times
7–8		Cast off to the L
		Repeat bars **1** to **8** contrariwise.

On bars **1** to **6** make a complete turn to the right.

Miss Gayton's Hornpipe

This dance was collected in 1959 from Miss Elizabeth Wallace of Kilmarnock. It is the one dance collected from oral tradition on the mainland of Scotland which bears the type of name which we noted in Chapter 1. This was the solo dance made up by dancing teachers for favoured pupils. Unfortunately we were unable to discover any details of the origin of the dance – it might be old but might equally be of more recent origin. The music occurs in *Kerr's Caledonian Collection of Highland Airs and Quicksteps, Hornpipes etc.*

Miss Wallace was a dancing teacher, aged 65, and was a member of the British Association of Teachers of Dancing and represented them on the Official Board of Highland Dancing and served on its technical committee. She followed her father, grandfather and grand-uncle in their profession. Her father, Joseph Wallace, Junior, was born in 1856 and died in 1932 at the age of 76. He had possessed a large number of the early ballroom guides and had an enormous repertoire of Country Dances. In addition, he had a large repertoire of solo dances, some of which he undoubtedly learnt from his own father and uncle. The list included:

Highland Fling	Miss Gayton's Hornpipe
Sword Dance	Jockey's Hornpipe
Seann Triubhas	Skipping Rope Dance
Sailor's Hornpipe	Skirt Dance
Irish Jig	Tambourine Dance
Highland Laddie	Various clog dances
Rock and the Wee Pickle Tow	Various fancy dances

The last six dances together with the Irish Jig and the Sailor's Hornpipe were taught by many teachers in the north of England as well as in Scotland; for example see our *Traditional Step-Dancing in Lakeland* (London, 1979).

Miss Gayton's Hornpipe was taught by Mr Wallace to his young girl pupils, usually aged about eight to twelve years old. They held their dresses slightly out to the side with their thumbs at the back. Three Morris dance type bells were sewn to a band of elastic at each wrist.

A step took about 22 seconds (16 bars) counting 1 & 2 & 3 & 4 & etc.

One movement needs to be described. This is a 'break' used to end an eight bar phrase in each step.

Break *(This is similar to the 'ronde' in Over the Water to Charlie)*

7	Hop twice on LF (counts 1, 2), taking RF through a very loose front leg position round and down to a rear 5th position (R toe under L arch) (count 3) and pause there for count 4
8	Perform bar **7** contrariwise.

1st step

Start in 3rd position with RF in front.

On bars **1–6** describe a complete circle in a clockwise direction, and the reverse on bars **9–14**.

1	1	Hop on LF and shake RF out from 3rd position to semi 4th low aerial position and back to low front leg position, moving slightly forward on the hop
	2	Repeat count 1
	3	Step forward on RF leaving LF on the ground
	4	Draw the LF along the ground past RF and then up into semi 4th low aerial position (the LF starts to move on count 4)
2		Perform bar **1** contrariwise, the RF coming back into low front leg position on count 1
3–6		Repeat bars **1, 2** twice
7, 8		Break RF
		Perform bars **1** to **8** contrariwise.

2nd step

I	I	Spring on LF and slide the ball of RF to semi 4th int position
	&	Keeping weight on LF and without hopping, brush the ball of the RF about 4 inches inwards towards 1st position
	2	Keeping weight on LF and without hopping, brush the ball of the RF back out to semi 4th int position
	&	Keeping weight on LF and without hopping, brush the ball of the RF about 4 inches inwards towards 1st position
	3	Continuing this inward movement, spring on to RF in 1st position (almost a drop rather than a spring) and at the same time slide LF on the ball out to semi 4th int position (so that both RF and LF arrive in position on count 1)
	& 4 &	} Perform bar 1. & 2 & contrariwise
2–5		Repeat bar 1, four times
6		Repeat 1. 1 & 2 &
	3	Beat with flat of RF in semi 4th int position (and pause there on count 4)
7, 8		Break RF
		Perform bars 1 to 8 contrariwise finishing with RF in rear 5th position.

3rd step

I	I	Hop on LF and point R toe in rear 5th position
	2	Hop on LF and place R heel in semi 4th int position
	3	Hop on LF and point R toe in 5th position (pause there for count 4)
2		Perform bar 1 contrariwise
3–6		Repeat bars 1, 2 twice
7, 8		Break RF
		Perform bars 1 to 8 contrariwise.

4th step

The dancer advances about six feet on bars **1–6** and retires on bars **9–14.**

1	1	Make a small spring to the R on RF (about ¾ of the way to 2nd position)
	&	Close LF to flat 5th position
	2	Beat with RF in flat rear 5th position
	&	Make a small beat with the LF about six inches to the left of flat 5th position
	3	Beat with RF on the spot
	&	Close LF back to flat 5th position
	4	Beat with RF on the spot
2		Perform bar **1** contrariwise
3–6		Perform bars **1, 2** twice
7, 8		Break RF
9	1 ⎫	
	& ⎬	As bar **1** counts **1 & 2**
	2 ⎭	
	3 ⎫	
	& ⎬	Perform counts **1 & 2** contrariwise
	4 ⎭	
10–14		Repeat bar **9** five times
15, 16		Break LF.

The action on bar **1** was known as a double pas de Basque. That on bar **9**.**1 & 2** is a simple pas de Basque made with more movement and more spring on count 1.

5th step

On the first six bars the dancers describe a circle anti-clockwise, then reverses this on bars **9–14**.

1	1	Keeping the L toe on the floor, make a springy step to the side and slightly forward, on to the RF. During the movement, swivel the LF on the toe and turn the R toe in, so that when the RF reaches the floor (on the count 1) both toes are turned well in, the weight being equally distributed on both feet
	2	Transfer the weight to the RF and swivel on the R toe to turn the R toe out and, at the same time, draw the L toe along the floor in to rear 5th position
	3, 4	Repeat counts 1, 2
2–6		Repeat bar **1** five times
7, 8		Break RF
		Perform bars **1** to **8** contrariwise.

During these movements the dancer's body is facing in towards the centre of the circle which is being described.

6th step *(Double toe and heel)*

1	1	Hop on LF and point R toe in rear 5th position
	2	Hop on LF and place R heel in semi 4th int position
	3	Hop on LF and point R toe in 5th position
	4	Hop on LF and place R heel in semi 4th int position
2	1	Hop on LF and point R toe in rear 5th position
	2	Hop on LF and place R heel in semi 4th int position
	3	Hop on LF and point R toe in 5th position and hold this position throughout count 4
3, 4		Perform bars **1, 2** contrariwise
5, 6		Repeat bars **1, 2**
7, 8		Break
		Perform bars **1** to **8** contrariwise.

7th step

1		As in 2nd step
2		As in bar **6** of 2nd step
3	1	Step to the R on RF
	2	⎫ Beginning to turn to the R,
	3	⎬ pivot on the R toe and,
	4	⎭ step on LF with L leg crossed over R leg
4		Pivoting on the toes, continue the turn to finish facing the front with RF in flat 5th position and hold this position momentarily
5, 6		Repeat bar **1** of 2nd step twice
7, 8		Break RF
		Perform bars **1** to **8** contrariwise
		Curtsey to finish.

12

Clog Dances

C log dances were well known in Scotland. In this chapter we give two versions of the dance, Liverpool Hornpipe. They are drawn from opposite sides of the country but are very similar in style. The first comes from Mr Thomas Shanks who learnt it in Wigtownshire in about 1900. The second is from Mr William Adamson of Kingskettle, Fife, whose father learnt the dance in about 1875. In addition we give the instructions for Mr Adamson's dance known simply as 'Clog Hornpipe'.

Wigtownshire-Liverpool Hornpipe

Mr Shanks learnt this dance from Mr Peter Marshall. Both Mr Shanks and Mr Marshall performed it in Highland dancing pumps. The dance involves the beating out of the rhythm and his pupils danced in clogs or hard-soled shoes. It was widely regarded as a 'clog dance'. For other clog dancing, Mr Shanks wore the special clogs noted in Chapter 6. Mr Shanks danced to a Scotch measure, at a speed of 8 bars in 13 seconds.

Only one movement in the dance was given a name by Mr Shanks; this was the 'treble' which in our terminology consists of 'flatter, drop and treble'. To avoid confusion we shall call this movement 'Flatter and treble'.

The special movements used in the dance are given below.

Treble RF

Count	&	Brush RF out towards 4th int position
	2	Brush RF in towards 5th position
	&	Beat RF in 5th position and transfer weight on to it
	3	Beat LF in rear 5th position. This is a very heavy beat.

Flatter and treble RF

This runs across the end of one bar and the beginning of the next. For example, where bars **5, 6** give Flatter and treble RF, LF, the first movement actually starts on the counts **4.4 & a**. We give below a Flatter and treble performed in bar **1**.

	4	Hop on LF
	&	Brush RF out towards 4th int position
	a	Brush RF in towards 5th position
1	1	Drop on RF in 1st position
	&	Brush LF out towards 4th int position
	2	Brush LF in towards 5th position
	&	Drop on LF in 5th position
	3	Beat RF in rear 5th position with a heavy beat as in count 3 of the Treble.

Close RF

This forms the last two bars of each step and starts with a Flatter and treble in bar **7** i.e. actually starting in bar **6**.

	4	Hop on LF	⎫
	&	Brush RF out towards 4th int position	
	a	Brush RF in towards 5th position	
7	I	Drop on RF in 1st position	Flatter and
	&	Brush LF out towards 4th int position	treble RF
	2	Brush LF in towards 5th position	
	&	Drop on to LF in 5th position	
	3	Beat RF in rear 5th position as count 3 of treble	⎭
	&	Brush LF out towards 4th int position	
	4	Brush LF in towards rear 5th position	
	&	Hop on RF	
8	I	Beat LF in rear 5th position and transfer weight to it	
	2	Step forward on RF	
	3	Close LF to 1st position.	

1st Step

1–6	Flatter and treble with RF and LF alternately, six times
7, 8	Close RF
	Perform bars **1** to **8** contrariwise.

2nd Step

I		Flatter and treble RF
	&	Beat LF in 5th position transferring weight to it
	4	Beat RF in rear 5th position transferring weight to it
	&	Beat LF in 5th position transferring weight to it
2	I	Beat RF in rear 5th position transferring weight to it
	&	⎫
	2	⎬ Treble LF
	&	
	3	⎭
3, 4		Perform bars **1, 2** contrariwise (actually starting on count **2.4**)
5, 6		Flatter and treble RF, LF
7, 8		Close RF
		Perform bars **1** to **8** contrariwise.

3rd Step

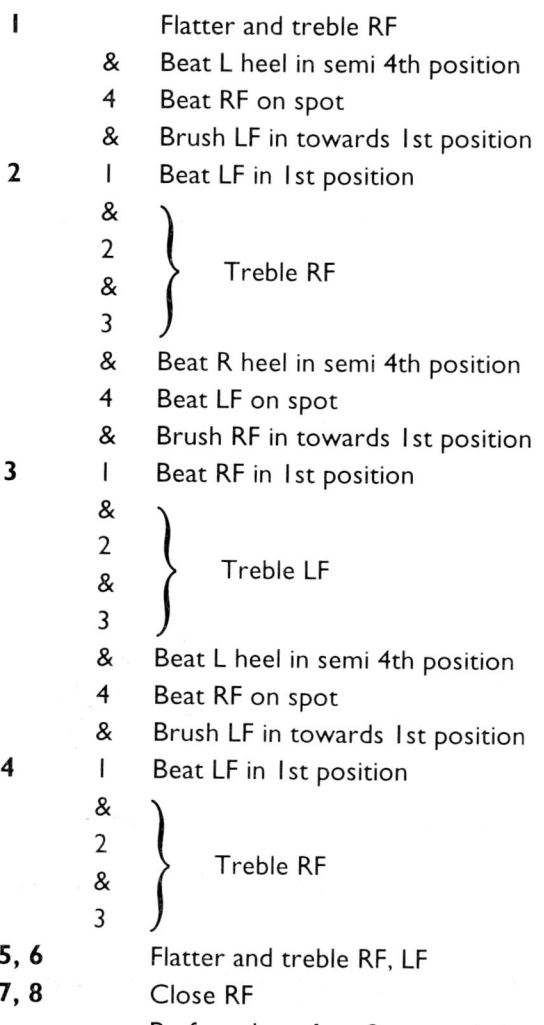

I		Flatter and treble RF
	&	Beat L heel in semi 4th position
	4	Beat RF on spot
	&	Brush LF in towards 1st position
2	I	Beat LF in 1st position
	&	⎫
	2	⎬ Treble RF
	&	
	3	⎭
	&	Beat R heel in semi 4th position
	4	Beat LF on spot
	&	Brush RF in towards 1st position
3	I	Beat RF in 1st position
	&	⎫
	2	⎬ Treble LF
	&	
	3	⎭
	&	Beat L heel in semi 4th position
	4	Beat RF on spot
	&	Brush LF in towards 1st position
4	I	Beat LF in 1st position
	&	⎫
	2	⎬ Treble RF
	&	
	3	⎭
5, 6		Flatter and treble RF, LF
7, 8		Close RF

Perform bars **I** to **8** contrariwise.

4th Step

I		Flatter and treble RF
2		Flatter and treble LF making one complete turn to L
3		Flatter and treble RF
	&	Brush LF out towards 4th int position
	4	Brush LF back towards rear 5th position
	&	Beat LF in rear 5th position and momentarily transfer weight to it
4	I	Beat RF in 5th position
	&	⎫
	2	⎬ Treble LF
	&	
	3	⎭
5, 6		Perform bars **3**, **4** contrariwise
7, 8		Close RF
		Perform bars I to **8** contrariwise.

5th Step

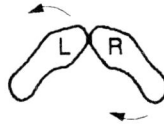 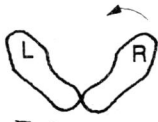 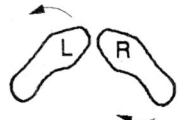

Count 1 to 2	Count 2 to 3	Count 3 to 4

This is a simple crab-walk, moving once round anticlockwise in a circle on bars **1–4** facing outwards.

I	I	Jump on to both feet with the toes turned well in and touching each other
	2	Swivel on the L heel and the R toe, turning the feet out to bring the heels in contact
	3	Swivel on the L toe and R heel, turning the feet in, to bring the toes together
	4	Repeat count 2
2–4		Repeat bar I, three times finishing on count **4.3**
5, 6		Flatter and treble RF, LF
7, 8		Close RF
		Perform bars I to **8** contrariwise.

6th Step

I		Flatter and treble RF
	4	Drop on LF slightly behind 1st position and at same time raise RF to a loose front leg position. The R knee should be well turned out, the R heel level with the bottom of the L kneecap, and the RF about 4" from the front of the L leg.
2	I	Drop on RF in 1st position
	&	⎫
	2	⎬ Treble LF
	&	⎭
	3	
3, 4		Perform bars **1, 2** contrariwise
5, 6		Flatter and treble RF, LF
7, 8		Close RF
		Perform bars **1** to **8** contrariwise.

7th Step

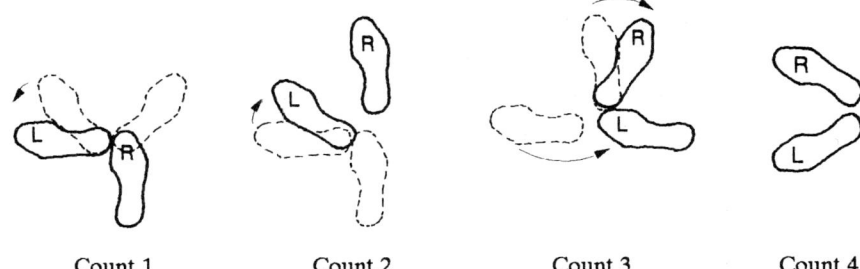

| Count 1 | Count 2 | Count 3 | Count 4 |

The dancer moves in a circle anticlockwise during bars **1–4**. The dancer faces outwards all the time. The positions given in the diagrams are only approximate.

1	1	Starting in 1st position, swivel the LF on the heel to the L, at the same time sliding the RF on the ball of the foot to rear 5th position. The knees are bent, and the L toe is well off the ground
	2	Swivel the LF on the heel back halfway to its original position, and slide the RF on the ball of the foot slightly to the L of 1st position
	3	Swivel the RF on the heel to the R and slide the LF on the ball of the foot to rear 5th position
	4	Swivel the RF on the heel and slide the LF on the ball of the foot to 1st position, but now facing to the L
2–4		Repeat bar **1**, three times finishing on count **4**.3
5, 6		Flatter and treble RF, LF
7, 8		Close RF
		Perform bars **1** to **8** contrariwise.

8th Step

The Close changes in bars **15, 16**. There is a exaggerated balancing action on counts **15**.3–**16**.3.

1–6		Flatter and treble with RF and LF alternately, making one complete turn to the L on bars **2–6** (one turn only, not one turn per bar)
7, 8		Close RF
9–14		Perform bars **1–6** contrariwise
15	1	Hop on LF, and point R toe in 2nd int position, with the toe pointed inwards
	2	Hop on LF and place R heel in 2nd int position
	3	Step back on RF in rear 4th position and lift LF off the ground
	4	Step forward on the LF on the original spot
16	1	Kick R instep against L heel
	2	Step back on RF in rear 4th position and lift LF off the ground
	3	Step forward on to LF on the original spot.

Fife-Liverpool Hornpipe

Mr Adamson could only remember 6 steps out of the original 10 steps and the description of the 6th step is not very precise so we only give the first five.

Mr Adamson wore Highland dancing pumps which had heels added to them made of several layers of leather. He regarded the dance as a 'heavy shoe' dance but stated that it could be danced in clogs. His pupils danced in clogs or hard-soled shoes. He taught his pupils to hold their hands by their sides with the fingers spread and slightly raised, arms swinging gently (also used in the Clog Hornpipe). Mr Adamson danced to a Scotch measure at a speed of 27 seconds per step (16 bars of music).

The special movements used in the dance are given below.

Catch in RF

This occurs either at the end of one bar running into the beginning of the next (counts 4 & 1) or in the middle of a bar (counts 2 & 3). Where bar **3** gives Catch in RF, Catch in LF, the first catch in starts on count 4 in bar **2**, as shown below:

Count	4	Hop on LF and take RF out to 4th int low aerial position
	&	Brush RF in towards 5th position
3	I	Beat RF in 5th position and transfer weight on to it.

Treble LF

Count	&	Brush LF out towards 4th int position
	2	Brush LF in towards 5th position
	&	Beat LF in 5th position and transfer weight on to it
	3	Beat RF in rear 5th position.

Cast-off RF

I	I	Step on RF in Ist position
	&	Brush LF out towards 4th int position
	a	Brush LF in towards 5th position
	2	Drop on LF in Ist position
	&	Brush RF out towards 4th int position
	a	Brush RF in towards 5th position
	3	Drop on RF in Ist position
	&	Brush LF out towards 4th int position
	4	Brush LF in towards rear 5th position
	&	Hop on RF
2	I	Step on LF in rear 5th position
	2	Step on to RF (in 5th position)
	3	Step on flat of LF in 4th position – weight backwards.

Heel Roll LF

Figure a   Figure b

I	I	Step on RF
	&	Beat L heel in position shown in Fig. a and immediately begin to swivel LF outwards on the heel
	2	Momentarily transferring the weight to the L heel, beat with RF on the spot, at the same time continuing to swivel the LF on the heel to the position shown in Fig. b

1st Step

1	1	Step forwards on ball of RF
	2	Step forwards on ball of LF
	3	Step forward on ball of RF
2	1	Hop on RF, place L heel in 4th position
	2	Hop on RF, place L toe in 4th position
	3	Hop on RF, place L heel in 4th position
3		Catch in LF, Catch in RF
4		Catch in LF and treble RF
5		Repeat bar **1**
6	1	⎫
	2	⎬ Repeat counts **2**.1, 2, 3
	3	⎭
	4	Stamp with LF
7, 8		Cast off RF
		Perform bars **1** to **8** contrariwise.

2nd Step

1	1	Spring on to RF and place LF in 2nd position
	3	Hop on RF, turning to R with LF in 2nd low aerial position
	4	Repeat count 3
2	1	Repeat **1**.3, completing turn to R
	&	⎫
	2	⎬
	&	⎬ Treble LF
	3	⎭
3, 4		Perform bars **1**, **2** contrariwise
5		Catch in RF, Catch in LF
6		Catch in RF
	&	⎫
	2	⎬
	&	⎬ Treble LF
	3	⎭
	4	Beat L heel in 4th position
7, 8		Cast off RF
		Perform bars **1** to **8** contrariwise.

3rd Step (Heel roll – our name)

1	1 & 2	Heel roll LF, making first beat with RF a stamp
	&	Bring LF back towards 1st position beating with LF in semi 4th position on the way in
	3 & 4	Heel roll RF
	&	Bring RF back towards 1st position beating with RF in semi 4th position on the way in
2	1 & 2	Heel roll LF
	&	Keeping weight on RF, pivot on toe of LF so as to turn L toe inwards
	3	Put weight on LF and close R toe to L heel as first beat of Heel roll LF
	& 4	} Complete Heel roll LF
	&	Bring LF back towards 1st position beating with LF in semi 4th position on the way in
3, 4		Perform bars **1, 2** contrariwise with just a beat on **3**.1
5, 6		Perform bars **1, 2** upto **2**.3
6	4	Beat L heel in 4th position
7, 8		Cast off with RF
		Perform bars **1** to **8** contrariwise.

4th Step

I		Catch in RF
	&	⎫
	2	⎬ Treble with LF, moving about 6" to right on final step with RF
	&	⎪
	3	⎭
	&	⎫
	4	⎬ Treble with LF again moving to R
	&	⎪
2	I	⎭
	&	⎫
	2	⎬ Treble with LF moving to R
	&	⎪
	3	⎭

3, 4   Perform bars **1, 2** contrariwise
5–8   Perform bars **5** to **8** from 2nd step including Catch in with RF
starting in bar **4**
Perform bars **1** to **8** contrariwise.

5th Step

I		Catch in RF
	&	⎫
	2	⎬ Treble with LF
	&	⎪
	3	⎭
	4	Spring on to LF, throwing RF out to 4th int low aerial position
2	I	Repeat 1.4 with spring on to RF
	&	⎫
	2	⎬ Treble with LF
	&	⎪
	3	⎭

3, 4   Perform bars **1, 2** contrariwise including first Catch in
5–8   Perform bars **5** to **8** from 2nd Step including Catch in with RF
starting in bar **4**
Perform bars **1** to **8** contrariwise.

Clog Hornpipe

Mr Adamson wore clogs with bells under the instep for this dance. He taught his pupils to hold their hands by their sides with the fingers spread and slightly raised, arms swinging gently.

The Clog Hornpipe was danced to the tune 'Navvie on the Line', widely known simply as the 'The Clog Hornpipe' played at a speed of 27 seconds for a step of 16 bars.

The special movements used in the dance are given below.

Treble RF

Count	&	Brush RF out towards 4th int position
	2	Brush RF in towards 5th position
	&	Beat RF in 5th position and transfer weight on to it
	3	Beat LF in rear 5th position.

Back Treble RF

	&	Brush RF out towards 4th int position
	2	Brush RF in towards 5th position
	&	Hop on LF carrying RF back towards rear 5th position
	3	Beat RF in rear 5th position

Cast-off RF (same as Fife-Liverpool Hornpipe)

1	1	Step on RF in 1st position
	&	Brush LF out towards 4th int position
	a	Brush LF in towards 5th position
	2	Drop on LF in 1st position
	&	Brush RF out towards 4th int position
	a	Brush RF in towards 5th position
	3	Drop on RF in 1st position
	&	Brush LF out towards 4th int position ⎫
	4	Brush LF in towards 5th position ⎬ Back Treble LF
	&	Hop on RF ⎭
2	1	Step on LF in rear 5th position
	2	Step on to RF (in 5th position)
	3	Step on flat of LF in 4th position – weight backwards.

Shuffle and Hop Back RF (our name)

I	I	Step on RF in 1st position
	&	Brush LF out towards 4th int position
	2	Brush LF in towards 5th position
	&	Hop on RF and,
	3	Beat ball or toe of LF in rear 4th position
	&	Hop on RF and,
	4	Beat with flat of LF just in front of 1st position.

1st Step

On bars **1–5** describe a complete circle to the right, finishing facing the front. Swing the L arm forward with the RF and vice versa.

I	I	With a pawing movement step out on R toe
	2	Drop on R heel
	3	With a pawing movement step out on L toe
	4	Drop on L heel
2–5		Repeat bar **1**, four times
6		Shuffle and hop back RF
7, 8		Cast-off RF
		Perform bars **1** to **8** contrariwise.

2nd Step

I	I	Stamp with R on spot
	& ⎫	
	2 ⎬	Back Treble LF
	&	
	3 ⎭	
	&	Tap RF out to 4th position
	4	Beat RF a further 6" diagonally forward of 4th position
	&	Tap with LF moving towards rear 5th position
2		Perform bar **I** contrariwise making first beat a tap with LF in rear 5th position
3		Perform bar **2** contrariwise
4		Repeat bar **2**
5		Perform bar **2** contrariwise
6		Shuffle and hop back LF
7, 8		Cast-off RF
		Perform bars **I** to **8** contrariwise.

3rd Step

In bars **5** and **6** keep body erect while lifting feet sideways.

I		Shuffle and hop back RF, making first beat with RF a stamp
2		Shuffle and hop back LF
3		Shuffle and hop back RF
4		Shuffle and hop back LF
5	I	Step on RF in 1st position and lift LF to L side and slap foot with L hand
	3	Step on LF and lift RF and slap foot with R hand
6	I	Step on RF and lift LF behind R leg and slap foot with R hand
	3	Step on LF and lift RF behind L leg and slap foot with L hand
7, 8		Cast-off RF
		Perform bars **I** to **8** contrariwise.

4th Step

I		Perform bar **I** of Cast-off with RF, making first beat with RF a stamp
2	I	Beat LF in rear 5th position
	&	Brush RF out towards 4th int position
	2	Beat RF in 4th int position
	&	Brush LF in towards rear 5th position
	3	Beat LF in rear 5th position
	&	Hop on RF
	4	Beat LF in 4th position
3, 4		Repeat bars **I, 2** contrariwise, making just a beat with LF on **3.I** not a stamp
5, 6		Repeat bars **I, 2** making just a beat with RF on **5.I**
7, 8		Cast-off RF
		Perform bars **I** to **8** contrariwise.

5th Step (*Double Heel Roll – our name*)

I	I & 2	Heel Roll LF (as in Fife-Liverpool Hornpipe) starting with stamp on RF
	&	Bring LF back towards Ist position beating with LF in semi 4th position on the way in
	3 & 4	Heel Roll RF
	&	Bring RF back towards Ist position beating with RF in semi 4th position on the way in
2	I	Step on RF in Ist position lifting LF slightly off the ground
	&	Brush LF out diagonally forward to 4th int low aerial position
	2	Hop on RF
	&	Bring LF in towards 3rd low aerial position, beating once with LF on way in
	3	Hop on RF
	&	Brush LF out diagonally forward to 4th int aerial position
	4	Hop on RF
3, 4		Perform bars **I, 2** contrariwise, starting with just a beat not a stamp on **3.I**
5, 6		Repeat bars **I, 2** contrariwise
7, 8		Cast-off RF (first beat hop with RF)
		Perform bars **I** to **8** contrariwise.

6th Step

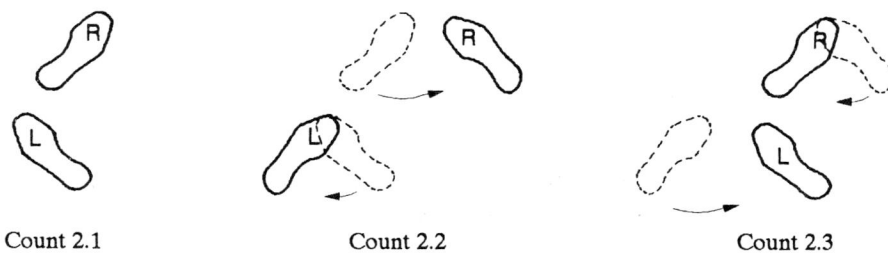

Count 2.1   Count 2.2   Count 2.3

1		Shuffle and hop back RF
2	1	Spring to land on toes with R in front of L, 4" between R heel & L toe, on toes, but with heels close to ground
	2	Pivot LF on L toe to turn toe inwards, at the same time sliding R toe about 10" to the right turning R toe inwards
	3	Close L to position as in **2**.1, pivoting on R toe to point toes outwards
	4	Repeat count **2**.2
3–6		Repeat counts **2**.3 and **2**.4, eight times ending with a stamp on count **6**.4
7, 8		Cast-off RF
		Perform bars 1 to 8 contrariwise.
		Actual distance moved sideways depended on dancing space.

7th Step (Double Crunch – our name)

I	I	Stamp on R on spot
	&	⎫
	2	⎬ Back Treble LF
	&	
	3	⎭
	4	Step on to RF about 6" to R side with heel in line with L toe
2	I	Cross LF over RF and step on to the ball of it
	2	Drop on to heel of LF
	3	Move RF as in count 1.4 placing weight equally on both feet
	&	Beat LF on spot
	a	Drop on to heel of LF
	4	Drop on to heel of RF
3, 4		Perform bars 1, 2 contrariwise, starting with just a beat on **3.**I
5	I	Repeat count **2.**3
	&	Repeat count **2.**&
	a	Repeat count **2.**a
	2	Repeat count **2.**4
	&	Step on ball on RF 6" to R of LF and in rear 4th position
	3	Beat LF on spot
	&	Drop on to heel of LF
	4	Stamp on RF in 4th int position
6		Perform bar **5** contrariwise
7, 8		Cast-off RF
		Perform bars I to **8** contrariwise.

8th Step

1	1	Stamp on RF
	2	Beat with flat of LF in 4th int position, using a pawing action with L leg, retaining weight on RF
	&	Brush LF out towards 4th int position
	3	Brush LF in towards 5th position
	&	Hop on RF
	4	Beat with LF in rear 5th position
2	1	Hop on LF
	&	Brush RF out towards 4th int position
	a	Brush RF in towards 5th position
	2	Hop on LF
	&	Tap RF in towards rear 5th position
	a	Beat RF in rear 5th position
	3	Brush LF out towards 4th int position
	&	Brush LF in towards 5th position
	a	Hop on RF
	4	Beat LF in rear 5th position
3, 4		Perform bars **1, 2** contrariwise, starting with just a beat on **3**.1
5, 6		Repeat bars **1, 2** ending with a stamp with LF in 4th int position on **6**.4
7, 8		Cast-off RF
		Perform **1** to **8** contrariwise

Back Treble LF (bracketed to the group: Brush LF out towards 4th int position / Brush LF in towards 5th position / Hop on RF / Beat with LF in rear 5th position)

9th Step

1	1	Stamp RF on spot
	&	Brush LF out towards 4th int position
	a	Brush LF in towards 5th position
	2	Hop on RF
	&	Tap LF in towards rear 5th position
	3	Beat LF in rear 5th position
	&	Tap RF in 5th position
	4	Beat RF in 5th position
	&	Brush LF forwards to 4th int low aerial position, beating once with ball of foot on way out
2	1	Hop on RF
	&	Brush LF in towards 3rd low aerial, beating once with ball of foot on way in
	2	Drop on L and move RF out to rear 4th int low aerial position
	&	Beat RF in rear 4th int position
	3	Beat LF on spot
	&	Brush RF forward to 4th int low aerial position, beating once with ball of foot on way out
	4	Hop on LF
3		Perform bar 1 of Cast-off
4	1	Beat LF in rear 5th position
	2	Cross RF over LF and step in crossed position
	3	Raise LF to 2nd aerial position, and bring RF up to kick feet together
	a	Drop on RF
	4	Bring LF to ground beside RF
5, 6		Repeat bars **1, 2**, starting with just a beat on **5**.1
7, 8		Cast-off RF
		Perform bars **1** to **8** contrariwise.

TMF noted that the movements on bars **3, 4** might be a bit dubious as he was unable to get Mr Adamson to slow this down.

13

The Dirk Dance

This is the dance as taught to us by Mrs Mary Isdale MacNab of Vancouver which she learnt from Mr D C Mather, a dancing teacher who emigrated to Canada from Scotland in 1899. The dance is quite vigorous and should be danced with a dirk, or replica, as it is used to emphasise the arm movements and is thrown on to the ground in the 4th step.

The dirk is held in the right hand with the point up as a sword would be held. In battle a dirk would have been clasped in the fist, with the point down in order to be used in a slashing movement upwards or in a jabbing movement downwards. We understand that a dirk would be custom made for its owner so that when held in the fist, the blade laid along the underarm, the point would not have protruded beyond the bend of the elbow.

We have used the points of the compass, indicated by N, S, E, W to identify the varying directions in which the dancer faces in the course of the dance. Arm and body movements are shown bold in square brackets.

The music used was 'Tha Biodag Air MacThomais' (Thomas' son wears a dirk) given below. There were originally about fifteen steps but we have only six. The first four are danced to slow tempo (about 10 seconds for 8 bars) and the last two are quick time (about 5 seconds for 8 bars).

1st Step (16 bars)

Stand in 1st position facing N, arms hanging naturally with dirk in right hand.

I	I	Spring forward on to RF with LF in 4th rear int aerial position
		[Flourish the dirk up across the front of the face to a position just above and slightly in front of the head with the back of the hand uppermost]
	&	Hold this position
	2	Balance on to LF with RF in 4th int aerial position
	&	Hold this position
2	I	Drop on to RF with LF in rear leg position
	&	Hop on RF with LF in front leg position
	2	Drop on to LF with RF in 4th rear int aerial position
		[Snap R arm out horizontally to R with dirk in line with arm]
	&	Hold this position
3	I	Hop on LF with RF in 2nd position
	&	Hop on LF with RF in rear leg position
	2	Carry RF in front of L leg and put it just to L of LF. Take LF to 2nd aerial position
		[Move W from 3.2 to 4.2]
	&	Spring L on to LF with RF in front leg position
4	I	Repeat **3**.2
	&	Repeat **3**.second &
	2	Repeat **3**.2
	&	Hold this position
5		Perform bar **I** contrariwise
		[On count 5.1 sweep dirk direct to position above head, on count 5.2 turn body to face NW but still looking to the N]
6		Perform bar **2** contrariwise
		[Turn body to face W but still looking to N, dirk points N from count 6.2]
7, 8		Perform bars **3, 4** contrariwise
		[Move N from 7.2 to 8.2]
9		Perform bar **I**
		[On count 9.1 sweep dirk direct to position above head]
10		Perform bar **2**
		[On count 10.2 flourish dirk above head]

11, 12		Perform bars **3, 4**
		[Turn three-quarters to L to end facing N in position occupied on 4.2]
13–16		Perform bars **5** to **8**.
		[Move E and slightly S to original position from 15.2 to 16.2. On 16.2 take dirk in teeth]

2nd Step (8 bars)

[Both fists on hips. Move to R on bars 1 and 3 and L on bars 5 and 7, on count 8.2 take dirk in R hand and let L hand hang naturally]

1	1	Step on to RF in 2nd position with weight on both feet
	&	Transfer weight on to RF
	2	Carry LF in front of RF and place it just to R of RF
	&	Pivot on both toes and make one complete turn to R
2	1	Spring upwards with legs out to sides
	&	Land with ball of LF in 5th position
	2	Repeat count **2.1**
	&	Land with ball of RF in 5th position
3, 4		Repeat bars **1, 2**
5, 6		Perform bars **1, 2** contrariwise
7, 8		Perform bars **1, 2** contrariwise.

3rd Step (8 bars)

1		Shuffle LF and RF
2	1	Drop on to RF in 5th position
	&	Step back diagonally on to LF
	2	Drop on to RF in 5th position with LF in 4th rear int aerial position

[From count 2.1 to 2.2 sweep dirk down and across body with elbow bent in a menacing movement, slowly at first quickening to a vicious slash on 2.2]

	&	Hold this position
3	1	Close LF under RF
	&	Step forward diagonally on to RF
	2	Close LF under RF and shoot RF to 4th int aerial position

[From count 3.1 to 3.2 sweep dirk back on same path as in bar 2, with same slashing movement]

	&	Hold this position
4	1	Turn to R with RF in 2nd position. Flex both knees and crouch slightly

[Swing dirk out to right and down to shoulder height]

	&	Take weight on RF, carry LF in to side of RF and pivot on RF a further quarter turn to R

[Continue to swing dirk down and in to position in front of body with back of hand down, the elbow is bent throughout]

	2	Drop on to LF with RF in 4th int aerial position. Complete full turn to R to end facing N

[Rip dirk up to original place above head]

	&	Hold this position
5		Shuffle RF and LF
6		Perform bar **2** contrariwise

[Sweep dirk across the face, down and back across the body to end out and back on the R hand side. The movement starts as a slow cutting slash and ends as a vicious flourish on 6.2]

7		Perform bar **3** contrariwise

[Sweep dirk back on the same path with the same kind of movement as in bar 6]

8   Perform bar **4** contrariwise.
               [Swing dirk as in bar 4]

4th Step (8 bars)

I   I   Drop on to LF with RF in 2nd aerial position (to NE of LF)
               [Face NW]

         &   Spring on to RF with LF in front leg position
               [Move NE]

         2   Repeat count **1**.**1**
               [Face NW]

         &   Repeat count **1**.**&**
               [Move NE]

2   I   Put ball of LF in 5th position

         &   Flex knees for spring

         2   Spring with knees high
               [Cut dirk below feet and back up to place, turn R to face S]

         &   Lift LF to front leg position

3   Repeat bar **1**
               [Move W]

4   Repeat bar **2**
               [As on 2.2 cut dirk below feet, turn R to face NE]

5   Repeat bar **1**
               [Move SE]

6   I   Repeat count **2**.**1**

         &   Repeat count **2**.**&**

         2   Repeat count **2**.**2**
               [As on 2.2 cut dirk below feet, turn R to face N]

         &   Lift RF to 4th int aerial position

7   I   Kick back of R leg with LF (in back leg position)

         &   Drop on to RF

         2   Repeat count **7**.**1**

         &   Repeat count **7**.**&**

8   I   Repeat count **7**.**1**

         &   Repeat count **7**.**&**

         2   Put ball of LF in 5th position.
               **[Move forwards on bars 7 and 8, on count 8.2 throw dirk on
               to the ground diagonally forwards to R]**

5th Step (16 bars quick time)

		[Hands on hips for Pas de Basque and up for High cuts throughout]
1, 2		Pas de Basque RF, spring with LF in 5th position, high cut RF
		[Turn once and a quarter R to face E, move 4–5 feet SE]
3, 4		High cut with LF, RF, LF, RF
5, 6		Repeat bars 1, 2
		[Turn once and a quarter R to face S, move 4–5 feet SW]
7, 8		Repeat bars 3, 4
9, 10		Repeat bars 1, 2
		[Turn once and a quarter R to face W, move 4–5 feet NW]
11, 12		Repeat bars 3, 4
13, 14		Repeat bars 3, 4
		[Turn once and a quarter to face N, move 4–5 feet NE to complete square]
15		Walk RF, LF
		[Hands hanging naturally, move to dirk and bend to pick it up]
16	1	Walk RF
		[Grasp dirk]
	2	Drop on to LF with RF in 4th int aerial position.
		[Straighten up and sweep dirk to position above head]

6th Step (16 bars)

1		High cut with LF, RF
2	1 &	High cut LF
	2	Drop on to LF with RF in 4th int aerial position
	&	Hold this position
3, 4		Perform 3rd Step bars **2** and **3**
		[Hands as in 3rd Step]
5–8		Repeat bars 1 to **4**
		[Hands as in bars 1 to 4]
9		High cut with LF, RF
10		Double high cut LF
		[Flourish dirk above head]
11		High cut with RF, LF
12		Double high cut RF
		[Flourish dirk above head]
13		High cut with LF, RF while making half turn right to face S
14	1 ⎞	High cut LF while making quarter turn,
	& ⎠	R to face W
	2	Drop on LF with RF in 4th int aerial position, while making quarter turn R to face N
15		Perform 4th Step bar **7** moving N
16	1 ⎞	Spring forward and land on both feet,
	& ⎠	making full turn to R on spot
		[Straighten arm above head]
	2 ⎞	Spring up and land on both feet,
	& ⎠	in 1st position.

Appendix

Step-Dancing in Cape Breton Island Nova Scotia

Frank Rhodes

C ape Breton Island is part of the Canadian province of Nova Scotia. It is about 105 miles long from north to south and about 85 miles wide from east to west. It lies to the north-east of mainland Nova Scotia, from which it is separated by the Straight of Canso. It is divided geographically by Bras d'Or Lake and the associated channels which focus on the central Grand Narrows; and it is divided administratively into the four counties of Cape Breton, Richmond, Victoria and Inverness. The last of these is on the west coast of the island. It faces across George Bay to the mainland town and county of Antigonish, and across the end of Northumberland Straight to Prince Edward Island.

The European settlements on the island were dominated by the French until the British forces destroyed the French fortress at Louisburg on the south-east coast of the island in 1758. The ruined town became the centre of a small British settlement until 1784. The development of the island was slow in comparison with that of mainland Nova Scotia and of Prince Edward Island. Then a separate Governor was appointed for Cape Breton Island and a location on the east of the island with good harbours was chosen as the capital, Sydney. The first flood of new settlers came from all over the British Isles to spread out from Sydney over the east of the island. At the beginning of the nineteenth century the west coast and the central part of the island round Grand Narrows were settled by immigrants from the Scottish Highlands and the Western Isles. Many of them spent their first winter in the established settlements, sometimes in Antigonish or Prince Edward Island, before starting out on their own the following spring. When the mineral resources were being developed in the middle of the nineteenth century a new wave of immigrants came to the island. These were mainly miners from England and Wales, together with Irish labourers. Nevertheless, for most of the nineteenth century large parts of the island were populated predominantly by Gaelic speaking Scottish communities.

Details of the early settlements in the west of Cape Breton Island are given in *The History of Inverness County* [50]. It is clear from these records, and from the memories of older people even in 1957, that dancing in the old Scottish tradition

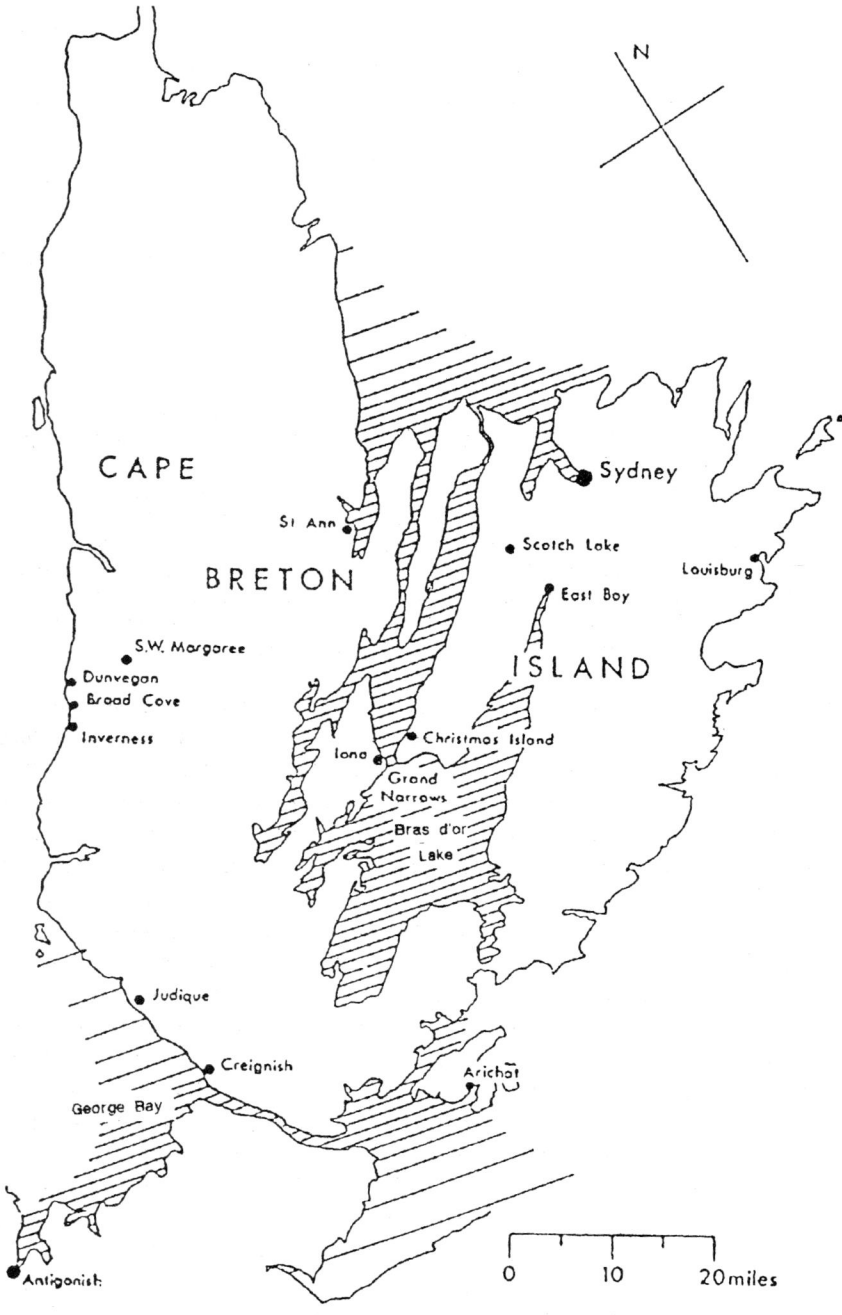

Cape Breton Island, Nova Scotia

had played a significant part in the social life of the Scottish communities. It is recorded that Lauchlin MacDougall emigrated from Moidart in 1807 and after wintering in Antigonish crossed to Inverness County. There he settled three of his grown-up sons, Alexander, Duncan and Archibald, side by side on the last 600 acres at Broad Cove Banks, and the last one, Hugh, a little further north in Dunvegan. Duncan had a son, John, 'a man of great industry and good judgement, a famous dancer, and withal a kind and genial host'; while Archibald had a son, Lauchlin, who 'was a particularly cheerful and pleasant man, with an immense fund of the old Scottish legends'.

However, it was another family that was particularly noted for dancing in the early days of Inverness County [50].

MacMillans (The Dancers)

Allan MacMillan was born in Lochaber, Scotland. About the year 1817 he came to America, landing at Pictou and spending his first winter in the new world with relatives at the Gulf shore of Antigonish. In 1820 he came to Rear Little Judique in the county of Inverness where he took 200 acres of land.

On the eve of his departure he was married by Fr. William Fraser (afterwards Bishop of Arichat) to Catherine Rankin of Lochaber. She was a Catholic and he a Protestant. He remained in the Protestant faith until his last illness, when he became a Catholic and received the last rights of the church at the hands of Reverend Alexander MacDonell of Judique. He was a celebrated dancer, and after coming to this country, kept a dancing class in both the settlements of Judique and Creignish. He had four of a family, namely John, Donald, Ann and Sarah.

The dances taken from Scotland to Cape Breton Island in the early nineteenth century seem to have been four-handed and eight-handed Reels with stepping, and some solo step-dances. There were also a few dance-games. The figures and the stepping for the Reels as they were danced in 1957 have been described in the appendix to *Traditional Dancing in Scotland* [48]. The various forms of the Reels are related to Highland and Hebridean forms of these dances. The stepping used in Cape Breton Island often involved a continuous marking of the rhythm with toe and heel beats. In some ways it resembled the 'treepling' which survived in East Lothian, Roxburghshire and West Berwickshire within living memory, and which is described in *Traditional Dancing in Scotland* [42]. The style certainly goes back in Scotland to the beginning of the nineteenth century. In his description of a country dance at a dancing-master's ball at Damally, Colonel Thornton notes, 'The company consisted of about fourteen couples, who all danced the true Glen Orgue kick. I have observed, that every district in the Highlands has some peculiar cut; and they all shuffle in such a manner as to make the noise of their feet keep exact time' [31]. The solo dances belonged to an old Scottish tradition in which the steps were low and close. In these dances also there was considerable beating of the feet marking the rhythm of the music.

The number of people who knew the solo dances diminished gradually between the two World Wars and rapidly after the second. The survival of the Cape Breton solo dances was affected by the introduction of modern Highland dancing. Until about 1939 Highland dancing was performed only by 'outsiders' to the island. The forms of Highland dancing then current in the Highland Games in Scotland had been introduced in Antigonish in the 1930s. For the first Gaelic festival at the Gaelic College at St Ann, Victoria County, in 1939, dancers came from Antigonish. Subsequently, there was a team of Highland dancers centred on the college. From that time, certainly up to 1957, many young people, mostly young girls up to the age of about sixteen, were trained in the modern style of Highland dancing. At first the descriptions of the dances published in Glasgow by D R MacKenzie [51] were taken as the standard. In 1950 most of the Highland dancers of the province, with the exception of those in Cumberland County, adopted D G MacLennan's descriptions given in his *Highland and Traditional Scottish Dances (op. cit.)*. The Scottish Official Board of Highland Dancing's textbook *Highland Dancing (op. cit.)* was published in 1955 and by 1957, some of the competition Highland dancers favoured D G MacLennan while others favoured the Official Board [Informant 1]. For a time the dancing competitions included Cape Breton solo dances, but they were dropped because of the difficulty of deciding on a standard for judging. The same difficulty with judging dancing competitions in Scotland had led to the publication of recommendations for judges by a conference in 1925 [52] and later to the Scottish Official Board's textbook in 1955.

From the time of the introduction of the modern Highland Games dances in about 1939 up to 1957, the form in which the Cape Breton solo dances were most frequently seen was as extempore continuous stepping. They were danced to fast strathspeys and to reels played on a violin. The favourite tune was 'Calum Crubach' (Miss Drummond of Perth). However, they were originally taught as solo dances with fixed sequences of steps, each dance having its own tune or tunes. The steps did not consist of continuous beating on the spot, but included wider movements with a 'beating' finish to each step. In 1957 there were many people who recalled seeing the old solo dances. It was still possible to find people who had themselves been to dancing classes at which these solo dances were taught, and others who has learned some of the dances within their families.

The music for the solo dances was usually played on the violin. The old tempo for strathspeys was about 44 bars per minute, with about 52 bars per minute for reels. One of the legendary Cape Breton fiddlers was Charlie MacKinnon who came from Scotland to the island about 1810. In 1957 there were still people who could recall his traditional style of playing [Informant 2]. People would also 'jig' the tune of a dance. 'Jigging' was the English word used on the island for a form of canntaireachd or mouth-music. This was originally a method of representing the notes and grace-notes of bagpipe music by vocable syllables.

Some dance tunes had their Gaelic dance-songs or puirt-a-beul. In particular, there was a puirt-a-beul for the favourite tune 'Miss Drummond of Perth'. That given in MacDonald's collection *Puirt-a-Beul* is 'An Gillie Crubach anns a'Ghieann' [53]. The Cape Breton puirt-a-beul for this tune is 'Calum Crubach' [Informant 3]. Since it differs substantially from the other it is given here.

Calum Crubach	*A rough translation is:*
Calum crubach anns a'Ghleann	Crooked Calum in the glen
Till a null na coraich chusainn	Return over the sheep to us
Calum crubach anns a'Ghleann	Crooked Calum in the glen
Till a null na coraich	Return over the sheep
Ged a tha do leth-shuil dall	Although one of your eyes is blind
Chi thu leis an t-suil udieile	You can see with the other eye
Ged a tha do leth-shuil dall	Although one of your eyes is blind
Chi thu lei an aonte	You can see with one
Calum crubach anns a'Ghleann	Crooked Calum in the glen
'Se 'na dheann asiarraidh mna	In a great rush looking for a wife
Calum crubach anns a'Ghleann	Crooked Calum in the glen
'Se a'bagairt posaidil	And him thinking of marrying

Puirt-a-beul, rather than fiddle music, seems to have been used for dance-games such as Marbadh na Beiste Duibhe (The Killing of the Otter), Cailleach an Dùdain (The Old Woman of the Milldust) and Tri Croidhan Caorach (Three Sheep's Trotters) [Informant 4]. Descriptions of these old Gaelic dance-games can be found in *Some Hebridean Folk Dances* [46]. Some special reels such as Ruidhleadh nan Caraid (The Married Couple's Reel) were also danced to puirt-a-beul. The puirt-a-beul for Ruidhleadh nan Coileach Dubha (The Reel of the Blackcocks) was sometimes used for Dannsa na Tunnag (The Duck's Dance), in which the dancers go down on their hunkers and throw their legs forward alternately [Informant 5]. The Reels are described in [42] and [48]. The Duck's Dance seems most often to have been danced by children individually, but a lady of ninety-three who demonstrated it in 1957, recalled seeing it performed at a picnic by a ring of grown-ups holding hands [Informant 6].

The members of the Gillis family of Gillisdale, South West Margaree [Informant 7] were able to recollect a number of the Cape Breton solo dances. Mr John Gillis's grandfather, who came from Morar, had been taught dancing as a child in Cape Breton Island by an itinerant tailor from Scotland, Donald Beaton. The dances had been handed down in the Gillis family and both John and his daughter Margaret could dance some of them in 1957. The Gillis family dances originally included the Fling (which was not called the Highland Fling), the Swords, Seann Triubhas, Flowers of Edinburgh (Dannsa nan Flurs), Jacky Tar, Duke of Fife, The Girl I Left Behind Me, Over the Hills and Far Away, Irish Washerwoman, Princess Royal, and Tullochgorm. Each of them originally had twelve steps.

The first seven of these dances were also included in the repertoire of the Kennedy family at Broad Cove [Informant 8]. As a young boy Ronald Kennedy had watched his father teaching them at dancing classes which he ran there up to about 1900. There also the dances each had twelve steps. Ronald had not been taught them formally by his father but had picked them up by watching. His father had learned the dances from his own father, John Kennedy. John had emigrated from Canna to Prince Edward Island in 1790, his wife giving birth to triplets on the way. He had run dancing classes in Broad Cove when he moved there from Prince Edward Island after a few years.

The name of Beaton appeared again in connection with dancing, for Ronald Kennedy recalled dancing classes run by a teacher, Angus Beaton, at South West Margaree and in the town of Inverness. Dancing classes in Creignish, run by Allan MacMillan 'the dancer' about 1820, continued to be held up to about 1910 [Informant 9]. Hugh MacKenzie, whose family came from Barra recalled that the classes attended by his grandmother at Christmas Island included Tullochgorm, a solo dance with fourteen steps [Informant 3]. These classes and the step-dance classes at nearby Iona went on until the turn of the century [Informant 10].

The main venue for dances was in peoples' houses. They had their 'kitchen rackets' and 'milling frolicks' [Informant 11]. Schoolrooms were also used for dancing until the first halls were built about 1920. Out of doors the wooden bridges provided the best smooth surfaces for dancing in small groups. Indeed Angus Beaton's dancing classes at South West Margaree were held on the bridge [Informant 8]. For summer weddings and picnics large wooden platforms were built specially for dancing.

The wooden houses of Cape Breton were larger than the crofters' cottages of the Highlands and Hebrides, but still did not give much room for dancers to spread themselves. Modern versions of the 'Hebridean' solos are performed in Highland dancing pumps, in the style of modern Highland dancing, with wide leg and arm movements which can be seen easily by large audiences. The versions collected in the Hebrides in the 1950s were performed in hard shoes. The movements were neat and close, with little or no arm movements, as is appropriate for dancing in confined areas. The dances were *heard* as well as seen.

Similar comments were made about this aspect of the style of the solo dances of the Hebrides and of Cape Breton Island. The notes of conversations in 1955 with Archie Monroe of Loch Boisdale in South Uist include, 'No special shoes were worn for dancing. The hands hung naturally or were placed on the hips. The dancer did not jump up; his body was absolutely still, and had he been dancing in a crowd with his feet obscured he would not have been picked out by the movement of his body. The style was the same for men and women' [Informant 12]. The notes of conversations in 1957 with Hugh MacKenzie who was brought up at Christmas Island, Cape Breton include, 'Ordinary shoes were always worn for dancing (other than modern Highland). For step-dancing people stood erect with hands hanging by side. Sometimes the whole upper body is held stiff' [Informant 3]. While the last two sentences bring modern Irish step-dancing to mind, the dances which Hugh MacKenzie mentioned by name were the Fling, Flowers of Edinburgh and Tullochgorm. The solo dances which I recorded in 1957 could be traced back through dancers of Highland or Hebridean descent and I found no indication of any influence on them by Irish immigrants.

The dancers used hard soled shoes with heels for their step-dances as well as for their social dances. The dancers 'all wore ordinary clothes and home made broguans. Ladies pulled up their long skirts a little to show their feet' [Informant 13]. The one exception to the statement about the use of ordinary shoes for dancing in Cape Breton was that given by John Gillis, who said that he had soft shoes for the Fling which he did not use for any other of the dances, even the Swords [Informant 7]. He used no hand movements in any of the dances.

The difference between the style of the Cape Breton solo dances and the modern Highland Games dances was emphasised frequently. In 1957 most of the old people knew of dances like Flowers of Edinburgh (Dannsa nan Flurs), Tullochgorm, Seann Triubhas and the Swords, which had special steps on the toes and on the heels. 'The modern style of dancing up on the toes is alien to these' [Informant 2].

The impression that step-dancing was tight and close is reinforced by another of Hugh MacKenzie's recollections [Informant 3]. He said that at the end of an evening of dancing the two men who had shown the most steps had to 'dance it out'. A block of wood about eighteen inches high and twelve inches in diameter was placed in the centre of the floor. The two men danced round it, then in turn jumped on to it and danced as many steps as possible there. The one who danced the most complete steps there won.

In the Cape Breton solo dances, including the Fling, the various setting steps alternated with a travelling figure called a 'Reel'. In this the dancer danced round in a circle clockwise during the first half of the music. The steps used in the Reel were often six chassés followed by two bars of stepping, though the dancers might mark out extra beats in the chassés [Informant 7]. The setting steps of each particular solo were danced to the second half of the music. In the old days the setting steps were not continuous beating; each setting step had some special movement followed by a beating end. The older form was for each setting step to be danced one way only; it was not repeated starting with the other foot as is usual in Highland and Hebridean dances. The phrasing of this alternation of Reel and setting step is the same as in the old West Highland circular Reel [42] although sometimes the second part of the music was doubled up on the violin to give sixteen bars for the setting step and eight bars for the Reel [Informant 14]. The sequence of Reel and setting step was repeated to the end of the dance. The dancing round the block of wood in the competition which Hugh MacKenzie recalled was probably just the Reel part of the solo dances, the setting steps being performed on top of the block. In Scottish solo dances, dancing round in a circle occurs in a very simple version of Over the Hills and Far Away collected in South Uist [Informant 15], in the first step of the First of August (see Chapter 9) and in the first step of most (but not all) versions of Seann Triubhas.

The common social dances of the 1950s included 'square sets' which appeared to be derived from the figures of the Lancers and Quadrilles, with American square dance influence. In the travelling steps, as well as in the setting steps, the rhythm of the music had come to be marked with the feet. Whereas in earlier times some people in a square set would be standing while others danced, it had become usual for all to step-dance for the whole of a square set. The practice of stepping through the travelling movements of four-handed and eight-handed Reels, on the few occasions when they were performed in the 1950s, had also crept in. However, the older tradition was to move with a quiet travelling step. That most commonly described was an easy flowing walk, sometimes with the foot brushing the ground as it swung forward. The chassé was usually danced without any distinct rise on the supporting foot as the other foot was swung through, though one version with a hop was like a neat and tight polka step. In all cases the movements were small and the indications were that the circles were small.

There were other tests of skill associated with step-dancing in addition to the dancing on the block of wood described earlier, including tricks with candles and lamps which were also known of in the Hebrides, see Chapter 2. In one version of Smàladh na Coinnle (The Smooring of the Candle) three candles were placed in a row on the floor and the best dancers tried to flick off the wicks without putting out the candles [Informant 13]. In another version, the dancers had to put out candles by snuffing them between their heels in the middle of a dance. Dancers would sometimes step-dance on tables, with glasses full of whisky on them [Informant 2]. However, it was said that anyone who could step to Tullochgorm need not be tested; they were sure to be good dancers [Informant 13].

Hugh MacKenzie had heard his father and Alan Quinn speak about Dannsaidh na Biodag, which he called the Dagger Dance in English [Informant 3]. It was said to be a dance in which a dagger was stuck in the ground, point upwards, and the dancer danced round and over it without looking down. It is not clear whether his father has seen such a dance, or whether the story derived from printed references to dancing among upturned swords and spears which are misapplied to 'Caledonians' (see Chapter 3). Hugh MacKenzie had not heard of a Dirk Dance in which a dirk was held in the hand, but Archie Kennedy [Informant 14] had heard old men talk about a Dirk Dance whose Gaelic name he gave as Dannsa no Pitock. In this dance a dirk was held and thrown down and picked up again. It was danced to either of the tunes 'Thompson's Dirk' or 'MacAllister's Dirk', for each of which his grandfather had canntaireachd. The description of the Dirk Dance fits one of the steps of the dance mentioned in Chapters 7 and 13.

In 1957 there were a few people who had recollections of a Sword Dance from before the introduction of the modern Highland Games Sword Dance to Cape Breton Island. It was danced over two crossed swords in a similar style to the steps of the Sword Dance which could be found at that time in the Highlands, not in the style of the Cape Breton solo step-dances. Three people each showed a step of the dance. Two of them said that the dancer went anticlockwise round the swords, while the third said that the direction was clockwise.

The first step started at the corner of the swords with two pas de Basque (stepping on to the right foot) moving to the next space to the right, and four points with right, left, right and left toes in the space. This was repeated four times to return to the starting position [Informant 7]. The movement round the swords back to the starting position was completed in eight bars rather than the usual sixteen bars. The second step started at the point of a sword, which we may take to be point 1 in the diagram below. In the first bar the dancer hopped four times on the left foot while the right toe touched the ground successively in the spaces D, A, D and A. This was repeated contrariwise in the second bar. In the next bar the dancer moved to position 4, turning three quarters to the left with two low travelling pas de Basque (stepping first on to the left foot). The dancer was 84 years old, and the steps in the last bar of the phrase was indistinct, but they seemed to be four points in position 4. These four bars were to be repeated four times to take the dancer back to position 1 [Informant 8].

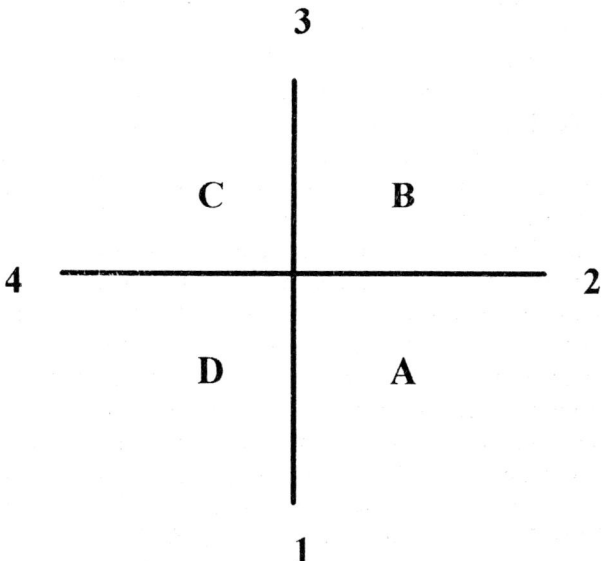

The oldest of the three sword dancers, Mrs MacDonald, was over 100 years old when she broke off from painting a shed door to talk about dancing [Informant 4]. She was soon demonstrating how the Sword Dance began! One step was a succession of simple pas de Basque at a point. The move to the next point to the right at the end of the four bar phrase involved some sort of pointing. The pointing part of one of her steps was over the swords as follows.

1   Hop on L foot in D and tap R heel in B
2   Drop on to R foot in A and tap L heel in C
3   Drop on to L foot in A and tap R heel in C
4   Drop on to R foot in B and tap L heel in D.

That is more than a centenarian should try to dance, and as much as I learned about the Cape Breton Sword Dance.

Instructions for the Dances from Cape Breton

The following versions of four of the Cape Breton Scottish solo dances were collected on a single visit to the island in 1957. Unlike the collecting in Scotland at that time, it was not possible to check the dances by repeated visits. Nevertheless, the dances as seen on that occasion help us to appreciate that the differences of styles of the Scottish solo dances were not as rigidly prescribed in former times as now. The Highland Games dances are now danced silently in soft shoes with defined arm movements and with wide leg movements. The collected versions were less formal in style. The other solo dances collected in the Hebrides and in the Highlands in the 1950s were danced with close leg movements. The arm movements, if they were used at all, were variable and informal. Hard shoes were worn, but the sounds made by them were subordinate to the movements in most of the steps of the dances. However, the sounds became more dominant when heel beats were used as well as toe beats, as in the treble in the Hebridean First of August. Indeed there are a number of steps in some of the versions of the First of August which are akin to some clog dance steps. The use of fast heel and toe beats in Aberdonian Lassie and in Scotch Jig is the closest one comes in collected Scottish solo dances to the Cape Breton step-dance style. The Scottish version of Flowers of Edinburgh also seems always to have involved fast beating steps.

In 1957, the Cape Breton step-dances looked very different from Highland Games dancing. However, one can see from the instructions for the dances how they are related to the solo dances collected in Scotland at that time. The overall impression is of a common collection of dance movements which had come to be danced very low on the ground in Cape Breton and much higher on the toes in Scotland. Some particular pairs of steps tend to reinforce this impression. The double ronde movement occurs in the 6th step of the Cape Breton Seann Triubhas and in the 6th step of the version of Highland Laddie from the Hebrides. The 'hesitation walk' forward at the start of the 6th step of the Cape Breton Flowers of Edinburgh is like the start of the 10th step of the First of August, while the first two bars of its 7th step are like a Scottish clog dance step. The first bar of the 4th step of the Cape Breton Fling has the same form as the heel and toe movement of the Forfar Shan Trews, which also occurs at the start of the 4th step of John MacLeod's Hebridean version of Highland Laddie, though at a different tempo.

The Cape Breton solo dances (with the exception of the Sword Dance) all involved fast beating steps. The first two steps of the Cape Breton Fling recorded below are beating versions of the Old Highland Fling steps. In the Scottish Fling step the dancer hops on the supporting foot while the working foot moves forward, back and forward, close round the supporting leg. In the corresponding step of the Cape Breton dance, the dancer beats with the heel of the supporting foot while the working foot is scuffed forward (brushed), back and forward, close to the supporting foot. The Cape Breton Seann Triubhas combines aspects of Scottish versions of the dance with steps which occur in the Hebridean dance, Over the Water to Charlie. The rapid heel and toe beats in the second bar of the 3rd step have the same form as the double heel and double toe beating at the start of the 6th step of the Scotch Jig. The other two Cape Breton solo dances use a step similar to the Catch in and Treble which occurs in the First of August, though the Cape Breton step uses one heel and two toe beats while the Scottish step uses three toe beats.

Most of the steps in the Cape Breton dances are low on the ground with the feet kept almost parallel throughout. The body is held upright and the arms hang loosely by the sides. There is almost no vertical movement of the body. Ordinary hard-soled shoes are worn. Often the weight is transferred from one foot to the other with no perceptible hop or jump. In some cases the weight is kept on the ball of one foot while the heel of that same foot makes a beat; the knee is bent in the movement, but the body is not lifted.

Anyone who is used to dancing high on the balls of the feet could start working on the Cape Breton solo dances by practising beating out the rhythm of a tune with the balls and heels of the feet, keeping both feet in contact with the ground. It may be found helpful to start sitting down, then to work standing with the weight partly supported by the hands holding onto something, before practising standing free.

Instructions are given below for some steps of four dances, the Fling, Seann Triubhas, Over the Hills and Far Away and, Flowers of Edinburgh. The tunes for the first two are strathspeys. They are slow 4/4 tunes with four beats to a bar, the first being a little stronger than the other three. The tunes for the last two have the tempo of reels. These are not smoothly flowing reels, i.e. with four almost equal beats to a bar, but have more of a bounce with two main beats and two subsidiary beats to a bar. In the eighteenth and early nineteenth centuries they were commonly called Scotch measures and that name will be used here.

In the descriptions of the steps given below the phrasing of the dance movements will be described by a system of counting the beats of strathspeys and Scotch measures. The four main musical beats of a bar of a strathspey are represented by the counts '1 2 3 4' which count the four crotchets in the bar. When two dance movements occur in one beat of music they are represented by counts '1 &' which correspond to two quavers. Three dance movements in one beat of music with the rhythm of a triplet of quavers are represented by counts '1 & a'. The four dance movements of 'Shuffle', which occur on the four semi-quavers of a beat, are represented by counts '1 an & a'. The two main beats and the two subsidiary beats of a Scotch measure are represented by the counts '1 & 2 &'. The four dance movements of the 'Triple' which fall in half a bar of a Scotch measure are represented by the counts '1 an & a'. Successive bars of music are denoted by numbers in bold face.

Reel

In each of the following dances the given steps are danced to the second half of the tune. Each step is preceded by a Reel which is danced to the first part of the tune. The Reel consists of six travelling steps round a small clockwise circle followed by a two bar close.

The travelling steps seem not to be fixed. They can be walks or chassés, with extra beats which are used to mark the tune. For example, in the walk, as each foot is swung through it can make one, two or three extra beats with the toe or heel before the weight is taken on that foot. The counting given here for the beats within a bar is that for a strathspey. For a Scotch measure the counting is 1 & 2 & a, 1 an & a 2 & a.

1	1	Step forward on RF
	2	Brush LF forward through 1st position
	3	Step forward on LF
	4 &	Brush RF forward making two beats with ball of RF
2	1	Step forward on RF
	& 2 &	Brush LF forward making one beat with heel and two with ball of LF
	3	Step forward on LF
	4 &	Brush RF forward making two beats with ball of RF

In the chassé all eight counts of the bar may be marked in the following way. Some of the beats may be omitted to fit the tune. Again the counts are given for a strathspey. The counts for a Scotch measure are 1 an & a 2 an & a.

1	1	Step forward on RF
	& 2	Beat with ball of LF and step on it in rear 3rd position
	& 3	Beat ball of RF and step forward on RF
	& 4 &	Beat L heel once and ball of LF twice bringing LF forward

The Reel ends with a two bar close which is adapted to the dance. The movements of the last two bars of the step of a dance make an appropriate close for the Reel for that dance.

Strathspey Setting Steps

No special names were given by the Cape Breton dancers to any of the setting steps. The names used below correspond to some used by dancers in Scotland.

A step like the pas de Basque is performed with a toe beat, or to obtain a stronger sound, with a heel beat in the middle. The middle beat is sometimes doubled up to two beats with the heel or the toe (strictly the ball of the foot). There is no extension of the leg at the end of the step: the form is that of version 1 of the pas de Basque given on page 111 of [42].

The 'double toe beat' step is a close version of the 'toe beat step' used in the Hebridean dance, Over the Water to Charlie. Single toe beat, single heel beat, double toe beat, double heel beat, and heel and toe beat versions of the step are used in the Cape Breton dances. The positions given for a beat with the ball of the foot is the position of the whole foot, which may not be the position in which the beat takes place. Thus for a beat by the ball of the RF in 3rd position the R heel will be next to the L instep and the ball of the RF will beat the ground to the right and in front of the L toe.

Single Heel Beat with RF

Count I Step on to LF in semi 2nd position
& Beat R heel in 5th position
2 Beat ball of LF in rear 5th position

Heel and Toe Beat with RF

Count I Step on to LF in semi 2nd position
& Beat R heel in 3rd position
a Beat ball of RF in 3rd position
2 Beat ball of LF in rear 5th position

In the 'single toe beat' the ball of the RF beats in 3rd position on the middle count. In the 'double toe beat' the ball of the RF beats twice on counts &a. To obtain more emphasis on counts 1 and 2 the beats can be made with the L heel, and the weight can be kept on the ball of the left foot.

The following step plays the same role in the Cape Breton Fling as does the 'fling step' in the Scottish Highland Fling. It was not given a name by the dancers in 1957, but will be called the CB Fling step here.

CB Fling Step with RF

Count I With both feet on the ground in 1st position with toes pointing nearly straight forward beat heels together (or, click L heel with R toe)

 2 3 4 With weight on ball of LF beat L heel three times while scuffing ball of RF forwards, back and forwards through front 3rd position

Double Shuffles with RF

Count I Slide LF back to take weight

 an Slide RF forward to 5th position

 & Slide RF back to 1st position

 a Slide RF forward to 5th position

Ronde with RF

Count I Hop on LF and lift RF a little above 5th position

 & Hop on LF and move RF back to above 1st position

 2 Drop on to RF in rear 5th position

Scotch Measure Setting Steps

In those Cape Breton dances which are danced to Scotch measures a movement similar to the Scottish treble is used. The treble occurs in the Hebridean dance, First of August, as well as in the practice of Treepling in Scotland (see Chapter XI of [42]). In the treble, three beats of the working foot lead to a strong beat of the supporting foot. In the corresponding Cape Breton movement, a strong beat of the supporting foot leads to three beats of the working foot. The difference of emphasis is less apparent when the movement is repeated than when it is performed once. The Cape Breton movement will here be called a 'triple'. The working foot making the three beats can move forwards or backwards in anticipation of the next movements.

Triple with RF

Count I Step on LF in rear 3rd position with beat

 an Beat R heel in 3rd position

 & a Beat ball of RF twice in 3rd position.

Cape Breton Fling

The four steps of the Fling recorded below were danced by John Gillis to the second half of the strathspey Stirling Castle at a speed of 40 bars per minute. There were originally 12 steps. Each step was preceded by a Reel danced to the first part of the tune.

1st step

1–6		CB Fling step RF, RF, LF, LF, RF, RF
7	1	Beat heels together with feet in 1st position
	2	Turn to left pivoting on both toes
	3	Step on to RF in 5th position turning left
	4	Step on to LF in 5th rear position turning left
8		Single heel beat LF, RF completing turn.

2nd step

1	CB Fling step RF
2	Heel and toe beat RF, LF
3, 4	Perform bars 1, 2 contrariwise
5, 6	Repeat bars 1, 2
7	Perform bar 7 of 1st step
8	Heel and toe beat LF, RF.

3rd step

1	1	Beat both heels in 1st position
	& 2	Brush RF forward and drop on it
	& 3	Brush LF forward and drop on it
	& 4	Brush RF forward and drop on it
2		Perform bar 1 contrariwise
3		Repeat bar 1
4		Turn L with single toe beat LF, RF
5–8		Perform bars 1 to 4 contrariwise.

4th step

1	1	Click L heel with R toe
	& 2	Scuff RF forward in front 3rd, slide LF to 1st position
	& 3	Scuff RF back to semi 2nd, slide LF to 1st position
	& 4	Scuff RF forward in front 3rd, slide LF to 1st position
2		Repeat bar 1
3, 4		Perform bars 1, 2 contrariwise
5, 6		Repeat bar 1 and perform it contrariwise
7, 8		Turn L with four single toe beats LF, RF, LF, RF.

The seven counts in bar 1 are marked by sounds. The last six of them were noted as scuffing sounds rather than as distinct beats with the heel or ball of the foot.

Cape Breton Seann Triubhas

The dance originally had twelve steps. The first seven steps recorded below were danced by Miss Margaret Gillis, while the eighth was danced by Ronald Kennedy. They were danced to the strathspey 'Whistle o'er the Lave o't' at a speed of 36 bars per minute. I was told that the same steps were danced to the jig 'The Irish Washerwoman' on St Patrick's Night, though this would require the steps to be modified to fit the tune.

1st step

1–3	Double toe beat RF, LF, RF, LF, RF, LF. In each bar count 1 & a 2, 3 & a 4. Circle each working foot from rear 3rd to 3rd position
4	Double shuffles RF, LF, RF, LF
5–8	Perform bars 1 to 4 contrariwise.

2nd step

1		Double toe beat with RF
	&	Step on to R heel in semi 2nd
	3	Close LF instep to R heel
	&	Step on to R toe in semi 2nd
	4	Close LF instep to R heel
2		Perform bar 1 contrariwise
3		Repeat bar 1
4		Double shuffles LF, RF, LF, RF
5–8		Perform bars 1 to 4 contrariwise.

3rd step

I		Heel toe beat RF, LF
2	I	Hop on LF
	& a	Beat R heel in 3rd and R toe before 3rd
	2	Hop on RF
	& a	Beat L heel in 3rd and L toe before 3rd
	3	Hop on LF
	& a	Beat R heel in 3rd and R toe before 3rd
	4	Beat LF
3		Heel toe beat LF, RF
4		Double shuffles LF, RF, LF, RF
5–8		Perform bars I to 4 contrariwise.

4th step

I	I–2	Double toe beat with RF
	&	Scuff RF to semi 4th in front of 5th
	3	Scuff LF to rear 5th position
	&	Scuff RF to semi 4th intermediate
	4	Scuff LF to rear 5th position
2	I–2	Double toe beat with RF
	3–4	Ronde with RF
3, 4		Perform bars I, 2 contrariwise
5, 6		Repeat bars I, 2
7		Double toe beat LF, RF
8		Double shuffles LF, RF, LF, RF.

5th step

I		Double toe beat then double heel beat with RF
2	I, 2	Double toe beat with RF
	3, 4	Ronde with RF
3, 4		Perform bars I, 2 contrariwise
5, 6		Repeat bars I, 2
7		Double toe beat LF, RF
8		Double shuffles LF, RF, LF, RF.

6th step

1	Double toe beat then double heel beat with RF
2	Ronde RF to 3rd and ronde RF to rear 5th
3, 4	Perform bars 1, 2 contrariwise
5, 6	Repeat bars 1, 2
7	Double toe beat LF, RF
8	Double shuffles LF, RF, LF, RF.

7th step

1	1	Drop on to both heels (or click heels together)
	2	Pivot on both toes and beat both heels on ground to left
	3 4	Heel beat with LF
2		Perform bar 1 contrariwise
3	1	Drop on to both heels
	2	Pivot on both toes, turn R, beat R heel
	3 4	Double heel beat with LF
4		Double shuffles RF, LF, RF, LF
5–8		Perform bars 1 to 4 contrariwise.

8th step

1		Double toe beat the double heel beat with LF
2	1 2	Double toe beat with LF
	3	Carry LF to 5th rear
	4	Step on to LF in 5th rear position
3	1 &	Beat ball of RF twice in front 5th position
	2	Beat ball of LF in rear 5th position
	3 & 4	Repeat counts 1 & 2
4		Double toe beat then double heel beat with RF
5	1	With weight on LF carry RF to rear 5th position
	2	Step on to RF in rear 5th position
	3 &	Beat ball of LF twice in front of 5th position
	4	Beat ball of RF in rear 5th position
6	1 & 2	Repeat counts 3 & 4 of bar 5
	3 4	Double toe beat with RF
7		Double toe beat RF, LF
8		Double shuffles LF, RF, LF, RF.

Cape Breton Over the Hills and Far Away

The six steps of the original twelve steps of this dance recorded below were danced by John Gillis to the second part of the Scotch measure tune of the same name at a speed of 44 bars per minute.

Four of the steps of this dance end with the following two bar sequence. The Reel is danced using six chassés followed by the same sequence.

Close

	& a	Beat ball of RF in 3rd position
7		Triple with LF twice with LF moving towards then back
8	1	Triple with RF forward from 3rd to 5th
	2	Triple with LF in rear 5th

1st step

	& a	Beat ball of LF in 1st and then in rear 3rd position
1	1	Triple with RF
	2 &	Beat ball of LF twice in rear 3rd position
2	1	Triple with RF
	2	Beat ball of LF in rear 3rd position
3, 4		Perform & a and bars 1, 2 contrariwise
5, 6		Repeat & a and bars 1, 2
7, 8		Close.

2nd step

I	I	Hop on LF
	an	Beat ball of RF in rear 3rd position
	&	Hop on LF and take weight on it
	a	Brush R heel forward through 3rd position
	2	Brush R toe back through 3rd position
	&	Brush R toe pointed in semi 2nd position
2	I	Beat R heel in 2nd position
	&	Beat ball of RF in 2nd position
	2	Beat R heel dropping on to flat of foot
	&	Close LF to 1st position
3, 4		Perform bars 1, 2 contrariwise
5, 6		Repeat bars 1, 2
7, 8		Close.

3rd step

	& a	Beat ball of LF in 1st and then in rear 3rd position
I	I	Triple with RF with backwards movement of RF
	2	Beat ball of LF
	an	Beat R toe pointed in rear 5th position
	& a	Repeat counts 2 an
2	I	Triple with RF with forward movement of RF
	2	Beat LF
3, 4		Perform & a and bars 1, 2 contrariwise
5, 6		Repeat & a and bars 1, 2
7, 8		Close.

4th step

I	I	Hop on LF
	an	Brush R heel forward through 3rd position
	&	Brush ball of RF back through 3rd position
	a	Beat ball of LF in rear 3rd position
	2 &	Tap R toe (pointed) twice moving to semi 2nd position
2	I	Beat R heel in 2nd position
	&	Beat ball of RF dropping on to flat of foot
	2	Beat ball of LF in 1st position
3, 4		Perform bars 1, 2 contrariwise
5, 6		Repeat bars 1, 2
7		Perform bar 1 turning left
8	I	Beat L toe in 1st position
	&	Beat R heel dropping on to flat foot
	2	Beat L heel dropping on to flat foot in 1st position.

5th step

I	I	Triple with RF
	2	Hop on LF
	an	Tap R toe in loose 3rd position with toe pointing in and heel out
	&	Beat R heel in semi 4th position, L toe pointing out
2		Repeat.bar 1
3, 4		Perform bars 1, 2 contrariwise
5, 6		Repeat bars 1, 2 turning left
7, 8		Close.

6th step

I	I an	Beat ball of RF twice in 3rd position
	& a	Beat ball of LF twice in rear 3rd position
	2	Repeat counts I an & a
2	I	Beat ball of RF in rear 3rd position
	&	Beat ball of LF in rear 3rd position
	2	Beat ball of RF in 3rd position
3, 4		Perform bars 1, 2 contrariwise
5, 6		Repeat bars 1, 2
7, 8		Close.

Cape Breton Flowers of Edinburgh
(Dannsa nan Flurs)

Miss Margaret Gillis danced the ten steps recorded below out of the original twelve. She danced them to the second half of the Scotch measure tune of the same name at a speed of 48 bars per minute.

Each step of the dance ends with the following two bar sequence. The Reel is danced using six chassés followed by the same two bar sequence.

Close

	& a	Beat ball of LF twice in 3rd position
7		Triple with RF twice with RF moving forward then back
8	I	Triple with LF
	2	Beat ball of RF in rear 3rd position.

1st step

	& a	Beat ball of RF twice in 3rd and 1st position
I		Triple with LF twice with LF moving forward then back
2	I	Triple with LF
	2	Beat RF in rear 3rd position
3, 4		Perform & a and bars **1, 2** contrariwise
5, 6		Repeat & a and bars **1, 2**
7, 8		Close.

2nd step

	&	Beat heels together by pivoting on toes
I	I an	Beat ball of RF twice ending in semi 2nd position
	& a	Beat ball of LF twice closing LF to RF
	2 an	Beat ball of RF twice ending in semi 2nd position
	& a	Beat ball of LF twice closing LF to RF
2	I	Beat ball of RF in 3rd position
	an	Beat R heel in 3rd position
	& a	Beat ball of RF twice in 3rd position
	2	Beat ball of LF in 1st position
	&	Beat heels together
3, 4		Perform bars **1, 2** contrariwise
5, 6		Repeat bars **1, 2**
7, 8		Close.

3rd step

I	I	Step on RF in 2nd position
	&	Close LF to 1st position
	2	Triple with LF
2	I	Triple with RF
	2	Beat ball of LF in rear 3rd position
3, 4		Perform bars **1, 2** contrariwise
5, 6		Repeat bars **1, 2**
7, 8		Close.

4th step

1, 2	As 2nd step, turning half circle to right
3, 4	As 2nd step, turning half circle to left
5, 6	As 2nd step, turning full circle to right
7, 8	Close, facing front.

5th step

1	1	Chassé diagonally forward to the right
2	1 & 2	Chassé diagonally forward to the left
	&	Beat ball of RF in rear 3rd position
	a	Beat ball of LF in rear 3rd position taking weight
3	1	Triple with RF moving RF forward
	2	Beat LF in rear 3rd position
	&	Hop on LF
	a	Beat ball of RF in 1st position
4	1	Triple with LF moving LF forward
	2	Beat RF in rear 3rd position
	&	Hop on RF
	a	Beat ball of LF in 1st position
5, 6		Repeat bars **3** and **4** with full turn to right
	&	Hop on RF
7, 8		Close.

6th step

1	1	Step on to R toe in 5th position
	2	Step on to L toe in 5th position
2	1	Step on to R toe in 5th position
	&	Step on to L toe in 5th position
	2	Step on to R toe in 5th position
3, 4		Perform bars **1, 2** contrariwise
	&	Step on to RF in rear 3rd position
	a	Beat ball of LF in 1st position
5	1	Triple with RF
	2	Beat ball of LF in rear 3rd position
	&	Hop on LF
	a	Beat ball of RF in 1st position
6	1	Triple with LF
	2	Beat ball of RF in 3rd rear position
	&	Hop on RF
7, 8		Close.

7th step

	& a	Brush ball of LF forward and back in 3rd position
1	1	Triple with RF bringing RF back
	2	Beat R toe pointing in semi 2nd position
	&	Beat R toe pointing further to right
2	1	Beat R heel in 2nd position (the R leg moves to the right for these 3 beats)
	&	Flap R toe before 2nd position keeping R heel on ground
	2	Beat ball of LF in 1st position
3, 4		Perform & a and bars 1, 2 contrariwise
5, 6		Repeat & a and bars 1, 2 with three quarter turn to the right
	2	Brush ball of LF forward through 1st position
	&	Hop on RF finishing turn to the right
	a	Beat ball of LF in 1st position
7, 8		Close.

8th step

	& a	Brush ball of LF out and in to rear 3rd position
1	1	Triple with RF bringing RF back
	2	Beat ball of LF in 3rd position
	an	Beat R toe pointing in rear 5th position
	&	Beat ball of LF in 5th position
	a	Beat R toe in rear 5th position
2	1	Triple with RF carrying RF forward
	2	Beat ball of LF in rear 3rd position
3, 4		Perform & a and bars 1, 2 contrariwise
5, 6		Repeat & a and bars 1, 2
7, 8		Close.

9th step

This step is similar to the 8th step with the toe points in the 5th position instead of the rear 5th position. The first two bars are followed by repeats as in the 8th step.

	& a	Brush ball of LF out and in to rear 3rd position
1	1	Triple with RF carrying RF forward
	2	Beat ball of LF in rear 3rd position
	an	Beat R toe pointing in 5th position
	&	Beat ball of LF in rear 5th position
	a	Beat R toe in 5th position
2	1	Triple with RF carrying RF back
	2	Beat ball of LF in 3rd position
3, 4		Perform & a and bars 1, 2 contrariwise
5, 6		Repeat & a and bars 1, 2
7, 8		Close.

10th step

	& a	Brush ball of LF out and in to 3rd position
1	1	Step on to LF
	&	Brush ball of RF forward through 3rd position
	2	Hop on LF
	&	Brush R toe from crossed leg through 5th position
2	1	Hop on LF
	an &	Beat ball of RF twice in crossed 5th position
	a 2	Beat ball of LF twice in rear 5th position
3, 4		Perform & a and bars 1, 2 contrariwise
5, 6		Repeat & a and bars 1, 2
7, 8		Close.

References

(A) Sources not cited in Full in the Text

1. Major Edward Topham, *Letters from Edinburgh written in the years 1774 and 1775* (Edinburgh, 1776), 338–45
2. A. Gibb, *A New Collection of Minuets, Medlies, High-Dances, ...* (Edinburgh, *c.* 1798)
3. Charles Stewart, *A Collection of Minuets, Cotillions, Allemandes, High Dances, Hornpipes etc.* (Edinburgh, *c.* 1805)
4. Archibald Duff, *Part First of a choice Selection of Minuets, ...* (Edinburgh and Aberdeen, *c.* 1812)
5. *Edinburgh Courant*, December 3, 1764
6. Felix MacDonough, *The Hermit in Edinburgh* (London, 1824), i, 30
7. *Scots Magazine*, lxiii (Edinburgh, 1801), 207
8. *Edinburgh Courant*, September 13, 1800
9. *Inverness Journal*, April 6, 1813
10. *Inverness Journal*, September 24, 1813
11. *Edinburgh Courant*, October 18, 1783
12. *Edinburgh Courant*, November 15, 1800
13. *Edinburgh Courant*, September 13, 1800
14. Robert C MacLagan, 'The Games and Diversions of Argyllshire', *Folk-Lore Society*, Publication no. 17 (London, 1901) 171
15. MS records of the Edinburgh Piping Competitions. See Chapter on Sword Dance.
16. *Scots Magazine*, lx (Edinburgh, 1798), 598–9
17. Sir Charles Petrie, *The Jacobite Movement, The Last Phase,... 1706–1807* (London, 1950) 18–19
18. William Stenhouse, Ed., *Illustrations* to *The Scots Musical Museum*, David Laing, Ed. (2nd edition, Edinburgh, 1839). [The *Illustrations*, i.e. notes, were actually printed in 1820 or 1821 for a new edition of the *Museum* but not published due to the ill health of the editor.]
19. Charles Compan, *Dictionaire de Danse* (Paris, 1787)
20. William Anderson, *New, enlarged and Complete Ball-room Guide* (Dundee *c.* 1894)
21. P Rameau, *The Dancing Master* (Paris, 1725)
22. Isobel Crambe, Ed., *Four Step Dances* (London, 1953)
23. J F and T M Flett, 'Some Early Highland Dancing Competitions', *Aberdeen University Review*, xxxvi (1956), 345–58
24. Robert Ridell, *Collection of Scotch Galwegian and Border Tunes* (Edinburgh, 1794)
25. J G MacKay, 'Widdershins; in Scottish Gaelic, Tuathal', *Folk-Lore*, 39 (1928), 283
26. William Chapell, *Popular Music of Olden Time* (London, [1855])
27. Andrew MacIntosh, 'English and Gaelic Words to Strathspeys and Reels', *Trans. Gaelic Soc. Inverness*, 28 (1912–14) 287–305
28. Cecil Sharp, MS collection in Clare College Library, Cambridge
29. Sir David Lindsay, 'The Works of Sir David Lindsay of the Mount', ed. D. Hamer, *Scottish Text Society* (Edinburgh, 1931)
30. Alexander Campbell, *The Grampians Desolate, A Poem* (Edinburgh, 1804)
31. Colonel Thomas Thornton, *A Sporting Tour through the Highlands of Scotland* (London, 1804), 171–2
32. J J H H S Murray, Duke of Atholl, *Chronicles of the Atholl and Tullibardine Families*, 5 vols. (Edinburgh, 1908) iv, 256

33. John Leyden, *Journal of a Tour in the Highland and Western Islands of... in 1800* (?, 1903)
34. James Logan, *The Scottish Gael*, 2 vols. (London, 1831) ii, 314–5
35. Barthélemi Faujas de Saint-Fond, *Travels in England, Scotland and the Hebrides*, 2 vols. (London, 1799), I. 281
36. Philo Scotus, *Reminiscences of a Scottish Gentleman* (London, 1861)
37. Henry Playford, *A Collection of Original Scotch-Tunes (full of the Highland Humours) for the Violin ...* (London, 1700)
38. Duncan Ban MacIntyre, *The Songs of Duncan Ban MacIntyre*, ed. Angus MacLeod (Edinburgh, 1952)
39. I Colquhoun and H Machell, *Highland Gatherings* (London, 1927)
40. *Inverness Courant*, October 3, 1848
41. Graham MacNeilage, *How to Dance the Eightsome Reel, Strathspey and Reel Steps...* (Alloa, 1900)
42. J F and T M Flett, *Traditional Dancing in Scotland* (London, 1964 and in paperback 1985)
43. K N MacDonald, *The Skye Collection of the Best Reels and Strathspeys Extant* (Edinburgh, 1887) Preface
44. J J H H S Murray, Duke of Atholl, *Chronicles of the Atholl and Tullibardine Families*, 5 vols. (Edinburgh, 1908) iv, 219
45. General D. Stewart, *Sketches of the Character, Manners, and Present State of the Highlands of* Scotland, 2 vols. (Edinburgh, 1822) ii, Appendix, liii
46. J F and T M Flett, 'Some Hebridean Folk Dances', *Journal of the English Folk dance and Song Soc.* (London, 1953) vol. 7 part 2
47. J F and T M Flett, 'Dramatic Jigs in Scotland', *Folk-Lore*, lxvii (London, 1956)
48. F Rhodes, Appendix to *Traditional Dancing in Scotland*, 'Dancing in Cape Breton Island, Nova Scotia' (London, 1964 and in paperback 1985). The appendix is reproduced in *Explorations in Canadian Folklore* by E Fowle and C H Carpenter (Toronto, 1985)
49. Allan Thomas, ed., *A New Most Excellent Dancing Master* (New York, 1992)

(B) Other References in the Appendix

50. J L MacDougall, *History of Inverness County, Nova Scotia* (privately printed, 1922)
51. D R MacKenzie, *National Dances of Scotland* (Glasgow, 1910, reprinted 1939)
52. *Highland Dancing: a guide to judges, competitors and teachers* (printed by a conference held in Edinburgh, 2nd April 1925). (A 15 page booklet, 98 by 132 mm.)
53. K N MacDonald, *Puirt-a-Beul* (Glasgow, 1901, reprinted 1931)

(C) List of Informants for the Appendix

All the informants were visited in Cape Breton Island in 1957 except for 12 and 15. These were visited in South Uist, Outer Hebrides, 15 in 1955 and 12 in 1956.

1. Major Calum Ian N MacLeod, Sydney. Gaelic advisor in the Adult Education Division of the Department of Education, Nova Scotia.
2. The Rev Father Stanley MacDonald, Big Pond. His grandparents came from Kinlockmoidart.
3. Mr Hugh F MacKenzie, Sydney. Brought up at Christmas Island. His family came from Barra.
4. Mrs Mary Sarah MacDonald, Scotch Lake. A centenarian whose grandmother came from Barra.

5. Mr James C MacNeil, Gillis Point, Iona.
6. Mrs MacTigue, Inverness.
7. Mr John Gillis and Miss Margaret Gillis, Gillisdale, South West Margaree, father and daughter. Mr Gillis's grandfather came from Morar.
8. Mr Ronald Kennedy, Broad Cove. His grandfather came from Canna.
9. Mr Donald A MacInnes, Creignish.
10. Mr Steve R MacNeil, Iona.
11. Mrs MacDougal, East Bay.
12. Mr Archie Monroe, Loch Boisdale, South Uist.
13. Mr Frank MacNeil, Big Pond. His grandfather came from Barra.
14. Mr and Mrs Archie Kennedy, Dunvegan. Mr Kennedy's great-grandparents came from Moidart.
15. Mrs Margaret MacAskill, South Boisdale, South Uist.

Index

Entries in this index which are bold, italic are names of dances.

215

Other books of interest

Parish Life in Eighteenth-Century Scotland: A Review of the Old Statistical Account
Maisie Steven; 1 898218 28 5

Scottish Lifestyle 300 Years Ago
Helen & Keith Kelsall; 1 898218 06 4

Robert Burns – A Man for All Seasons: The natural world of Robert Burns
compiled by John Young; 1 898218 60 9

Isabella Bird and a Woman's Right
Olive Checkland; 1 898218 33 1

The Democratic Muse: Folk Music Revival in Scotland
Ailie Munro; 1 898218 10 2